P9-CET-294

Split at the Root:
A Memoir of Love and Lost Identity

Catana Tully

For Kim,
Congratulations are
in order — on so many
levels! All the very
best! Catana!

Ⓒ Completion Enterprises, LLC

Sedona, AZ

Split at the Root is a work of nonfiction.
Some names have been changed.

Copyright © 2012, Completion Enterprises LLC.
All rights reserved. No part of this book may be
reproduced or transmitted in any form or by any means,
electronic or mechanical, including photocopying,
recording or by any information storage and retrieval
system without permission in writing from the author.

Cover photography: Family archive
Image adapted by Brenda Steves

Published for the author by
Completion Enterprises LLC,
PO Box 21482, Sedona, AZ 86341

Printed in the United States of America

About the Author

Catana Tully
Autumn 2012

Dr. Catana Tully grew up trilingual (German, Spanish, English) in Guatemala where she attended elementary and middle school. In tenth grade she entered a boarding school in Jamaica, WI and received her Advanced Level Higher Schools Certificate from Cambridge University, England. Expecting to become an international interpreter, she continued her studies at the Sprachen und Dolmetscher Institut in Munich, Germany. However, she was called to work in a play and discovered her affinity for the dramatic arts. She became the actress and fashion model Catana Cayetano and appeared in Film and TV work in Germany, Austria, and Italy. In Munich she met and married the American actor Frederick V. Tully and ultimately moved to the United States. They have a son, Patrick. In Upstate New York, she completed the BA in Cultural Studies, an MA in Latin American and Caribbean Literature, and a DA (doctor of Arts) in Humanistic Studies. She held the position of tenured Associate Professor at SUNY Empire State College from which she retired in 2003. She returned in 2005 for part time work in ESC's Center for International Programs, where she served as Mentor and instructor in the Lebanon program, and as Interim Program Director for the Dominican Republic. In 2011 she retired completely to dedicate herself to publishing Split at the Root. She is currently preparing an academic version discussing the psychological issues imbedded in the memoir.

For Patrick

My story is his, too.

ACKNOWLEDGEMENTS

I am indebted to my beloved Fred, for his ever-present support in life, and for gifting me with my Black skin in death; to my son Patrick, whose wisdom, remarkable talent, and profound insights brighten my existence. Indebted to innumerable friends and colleagues who through the years have encouraged me to publish my story; indebted to Constance Morgan for the guidance that strengthened my backbone, and sharing with me the notes of our sessions; to Anita Bucherer Godeffroy for precious hours of intense, other-worldly discussions; to Tristine Rainer for her enduring friendship through the years, her wisdom, insight, and contagious optimism; to Marion Roach for her excellent writing suggestions, to Sandi Gelles-Cole for recommending I re-write the story chronologically; to Joyce Elliott Ph.D for assuring Reassignment time to write and re-write the manuscript, to Marjorie Lavin Ph.D, Marc Cirigliano Ph.D, and United University Professions for four Faculty Development Awards that supported my research.

TESTIMONIALS

Split at the Root is a portal to Catana Tully's exotic past and an absorbing account of her search for identity. She laces this journey of self-discovery with the suspense and mystery of a compelling detective novel. We turn the pages immersed in her story as she strives to uncover the truths of her past. We witness her struggle to reconcile her racial displacement with her multiple roots. We celebrate her ultimate embrace of her heritage. An engrossing and moving tale filled with psychological and social insight, this memoir shows us what it means to be whole and how that wholeness makes us fully human.

Richard Gotti, PhD, MFA
Professor and Psychotherapist

Praise for *Split at the Root: A Memoir of Love and Lost Identity*
This book shows us how precious and fragile one's sense of identity can be. For some people, questions about their sense of self, their family roots, and their place in society, never come up. There is an unspoken assurance that who they are and how others see them, and how they see themselves are right out there in the open for everyone to see. Split at the Root represents a gradual and then radical departure from that kind reassurance of self. Catana Tully's memoir is a wrenching, painful and necessary excavation for a woman of color who spent her formative years growing up as a "younger daughter" in a German-Guatemalan family. How Catana unearths the many sided truths of herself and her racial and cultural inheritance is the core of this moving narrative.

Beverly Ann Smirni,
Associate Professor, Social Studies

Firstly, this is a riveting oral history, autobiography, detective story, as well as a family history and an individual's striving for knowledge, personal identity and closure. Catana Tully combined an impressionistic study of her natural environment with an impressive research effort to re-assemble her origins. The story resembles a palimpsest, a parchment that has been written on, partially erased, then written on again. While the German historian, von Ranke raised the bar of his profession by striving for Geschichte wie es eigentlich gewesen (history as it actually happened), Catana has arrived at a certitude that has allowed her to assert ownership over her own history and life. She has reached a very high plateau of historical understanding and re-creation while raising the bar for anyone who aspires to follow in her footsteps. The writer was actually "uprooted' from her birth family and, in a sense orphaned because the German family never shared their name with her through adoption; rather they colonized her mind and Mutti s/mothered her with a dutiful love aimed at producing a trophy child who could bring honor into her unfulfilled life. There may be no second acts in life, but Catana has empowered herself and others to compose an epilogue that captures the essence of their personal histories – while raising the bar for this genre. Those who control the present control the past, and those who control the past control the future. When the German family expelled her birth family from her life, they erased Catana's memories to control her life. The guilt she felt about this reality was mostly sadness over being apparently abandoned by Rosa, her birth mother, and consequently encouraged to deny her own roots. However, she became the beneficiary of greater opportunities for worldly success, but also a victim (of captivity) and an accessory to a crime of rejecting/abandoning her origins. It explains why Mutti disapproved of the Haitian artist's portrait: its colorfulness was too accurate a depiction of her genuine cultural roots. Catana's soulful re-creation of the first three years with Rosa was brilliant as was the excellent use she made of her multi-cultural heritage with her students in Albany.

Frank Rader, PhD
Professor, Historian

Catana Tully's book goes beyond narrating an unusual life's story with a global backdrop. She explores issues of identity and cultural influences on a deeply personal level. The honesty and clear voice in her writing made this book a pleasure to read and an inspiration.

Patricia Hoisch,
Artist, Musician

This is the compelling life story of a young Carib child, torn from her roots in an obscure coastal town and raised by wealthy German expatriates in Guatemala City, who struggles throughout a lifetime to reconcile her European upbringing and white identity with her dark skin. Her story takes us on a multi-cultural journey from Central America and the Caribbean through Europe and then the United States, offering profound insight into the relativity of racial identity and cultural assumptions. The style of this autobiography is vivid, dramatic, and moving. Particularly noteworthy is the lush and powerful way in which she evokes the immediate sensory experience of her childhood – the colors, tones, tastes, textures and scents etched upon her sense of the world. The narrative is wonderfully dramatic, at many points almost cinematic, as she lays before us the scenes, the people, words and gestures that shaped the unfolding of her mind and spirit. Particularly compelling is her portrait of her German mother, a strong woman of mature years, honed through difficult experience to face life squarely and independently, who struggles to prepare her Mohrle (little Moor) to find a place in educated and sophisticated society where her radiant spirit and keen intellect will outshine her dark skin. She teaches Mohrle the importance of the proper "frame," and we see Mohrle build a series of protective frameworks in both her inner and outer worlds. We see her shape and play a role in life, and do not wonder but only cheer at her success as an actress of European stage, cinema and television. A move to the United States challenges all her protective frameworks as she discovers the difference between having dark skin and being Black in America. Brought into vivid relief by the racism of American culture, the deep contradictions and fears which lurk at the root of her identity prod her eventually to seek out her roots and to reclaim the birth mother whom she had rejected, in fear and confusion, as a young child. The image of her birth mother's last visit and the recollection of her last words haunt the last part of the story, as Mohrle, now a professor of cultural studies, stops merely playing roles, albeit with consummate skill, and begins examining them. Throughout this story, vivid scenes of lived experience alternate with insightful commentary. The questions it explores strike at the heart of all of our lives: How do we frame the persona we present to the world? Ho do we reconcile the self-image we create and defend over a lifetime with the image we see in the mirror? How do we come to love and honor all of our mothers, and all of our heritage?

First Review for the electronic version of Split at the Root on
Amazon.com: October 12, 2012
Carolyn D. Broadaway PhD.

Table of Contents

We are, all of us, molded and remolded by those who have loved us, and though that love pass, we remain none the less their work – a work that very likely they do not recognize, and which is never exactly what they intended.

Francois Mauriac, *The Desert of Love*

Catana with Mutti in Livingston.

Catana, 4 1/2 years old

PART ONE

The First Twenty Years
1940-1960

Fact and Fiction

I was born at the mouth of the Rio Dulce, a Central American jungle river that slowly makes its way to the ocean through dense tropical rain forests in a part of the world where, it is said, the great mysteries of the Land of Mu and Atlantis wait to be re-discovered. Even as I write today Livingston, the remote village of my birth, is only accessible by boat: no roads connect it to the rest of Guatemala.

As the sun pierced the horizon my new voice joined that of the village roosters in welcoming the day. I was born at sunrise, in a humble village hut; the first child of a young Black woman named Rosa. I didn't grow up with her and although I knew her, it would take years before I would begin to remember her face.

I was told that, days after my birth I was brought to live in the Casa Grande, a mansion on the hill overlooking the village, the river, and the ocean. It belonged to don Pablo, a German exporter who lived there with his wife, doña Esther, and her daughter Miss Ruth. When they were forced to move to Guatemala City they took me with them because, doña Esther (whom I called Mutti, mommy in German) would tell me, she had fallen in love with me and couldn't leave me behind. I don't remember the village hut or the mansion on the hill for that matter, and only recall the family stories of what happened long ago.

"Tonight, I have a little story for my beautiful baby," my German mother murmured in my ear on a hot tropical evening when I was very young, and began to spin the first of many tales she would weave entirely for me.

We sat in the cool of the terrace - me in the fold of her arm - and observed day slip into night. Two long-tailed birds drifted across the sky in the fading light as a solitary canoe glided into darkness on the river below. Surrounded by the quiet of the jungle, the vast, leaden Atlantic spread before us. In the comfort of her arms, I absorbed the darkening landscape and listened to the sound of distant waves unfolding on the beach. I lived for those moments, when I shared the solace of the waning day with her; I yearned for her closeness, her generous, soft breasts, the way she smelled. I loved to hear her refined German voice as she shaped her words.

"One morning not so long ago, I woke up very early," Mutti whispered in my ear, "so early, it was still dark outside. I peeked into Ruth's room and she, too, was already awake. So we decided to come out and sit on the terrace and wait for the sun to rise. The grass was wet with dew and the breeze rustled in the palms, just like now... The whole world smelled fresh and new, like the very first morning of the very first day." Overjoyed, I looked at her, my little face beaming. This was already a wonderful story. "Suddenly, in the gray of the water," Mutti pointed to the distance, "we saw a big, round leaf slowly floating down the Rio Dulce. And guess what," she said, enlarging her eyes in amazement. "Right in the middle of this thick, beautiful leaf, sat a little brown baby."

"Oh," I said breathless and sat up to face her. "And then?"

"Then, Ruth and I ran down the hill as fast as we could, and..."

"Who won?"

"We both got there at the very same time," Mutti said, gently kissing my forehead. "And I pulled the leaf ashore, and picked up the baby and cuddled it in my arms, like this... and I kissed the little baby, like this... And then I said: Oh, what a beautiful little Mohrle, this is!"

"That's me!" I shrieked with joy.

"Yes!" my mother said with a broad smile on her face, "that's how you became my darling child."

My first story was so thrilling that it never occurred to me to ask who had put me on the leaf, or what would have happened if Mutti and Ruth hadn't seen me.

For as far back as I can think, I have been Mohrle, an endearing term in German: 'little Moor.' After more than half a century, I am still 'Mohrle' to those who knew me as a child.

IN PHOTOS OF MY EARLY DAYS in Livingston, I am a well-groomed tropical baby in piquet shorts and a ribbon around my head. I sit on Mutti's lap looking thoughtful while she smiles proudly into the camera. Sometimes I'm by myself with only the cloudless sky in the background; to that Mutti would say, "Mohrle you look like the happiest little cherub brought by angels and placed on the grassy hill." In spite of the imprint of the coastal sun on my skin, I became in every way Mutti's German child.

Esther, my German mother, was a sophisticated, sociable woman. She was 52 at my birth. In pictures of her youth her auburn hair is gathered in a bun at the nape of her neck. By the time I begin to see her, the hair was gray and wavy and kept short. Her eyes were deep hazel with a mischievous twinkle that betrayed a fine sense of humor. She had delicate, well-shaped lips and a large gently curved nose. Occasionally she longed for the wine country of southwest Germany where she was born. Hers was a powerful presence that gave me a profound sense of invincibility and security. Above all, I sought to please Mutti, and yearned for her approval long after I no longer needed to prove anything to anyone.

Of average but pleasant appearance, Mutti's daughter Ruth, who was 30 at my birth, was light in structure and elegantly thin. She lacked Mutti's effervescent personality but was gentle - a nurturer by nature - who complied with all her parents' wishes. I still remember her bathing and dressing me and combing my hair when I was little. At night, after my evening toilet, she fired my imagination with fairytales extolling the virtues of honesty, patience, and cleanliness. Then she would ask me to fold my hands and together we recited the prayer "Ich bin klein, mein Herz ist rein" (I am young, my heart is pure). After tucking me into bed and a gentle good night kiss on my cheek, she rejoined the others in the living room, always leaving my door slightly ajar so a ray of light from the hall entered my room and carried me to peaceful dreams. As a child I loved her dearly and called her Mama until she had children of her own, which was after she married a man named Rudolf. Then I began to refer to her as "my sister Ruth." I remember well how much I loved being with her, and how things were before she married.

The child of two doting women, I was also the daughter of an aging, moody man: Mutti's husband, Pablo Doescher. I called him Vati, daddy in German. His eyes were cornflower blue and when he laughed he displayed a row of perfect, shiny teeth that seemed even whiter against his brawny skin. Mutti told me he was blond, strong, and agile in his youth, so he came to figure in my mind as a powerhouse, a giant of a man. In reality, though, I only knew him as a physically incapacitated, corpulent, elderly gentleman.

Vati was born in Hamburg in 1886, and belonged to those German coffee growers and exporters who settled in Latin America in the late nineteenth, early twentieth century to see that local produce found its way to Europe. Some belonged to well-established families of importers from Hamburg or Bremen, younger siblings who were sent overseas to participate in their families' company affairs. Others, like Vati, left Germany in the employ of already established companies. Many were adventurers of the legendary, trailblazer sort, the devil may care type of men who with the help of machetes, Indians, and mules cleared their way through dense tropical vegetation and claimed arable land for their farms.

Vati arrived in Guatemala aged 21 in 1905 and settled in Livingston two years later. He worked for the Ferrocarril Verapaz, a German-owned railroad company founded in the late eighteen hundreds. The steam-powered engine was a charming relic of early private railroad enterprise. The line ran from Pancajché in the highlands, where the coffee was loaded, down to Panzós on the Rio Dulce and from there by barge to the port of Livingston on the Atlantic. "When a deadline had to be met," Mutti would tell me, "Vati took his shirt off and worked together with the natives loading and unloading the cargo. He never expected anyone to do what he himself couldn't. He may not have been easy to work for but he dealt fairly with everyone, and everyone deeply respected him." Livingston was not peripheral when exports to Europe boomed.

My father was on his first vacation in Germany when WWI broke out in 1914, and was drafted into the German army. It was during that time he met Mutti and fell in love with her. When he returned to Livingston in 1920, she was a bride at his side. Shortly after his return, Pablo Doescher was appointed Honorary Consul of Germany in Livingston. As such, his responsibilities were not diplomatic but commercial, and necessary primarily with regard to shipping and loading issues and permits.

As removed geographically as my parents were from Germany, so too were they distanced from the atrocious political and social goings on there. Because of the charged period in history, and because it is a general misconception that all Germans in Latin America were Nazis, I must mention that neither Vati, Mutti, or Ruth had the minutest sympathy for the political or philosophical aspirations of the National Socialist Party. Vati was aware of the activities in Europe and abhorred the developments in his home. When Hitler was named chancellor with dictatorial powers in 1933, Vati renounced his consular position. The German Ambassador in Guatemala City, a Herr von Kuhlman, also an avowed anti-Nazi, beseeched Vati to stay at his post, which he ultimately did in support of his friend. Neither had wanted to gamble as to who would be sent as Vati's replacement.

World War II would cause great difficulty for Germans living in Latin America. After Pearl Harbor, Guatemala, like most Latin American republics, joined the cause of the allies on the side of the United States, and German property was confiscated just about everywhere. My parents were given a few weeks to pack their belongings and move inland to Guatemala City. Then the United States demanded that German men be incarcerated, or if the prisons were inadequate, be shipped to US internment camps. After we had left Livingston in January 1942 and settled in Guatemala City, my father, together with the other German men, was deported like a criminal to a camp in Mc Allen, Texas.

The postcards addressed to Mohrle Doescher came with regularity and have yellowed in the decades since I received them. "Mein liebes kleines Mohrle," (my dear little Mohrle) Vati writes to me in one, "I just received your pretty paintings and Mutti's letter telling me what a wonderful child you are. I can tell that you are very careful and tidy. The minute your envelope arrived, I got this card so I could thank you right away. I miss you so very much. Soon I will be back to play with you and Schaeffi. Please give Mutti a hug for me, little Mohrle. I love you with all my heart, Vati." After Mutti read those words to me, I hugged her really tight. In those moments of sheer joy, I was the happiest girl in the world.

While in the camp, Vati contracted a nervous disorder that left him partially paralyzed and barely able to walk. I was almost five in 1945 when Vati came home, lying on a stretcher. My memories of those early days after his return are quite clear, for I kept him company and accompanied him on slow walks with our dog. Eventually he learned to move about quite well using a cane. On most unusual occasions when the maids had the day off and neither Ruth nor Mutti were home, Vati made my dinner: pancakes. I would find the bowl wherein he mixed flour, milk, and eggs; and I got the frying pan from the low cabinet because he could not bend down and keep his balance. I can still taste those delectable morsels today: a little burned on one side, on the other just right, sprinkled with cinnamon sugar and served with a glass of cold milk.

THE WOMEN IN THE GERMAN COMMUNITY, whether they liked each other or not, forged strong ties and held together like family. A young mother of 3, who had married a significantly older man, was left somewhere in the nowhere lowlands of Guatemala trying to make ends meet with her broken Spanish. Hannali, the middle child, was my age and came to stay with us several times a year for months at a time. As dissimilar in appearance as two individuals can be, Hannali and I were one in thought and action and could well have been one soul that came to earth through two different mothers. So much so, that people sometimes wondered whether Ruth perhaps wasn't pulling their leg when she said we were her twins.

Sometimes Hannali caught me observing her. "What?" She'd ask, as I looked and just looked at her.

"Nothing," I'd answer, embarrassed at being caught staring. I loved the freckles on her nose that looked like caramelized specks of sugar, or how her deep blue eyes turned purple when she got mad. But above all, I loved her straight, flaxen hair that flew around her head bending to the slightest breeze. I had no freckles, my eyes did not change color when I got mad, and my hair, in contrast to hers, was always immaculately well arranged. But my invariably perfect presentation came at a price, and Hannali commiserated with me every morning by sitting next to me on the bathroom bench while Ruth opened the four braids she had carefully woven the previous day. Meticulously, she combed through every bit of my kinky hair. "We'll be done sooner if you hold still," Ruth would inevitably say, "it hurts me more than it does you, Mohrle." Of course it was never soon and it's debatable who suffered more, but in the end my four braids were held in place with silver clasps and I looked as perfect as a doll. One thing was certain: having my kind of hair may have been painful, but I looked well groomed all day. I would have given anything, however, to have had the sort of hair that required the inconvenience of having to fix clips to hold it in place when the wind disheveled it. Many years later, I painted freckles on my nose with an eyebrow pencil.

When Cold Winds Began to Blow

Guatemala City is only 15 degrees north of the Equator, but at five thousand feet above sea level the altitude allows for November, December, and January to be cold dry months. Cold, of course, is relative where the world is in full bloom, where hummingbirds hover at golden honeysuckle blossoms and lizards, ants, and lady-bugs scurry along sun-warmed patio tiles.

Once the rainy season ended and November winds began to blow, our home released the scent of allspice, cardamom, nutmeg, and cinnamon: German spice loaves and Christmas cookies were being made. Sometimes Marta, our cook, tied an oversized kitchen towel around my neck and sat me at the pantry table where Simeón, our houseboy, was shelling nuts. Rather than stare at people working, I could blanch the almonds soaking in warm water, which meant squeezing the soggy skin at one end to make the nut shoot out the other.

There were chocolate spirals, anise stars, jelly filled sugar cookies; powdered almond moons, crispy walnut crowns, lemon glazed hazelnut balls, candied fruit clusters. Marta grouped them in large airtight glass containers and placed them on top of the pantry cabinets. Every time I saw them I thought: jewels in jars. At Christmas they would be arranged on trays and given to our friends as gifts.

Partly as a family tradition but also because the war had limited our resources, we made our presents. During afternoon tea, with the voices of the Vienna Boy's Choir flowing out of the gramophone and the active fireplace warming us, Mutti and Ruth knit while my young fingers molded clay or embroidered gifts requiring little supervision and less accuracy.

December sixth was Nikolaus, day of the generous saint who wandered through the night leaving a little something - a red imported apple, or a juicy orange, or perhaps some crayons - in a shoe I placed outside my bedroom door before going to sleep.

On afternoons, when the winds were less severe, Mutti and I might take our German shepherd, Schaeffi, for a walk along Avenida de la Reforma. We lived on a broad, tree-lined avenue with sidewalks, bridle paths, and paved streets for vehicles, each separated by grassy islands, pink oleander bushes, and towering cypress trees. Our steps would take us past the homes of friends to the outlook post where we admired the volcanoes: the dormant majestic Agua; the four-coned Pacaya, smoldering like an impaled dragon set to disgorge its fiery insides; the double-headed Acatenango; and lastly, true to its name, eternally spewing ashes and smoke, the Fuego. The air, crisp and clear and sharp as a knife, smelled of cypress and eucalyptus.

The setting sun lit up the sky in a series of blazing shades of tangerine, magenta, to ever-deeper crimson. Invariably the firmament reminded me of our oven at home when we opened it to retrieve the cookie sheets. I believed at times, when the sky seemed particularly inflamed, that angels in heaven were busy, not making Christmas cookies as we were on earth, but baking people. Those individuals who were closer to the heat became darker than the ones who had been farther away. That was my very own theory of creation; through it I explained to myself why I was darker than those around me: I had been closer to the fire.

My active participation in the feast began when Ruth brought out an old leather-bound volume of nineteenth century German Christmas poetry. We read some poems and I would choose one to memorize and recite on Christmas Eve. I treasured the heavy old book, its musty smell, the brittle, mustard colored pages, and I'd lose myself in the delicate drawings of snowy landscapes and scenes of yesteryear, imagining myself walking in the Black Forest, in Güntherstal perhaps – where Tante Gustl, Mutti's older sister lived – or stomping, knee deep in the snow of a wintry landscape. Or I'd admire a booth at the Christmas market in Freiburg; perhaps I was part of a chapel's choir singing O Tannenbaum. Whether I was five or eight or twelve, the book made me nostalgic for a Europe I had never known, and for a feast that was not part of my culture.

On Christmas Eve, that most special of days for a German child, I was not allowed to enter the living room until we exchanged our gifts in the early evening, as Christkind and angels were decorating our tree, and only adults were allowed in. Whenever I tiptoed by – I don't know how they sensed me coming – they went whoosh... whoosh... and moved the drapes, pretending that the heavenly helpers had flapped their huge wings as they flew out of the room. Ruth then appeared and accompanied me to the bathroom or out of the area.

At five-thirty, wearing my newest white dress, I waited in my room until Ruth came for me. "Want me to hear your poem one more time?" She'd ask, and I'd run through the verses just to make sure I knew them. Hand-in-hand we walked out of my room, past all the lit candles in the hall, to the drawn drapes. A gentle squeeze, and Ruth let go my hand before slipping through the drapes to join the adults.

My heart beat hard in my chest as I waited to be invited in. Then came the Christmas bell's silvery chime, and ever so slowly the drapes drew aside revealing a room aglow in candlelight. In the far left corner, a long-needled Guatemalan pine reached the ceiling. Its branches, covered with sparkly snow-like powder, held white candles, white stars, white pine cones, glass icicles: it was a symphony in white. Our cellophane-wrapped gifts, like giant sapphires, emeralds, and rubies, reflected in myriad colors the lights in the room. On silver platters were dates, figs, Christmas Stolen, cookies, red apples from Oregon, and large red California grapes.

All eyes, however, were on me. I waited for Mutti's nod. Then a step forward, a curtsy, and I began my recitation. I never stumbled, never erred, not with a single word. "That was beautiful," Mutti always praised, her face glowing with pride as she came toward me. Taking my hand, she slowly led me across the room to the tree. When I was little, she picked me up so I could see the decorations at the top. "What do you think, Mohrle?" she whispered. I was always breathless. "It's just beautiful... so beautiful, Mutti," I murmured amazed. It was the same every year.

Mutti led me to a table from which gifts spilled to the floor. Someone offered a few appropriate words of gratitude while Stille Nacht, Heilige Nacht played in the background. The adults raised their champagne cocktails and we wished each other "Frohe Weihnachten." My glass had bubbly lemonade and a maraschino cherry in it.

The Christmas pageantry, created for me alone, was so convincing that I already had little breasts and was menstruating when Mutti found it necessary to tell me Christkind, Nikolaus, and the angels did not really exist.

AS I LOOK BACK AT MY CHILDHOOD, I try to find a moment in time or space when I could have felt, or would have wanted to feel any different about myself. The festive Christmas seasons were only part of the powerful experiences that seduced my soul and transformed my spirit into becoming a German child.

The Child in the Potato Box

In 1946 we bought Chalet Catalina, a recently finished, modest house that accommodated us perfectly. We were already living there on the day I accompanied Ruth and the maid to the busy smelly market. I was not yet six, but even blindfolded could have pointed to saddles, knives, and umbrellas and told you they were next to chili peppers, garlic, and tomatoes. Stands of sticky mangoes, over-ripe bananas, and honey-sweet pineapples were across from those where fried tacos, refried beans, and braised pork were being prepared. Many eyes followed me, and not because I was the only clean child in the place. People as dark as me were an uncommon sight in Guatemala City, and it was obvious by my demeanor and by the language I spoke with Ruth that I belonged to her.

I was born with an inherent dislike for dirt and disorder and that place had too much of both. The dirt that accompanied poverty, the vendor children who came too close for my liking; their sticky, unclean hands, their uncombed, dusty hair with pieces of dried grass in it, the limp rags they wore which, like their bodies, had not been washed in days, all disgusted me. We reached a grimier stand than most, where in a crumbling, moist, cardboard box, half filled with potatoes, a particularly filthy child cried desperately. He stretched out his pasty arms at everyone hoping someone might take pity and release him from the misery of his predicament. Body fluids oozed out of every orifice: the little nose was caked with mucus, saliva ran from the open screaming mouth, tears left a wet trail on the dusty child's face, and the contents of the rags hanging around his hips streamed down short toddler legs soaking the feet. I stood there, revolted by his shrieks and sickened at the sight of him. When Ruth saw my disgusted face, she simply took my hand and moved us on.

Once at home, I played in my sandbox until it was time to wash for lunch. I was called to table but wasn't hungry. No matter how much they tried to talk me into eating, I stubbornly refused. At her wits end, Mutti declared I should not be given food until dinner, which suited me just fine. But I soon forgot.

After my nap I went to the pantry looking for my crackers and milk. The maid reminded me that I was punished and sent me off for get permission to be given food. When I asked Mutti if I could have my snack, she told me to apologize for the scene at lunch.

"I hate that horrible ugly food! I'm never going to eat vegetables! I'm hungry now, and I want my Saltines with marmalade!" I reacted furiously.

Ruth walked by. "Dear me," she chimed in, "What is this? Where is our dear sweet Mohrle?" She came into the room with an expression of shock. "I must have left our Mohrle at the market!" she exclaimed. "This is the horrible child from the potato box!" With that, she made two big steps toward me and grabbed my hand. "I have to take this awful child back to the market and find our darling Mohrle," she said and began to drag me out of the room.

It took several seconds before I realized what was happening. In panic I shrieked: "No! No! I'm your Mohrle. It's me! I'm here!"

Ruth stopped, looked at me as the tears poured down my face. "Oh, I... don't... think... so..." she said slowly, "our Mohrle would never make such a spectacle; our Mohrle would apologize."

"Looook at meee!" I screeched, almost delirious. "You know it's me! Can't you see it's me? I'm sorry, I'm sorry," I sobbed.

An apology had been extracted and I was no longer in danger of being exchanged for the horrible child in the market. All was well again. I wiped away my tears and whimpered as I sat at the table in the pantry eating my crackers with butter and orange marmalade. Each time I swallowed, the lump in my throat threatened to choke me.

The episode remained in my memory as funny, because Mutti

and Ruth sometimes brought it up and we would laugh long and hard about it. Even though there was no malice intended and it was meant as a joke, I now understand how appalling and agonizing a shock it must have been to me as a young child, that the people closest to me and who I trusted most, could mistake me for someone else. My friends knew they could never be confused with a child in a filthy potato box at the crummy market. Without a single word, they recognized their genetic kinship with their parents and siblings.

I had no such reference.

Various Shades of Dark

I figure my birthmother, Rosa, was 21 or 22 at my birth and 9 or 10 years younger than Ruth. Agatha, Mutti's housekeeper in Livingston, was Rosa's godmother. It was customary then, and might perhaps still be so, that a well-situated godmother cares for her godchild. That's how Rosa came to live in the German household. She was, however, not employed by the family. Mutti, Vati, and Ruth knew her very well and liked her a lot. Above all, they admired her remarkable talent for languages. Just by listening to conversations of people around her, Rosa became comfortable speaking German and English in addition to her native Spanish.

According to Mutti, when Rosa found herself pregnant and unmarried, she assured Rosa that if the baby was a girl, she, Mutti, would raise the child. "See," Mutti would say to me smiling and pinching my cheek, "you wanted me to be your mother because you came out being a little girl."

"You would not have kept me if I'd been a boy?" I asked Mutti. How horrible... where would I be? Where the Black people lived! What a terrible thought! It's not that I had reason to worry. I just wondered...

"Now Mohrle, what would I have done with a little Black boy?" Mutti said raising her eyebrows and shaking her head. And so, without another word, it was absolutely clear in my child's mind that something was seriously wrong with Black boys. In my evening prayers I made sure to add a silent one thanking God for giving me a vagina.

After telling me stories of how I arrived in her life, I also heard that the carpenter made a crib of shiny rosewood as a gift for me. The sheets covering the mattress were made of imported white linen with white lilies embroidered around the edges. The little crib was placed next to Mutti's bed, so she would be first by my side if I cried during the night. Thus, I had to understand that I was in every way Mutti's child.

On one occasion, my birthmother Rosa took me to the village to show me to her friends. Whatever some well-meaning woman gave me to eat or drink made me sick, and I was burning up with fever by the time we returned home in the evening. "When I saw you," Mutti said with an alarmed expression, "I quickly wrapped you in ice-cold towels to bring the temperature down. Had I not done that, Mohrle, you would have died." A pained look clouded her eyes as she recalled the scary night. That was probably the last time anyone in the village laid eyes on me.

I CAN'T RECALL EVER SAYING "mother" to Rosa. She was plain Rosa, someone who would ruin my day each time she showed up. I don't remember ever having a conversation with her and can't recall anything she said to me, or to anyone else for that matter. I was Mutti's child, and the dark woman with the sad black eyes filled me with profound fear. I had only one picture of her. In it we are playing with water in an enameled pan. She's laughing, but she's looking down at me, so one can't see the features of her face. I'm surprised I never tore it up. I probably looked like her, and I dreaded the thought that she might intend to snatch me and take me to the place where she and all the other Black people lived. I probably even looked like all of them and no one would have known I was different. The thought gave me goose bumps and chills ran down my spine. I made sure I stayed at least three arm's length away from her so I could outrun her if she tried to grab me. Although she never did anything to justify such a feeling of mistrust, I lived with a certain degree of apprehension when I saw the woman who had brought me into this world. It upset me that she was Black and powerless: I didn't want to belong to her. If she had a child, I didn't want to be it. She depressed me. Why did she come? Ohhh! Why did she come to see me?

Why had she always come? Why would she visit, even when she knew I preferred not to see her? Why was there always tension when she was around? Was it only I who became apprehensive at her presence, or did she also affect Mutti and Ruth? I was so embarrassed and ashamed at having her as a mother that it never occurred to me to see whether she made others uncomfortable, too. She must have. She did. I can feel it in my gut: she did... I can feel her heart speaking volumes each time it beat, and that she'd have screamed had she not remained silent.

GIL WAS MY BIRTH FATHER'S NAME. I think he came by when I was four or five, but I don't remember him. He was one of several children the American Honorary Consul for the area had with a village woman. Gil's father was White and had lived in the tropics all his life. Mutti said his face was always as red as a boiled lobster under his broad-rimmed Panama hat. She called him Old Man Reed. I don't know why, but I gathered Mutti thought less of him and not necessarily because he didn't have a lovely tan like Vati's.

That's what I knew about my genetic parents from hearsay and experience.

SOMETIMES BLACK MEN CAME FROM THE COAST to visit. I also kept my distance from them. They invariably brought live shrimp and lobsters, and fresh fish frozen in a block of ice: special delicacies for the cook to prepare. We sat on the verandah drinking ice-cold lemonade with sprigs of mint leaves, listened to how much life in Livingston had changed and how everyone missed don Pablo and the secure existence he had provided. I only remember one of those men by name, Chico Blanco, for I associated the wiry man with colors: his skin was dark brown, his eyes were green like Prell shampoo, and his name was white.

When I sat at the dinner table to enjoy the heavenly gifts from the sea, I flat out failed to associate the delicious meal with those who had brought it. What was a delicacy for us, I realized later, the Black people on the coast enjoyed regularly.

Power and Ownership

My apprehensions did not go unnoticed, so Mutti found it necessary to appease my fears by telling me that as soon as we had settled in the city she requested an audience with the President. I was probably three when I heard the story for the first time.

"I wanted to make sure he knew you are my child," Mutti said, and showed me the dark blue dress with white pinstripes and the blue and white pumps she wore for the occasion. She recounted her nervous walk up the steps of the presidential palace and how two soldiers of the guard accompanied her through one wood-paneled salon after another until, at the end of a long dark hall, she was asked to wait in front of a massive door while her arrival was announced to the President of the republic. Once inside the governing chambers, she implored him by saying that if he had intentions of also deporting German women and children, he allow her to keep little Mohrle: "I've been her mother from the day she was born, and I won't survive the separation," she said to him. Then, in an imposing, deep voice he answered, "Gentil señora, Doña Esther, usted no se preocupe" (don't you worry about a thing). Mutti would look at me and conclude slowly and in a calm voice: "He is a sensible man, Mohrle. He knows that with me you have a better home than with anyone else in the world. The main thing," Mutti impressed upon me, "is that we will never be separated. You will see, my little darling," she concluded embracing me and chirping lightheartedly like a morning bird, "he will keep his word. You are my child forever."

The highest word in the land had decreed I was forever Mutti's child and she had every right to keep me. No one was allowed to separate me from her. No Black people, no political situation. If Mutti and Ruth had to join Vati in the imprisonment camp, I would go with them. It was a powerful story that, as she repeated it through the years, never changed.

A Little Girl Dreaming

"Really?" was Mutti's answer when I told her at breakfast that I had seen my husband. "Well, what was he like?" She asked, not very interested in my exciting dream. After all I was only six or seven years old.

"He has brown hair, very pretty thick eyebrows, and his eyes are light green. He is very, very good looking, and he makes me laugh," my face glowed as I recalled the handsome apparition.

"Oh, is he kind and loving, too?" came a perfunctory response as she placed a dollop of marmalade on her buttered roll.

"He loves me as much as Vati loves you," I beamed, "and he is very kind, and very funny. We go for walks and throw stones into puddles. And he sings silly songs so I laugh. We like to laugh and laugh."

Mutti smiled. "That's just wonderful, Mohrle! He sounds like a very nice, friendly husband. How old is he?"

"Oh, he's much, much older than me. Probably 16," I figured after some reflection.

Every time variations of the dream recurred I spent the day swooning and telling everyone in the house I'd again seen my beautiful husband.

At some point after one of the apparitions, Mutti felt she had to bring some reality into the situation. "Mohrle," she took one of my hands, "he may be handsome and funny and generous and all the wonderful things you see in your dreams, but real men aren't that perfect, child. How about painting him on the wall? You go ahead and paint him on the wall, that way he will always stay as lovely as he is in your dreams."

How could I ever do his beauty justice? That was silly. I

didn't paint him on the wall. What I did, was not talk about him anymore. But I could not interfere with the phantom's nocturnal visits, which lasted years and ended in early adolescence.

Body and Soul: Philosophy

Once in Catalina, we became neighbors with a German family whose three daughters were close to me in age. Putzi, the youngest, wandered over to our house most often. We giggled and laughed, shared secrets and got into all sorts of mischief, and became inseparable. When one was punished the other also suffered the consequences. In a family of Hanseatic blondes, my friend was the fairest. Her features seemed chiseled in alabaster; her hair, thin and shiny like finest silk, was cut in a pageboy. When she laughed, light, caught like ripples on water, sparkled in her pale blue eyes.

It must have been a special day when Ruth bought me a Brownie camera that took black and white photographs. She showed me how it worked and then took pictures of Putzi and me. A week later, we saw the photographs. They came in a double-sided envelope with the positives in one side and the negatives in the other. In the positive images, as in reality, I was dark and my friend light. We discovered, however, much to our amazement, that in the negatives, I was light, and she dark.

"Maybe, the camera captures a picture of our soul," Putzi whispered mysteriously cupping a hand to my ear. "Maybe white people in reality are devils and dark people angels," she added and we curled up giggling. Just then Marta walked by with the freshly ironed laundry.

"I wonder how she looks in a negative," I whispered to Putzi. We looked for Ruth and finding her, asked her to capture our faces with caramel-colored Marta. On seeing the negatives, Putzi decided that Indians were saints in purgatory because their jet-black hair glowed like a halo invisible to regular eyes.

Such was the nature of our observations and our early

philosophical conclusions regarding skin color, angels, and purgatory.

Mischief in the Kitchen with Vati

Early one Sunday morning - it was so early, not even the maids were up - I heard my father's uneven step go by my room. I sat up to listen and heard sounds coming from the pantry.

I got out of bed and tiptoed out to see what was going on. Sure enough, Vati was in the kitchen, and he was wearing his faded red and gray plaid don't-mess-with-me-today shirt. I stood in the shadows and watched him close the refrigerator door and wobble to the counter with something wrapped in white paper. Then he noticed me.

"Ah, Mohrle," he whispered, greeting me cheerfully. "I'm going to make the best Sunday breakfast there is, and I invite you to be my guest."

"Why are you up so early?" I asked softly. "It's still dark outside."

"I am the only one who can prepare this," he winked at me and grinned sheepishly. "We'll have finished cooking and eating by the time the others even realize we were here." Then he opened the package and displayed the delicacy: an oily, golden fish. "Smoked herring! Imported smoked kippers: the best I've seen in a long time." Vati explained proudly. "Can you scramble eggs?" he asked me, almost as an afterthought.

"I can beat eggs really well," I said quickly, eager to be recruited.

"Good. Go find six and beat them up in something. And add a little milk and pepper, no salt," he instructed. "When the fish is fried to a crisp, we'll pour the eggs over it and let the whole thing set. Then," his deep blue eyes sparkled with anticipation, "it will be ready to eat." Without another word, he turned, picked up the knife and sharpener and crisscrossed the instruments in rhythm, like a magician. Carefully, he pared the leathery, golden skin off the fish.

As his accomplice, I also found the big frying pan and showed him where the oval serving platter and the dishes were kept. Then I set the dining room table for two, with fish forks and knives, as he directed.

"We need brown bread for this, do you know where they keep it?" He asked. I did, and also took it to the table.

The fried kippers and scrambled eggs melded in my mouth as the most delicious food I had ever tasted in my life, and I knew for sure that my father was absolutely the best cook in the world. He washed his fish down with a beer and a shooter of schnapps. I had ginger ale. It was not even five-thirty and we had eaten every last crumb of the best imaginable breakfast. I looked at my father's pleased face and somewhere in my young mind understood that the smell and taste of this Nordic dish had returned him to the winters of his youth, in that far away, gray, cold Hamburg.

Mutti heard an earful from the maids, of course; they had to clean up the oily kitchen and live in the smell of stale fried fish for days. Everyone had enough to say, and Vati wore his don't-mess-with-me-today shirt until the odor had left the house and the comments behind his back ended.

School and Scholarship

In addition to doing the necessary sewing for the household Zoilita, our seamstress, was also my first academic teacher. Sometimes in the afternoons she had me practice drawing straight and curved lines in calligraphy notebooks. Under her tutelage I learned how to read and write in Spanish. Zoilita also taught me arithmetic, so by the time I entered first grade at six, I was ready to engage in advanced class work.

My German friends went to a school that was immediately behind Catalina. It would have been logical for me to join them, but I had to walk eight blocks to a different school because the director, a haughty woman named Reyes Guerra, had in fact refused to accept me. "We can't have your negrita here; we have to keep our standards." I heard Mutti tell Vati and Ruth what had been said, and they were furious with the ignorant woman. I stood in the shadows, pale with shame and deeply humiliated that my mother had been treated with such disrespect because I was Black. I tiptoed to my room, and sat at my desk and cried a little bit. My young heart ached, lonely and forlorn, in a world where no one knew about or could have anticipated the hurt. Deeply embarrassed to talk to anyone about what I overheard, I resolved never to greet Reyes Guerra.

Had Rosa or my father Gil been around, and had I trusted them with my secret, I would probably have received a healthy perspective on prejudice and racism. I would have understood that it had only been Mutti's ego that got a dent, and that she was resilient.

Fortunately for me, I was accepted in a fine school run by German Jews, and received the very best elementary education a child could access in the Guatemala of the 40's and 50's.

On my first day of school, Ruth neatly combed my hair and arranged it into four braids as usual. Zoilita had made a light blue dress with puffy sleeves and a sash that tied into a bow in the back. Over it I wore the blue sweater with mother of pearl buttons Mutti had knit for me. Mutti held my hand as we walked several blocks over a sweet-smelling carpet of mauve jacaranda petals that covered the sidewalks.

The school, a wooden two-story building with many windows, sat in the middle of a large block. As soon as we entered the grounds, Miss Lehnsen came out of the building to greet us. She shook my hand and said to Mutti that it was a particularly special day for her and brother, the director. They were honored to have Catana in their school. We were all smiling. Then Mutti kissed me good-bye, and Miss Lehnsen took my hand and accompanied me to my classroom.

The Lehnsens had fled Hitler's Germany and had many Jewish children in the school. When Mutti talked to them about enrolling me, they were overjoyed. Accepting me could be seen as a gesture they bore no ill feelings toward the Guatemalan German community. I was, and yet was not, a German child. Being a German child was a distinction I particularly cherished.

My grades were excellent throughout, and I burst with pride at report card time when, during cocktails and before dinner, the remarkable grades and the teacher's positive comments were discussed in detail. One day, early in third grade, I heard Mutti say that such consistent excellence should be rewarded with a scholarship. She told me it would be an honor and I gathered that she really wanted me to receive the distinction. Soon enough I ended up horrified at discovering that students with scholarships went to school for less, sometimes no money. I related that to poverty and certainly did not want the association. Poor people had dark skin. It was a feature of mine I resented. I didn't want anyone to think I belonged to the poor as well. And so: my grades began to slip. Eventually I was so successful at being a mediocre student that I was in serious peril of having to repeat fourth grade. A little more effort in my work, and the grades improved and I passed easily. It was no big deal for me, but a great relief for Mutti, who never found out what had caused the academic deterioration.

As all children, I interacted with society according to my parent's social standing, and I figured that in order to be as White as my German friends I had to be mediocre, as I sometimes heard they were. It became etched in my psyche that White people excelled by being and connections, not by effort, certainly not knowledge. I had heard that this one or the other one was not particularly smart. From what I saw, this one or the other one was living in a nice house, had servants, drove a car. Those of whom I'd heard comments regarding superior intelligence were maids or gardeners. Yet they had nothing but long hours of tiring work to show for it. By the time I was 8 at most, it was clear to me that only dark people had to work hard, and in spite of that they would never achieve the social rank commensurate with the effort they expended. Neither their loyalty to the boss nor the integrity of their work, nor the keen knowledge in their field ever mattered: they were inferior because of their color. They were not paid more for their expertise and they could never leave the conditions into which they had been born.

I had to become White in every aspect. I saw myself as belonging fully to the privileged social class in which I was growing up. Being White became part of my fabric; as long as I was German I'd have everything I needed flowing to me from invisible channels, forever.

No scholarship for me, my parents had to pay for my education.

Injury

Europe had been at war. Germany was burning, or had been. I was too young to understand the dimensions of the devastation and too removed to be affected by it. But the war had separated Ruth from her love, a man named Rudolf, who was stuck overseas and couldn't return to Guatemala to marry her. Until he actually came back in 1950, my evening prayers ended, "Please, dear God, let Mama's novio come back." He was the 'novio,' the fiancé. Twice a month I saw Ruth in the pantry lovingly prepare a "care package" she would send to him. I knew him only in imaginary terms. However, if I ever had a wish, from the time I knew what wishing was about until his arrival when I was ten, it was always: "Please have Mama's novio return." At night, hoping to catch a falling star, I'd stretch out of my window to scan the sky above the somber silhouettes of the cypress trees, or when the setting sun fired the sky in bright magenta, I knew where to find a barely visible silvery Venus: seeing the evening star and casting one's desires on it would surely make them come true. Or, when driving with Ruth from the suburbs to the city, a train might be crossing over the bridge on seventh avenue just as our car drove under it and Ruth would say: "Quick, make a wish!" And I'd shut my eyes real tight and in my mind formulate my only request. I never wanted anything for myself or for anyone else. I loved Ruth so dearly that her innermost longing also became mine.

According to Mutti, Vati had once already derailed Ruth's

intentions to marry Rudolph, and the war had been on his side, for it caused a ten-year interruption in the lover's lives. No one could tell what was worse for Ruth: Vati's dislike for the man she loved, or the disruption the war brought by keeping them apart.

It was a Thursday in 1950. I know that detail because the maids have Thursday afternoons off, so that only Vati, Mutti and I were in the house. I was in the hall going toward my room, chewing the first bite I'd taken out of an apple, when Vati's voice exploded like a sonic boom that caused Catalina's thick walls to tremble. Oh, my God! My heart almost stopped beating. I could hardly breathe and my hands broke out in sweat. What was he saying? It was a loud guttural roar; the words made no sense. It was all horrible gibberish! Once in a while I heard Mutti's voice coming through the ruckus, and for the first time in my life I feared for her wellbeing. It was all so loud and scary that I couldn't think, much less act. I quickly slipped into my room and threw myself on the bed, holding on to the apple for dear life and feeling sick to my stomach. That's how Mutti found me.

"Mohrle, it's not so bad. Vati's just having a fit," she said helping me to sit up. Tears of fear and confusion welled up in my eyes. I felt alone and forsaken even though Mutti was next to me. And she was next to me smiling as if nothing was going on! She hugged me again and held me close. Still grinning broadly, she handed me a piece of paper. My hands trembled as I took it, while two fat tears plopped on my lap. I was too distraught to understand that the telegram was signed "Los recién casados" (the newlyweds).

"Mohrle," Mutti continued cheerfully, "don't you see? Ruth and Rudolf have married. Rudolf got off the ship in El Salvador and Ruth went there to meet him. It was a big secret, and now they're already husband and wife!"

"I thought that was good," I stammered, nauseated at the news and totally confused by the situation. Here Mutti was sitting next to me, acting as if the world were colored baby pink and smelled of roses, and there was Vati in his room, bellowing like a deranged Orangutan.

"Of course it's good news," Mutti said sealing her words with another hug. "Vati's having a fit just for the sake of having a fit."

With a graceful wave of her hand she dismissed his tantrum. "Please don't cry any more little one, everything is fine. We should be happy for Ruth; she's missed Rudolf for many, many years."

Vati would quiet down, and I sighed with relief that it was over, but he was only catching his breath to take up hollering again. My tears dried, but my heart ached and it hurt to breathe. I hoped Marta might have returned early, but there was no one in the back of the house. Where was Ruth when I needed her? She was with Rudolf... and a foreboding feeling seeped into me as I knew Ruth would never be the same again.

Preparations for a small reception were soon underway. Vati got over his fit and began to act with more civility. He was in charge of the beverages and to include me in the celebration, bought two small bottles of my favorite grape-flavored soda. Hors d'oeuvres were prepared, champagne cocktails would abound for friends who were expected to come by and welcome the new couple. The late morning arrival was accompanied by great overall excitement in Catalina.

I was the only child among the welcoming group at the airport. I wore my prettiest cream-colored dress, and my hair was neat with silver clasps holding my braids, as always. Ruth was all smiles and hugged and kissed me and said I looked as perfect as a pearl in an oyster. Rudolph? Never as much as looked at me. Not once, during the entire time. I had not taken my eyes off him and knew that he had not as much as thrown a glance in my direction. By the time we arrived in Catalina, I had accepted his dismissal as rejection and was deeply disappointed.

Everyone settled in the living room. Vati served cocktails and the maids, in pink and white uniforms, went from person to person, offering hors d'oeuvres. I chose to sit on a stool removed from the commotion and chatter. As a matter of courtesy, Marta asked me what I'd like to drink. No one was paying any attention to me, whatsoever. I answered in a low voice, "A Grapette, please."

The man who had ignored my presence, who in the past two and a half hours had not as much as glanced at me, threw me a cursory, split-second look and, instantly dismissing me, said, "So you, too, drink that kind of dirt."

All blood drained from my body; I turned to stone, or so it felt. I was injured beyond words. His comment was the single most shocking affront I had ever experienced. Never had anyone made me feel so humiliated. I had suspected it, but now I knew why he had so blatantly ignored my presence: I belonged to the people one doesn't see, and I had proven him right for I had asked for a colorful, sweet drink, something Europeans would not have ordered. My taste had betrayed who I was: a child of "those brown or Black" people who guzzle beverages that are too sweet, too orange, too pink, too purple. How tasteless of me!

The wound had been inflicted, and I began to hate him with every fiber in my body. He had taken my Mama, had used up all my innermost desires and wishes, and then he rejected me. And he did so because I was Black. All my shooting stars had culminated into a single monumental, painful disappointment. I was left with nothing more to wish for, so I stopped wishing, sadly aware that innermost desires can, when granted, turn into unbearable heartache. Rudolf was the first European individual who had, palpably and to my face, made me feel inferior. I never forgave him. I began to see him as an arrogant pathetic fortune hunter. In that, I must have agreed with Vati. I understood with a child's visceral senses that, although Mutti acted as if she were happy, she was only relieved that Ruth was finally no longer single. Rudolph had a fine education and knowledge of business, and instead of staying in Europe and re-building that part of the world where he belonged, he figured correctly that he could move ahead faster in an underdeveloped country where his White skin placed him in an advantaged position. After one night (or was it two?) Vati had enough and kicked him out. I remember looking out the window and seeing him walk away, suitcase in hand, toward the gate en route to the bus stop. As long as Vati lived, Rudolf never slept in Catalina again. He found employment with acquaintances in Retalhuleu, and soon he and Ruth moved there. My Mama embarked on her married life in another town and my world, as I had known it, had indeed come to an end.

Bigger Changes Were in Store

Five days before my eleventh birthday I left for school in the morning, as usual. Mutti and Vati were in Cobán visiting friends, so I thought nothing of it when Tante Annemarie picked me up at school in the afternoon. I would spend the rest of the day with her children, she said, and if I wanted I could stay for dinner. Dinner at her house meant Spaetzle. I loved Spaetzle. As my parents were not Swabian like Tante Annemarie, the dish was never prepared in our home. I spent hours laughing, chasing and being chased, hiding and seeking in and out of closets, in and out of the house.

It was dark when I saw our Ford pull up. Someone opened the back door and I got in, and that someone told me, as the car was driving home, that Vati had died during the previous night. I don't remember who drove. But someone sitting in the back with me, probably Ruth, told me. I must have stopped breathing, and it must have felt as if my heart should stop beating. But I didn't cry; I showed no emotion. That much I remember.

The house was somber when I entered. I had seen houses where someone had died. They were filled with flowers and wreaths and more flowers. But all the flowers in Catalina had already followed the coffin, and only the maids were still wearing black. Mutti would later tell me that, shortly after going to bed on that fateful night, Vati called out for her, and when she reached him he only had time to whisper, "I love you, Esther" before inhaling for the last time. The end comes swiftly when the aorta ruptures, and it all seems more abrupt in the tropics where burial must occur within twenty-four hours of death.

I don't know if I wept for Vati then. I guess I must have when I was alone and no one could see me; when I realized I would never see him again, never hold his hand and go for walks with him again. Things went on in the family as if nothing had happened. My birthday party was canceled, of course, and I have never celebrated my birthday since.

Vati was loving and patient with me. Although he suffered from vicious mood swings, his foul mood was never directed at me or at my friends. I miss him to this very day and have always compared every man I've fallen in love with to him. Was he as charming? Was he as powerful? Could his voice make people tremble; could his word and a single look demand instant attention and be enough to have things done at once? But above all: would he love me as much as Vati had loved Mutti? Vati was splendid in every way. I loved that father. I was his Mohrle in the dearest, gentlest way one can be someone's beloved child.

As fate would have had it, Vati's death came a few months after the marriage. He had hated Rudolf with every fiber of his being, and Mutti likewise never stopped mistrusting the man to the very end. I had to bury my hurt and my hatchet and accept the grumpy man who had entered my life. In time, however, I recognized that someone I had deeply despised was probably not that bad a person after all. We managed to establish a cordial, though somewhat distant relationship. What delighted me most about Rudolf was the brilliantly striking wit he sometimes coupled with a naughty sense of humor. He twisted his mouth into a crooked grin and his grey eyes had a wicked sparkle when he laughed. It wasn't often that I did, but he liked to see me "get" his jokes.

Vati knew I had two secrets. First, that I wanted to have a Bible; and second, that I was enamored with Humperdinck's opera Hansel and Gretel after seeing it being performed in Guatemala. On the Christmas after his death, among my presents in that festive room aglow with candlelight lay, unwrapped, a white leather-bound gold leaf Bible and, hidden under a pile of gifts was the complete recording of Humperdinck's opera. I was told Vati had ordered them for me in the States before his death, and Vati's saintliness became even more cemented in my love for him. Many, too many years later, I learned by chance that it was Rudolf who had ordered the Bible and the opera for me.

Rudolf began to shape my early intellectual tastes by generously exposing me to what nourished his own spirit: German literature, music, and art. Sometimes when I caught him coming through the garden toward the house, I could tell by the bounce in his gait that a book he had ordered for me at the bookstore had arrived.

I lived in a colorful, sensuous world, where volcanoes are chiseled into a cobalt blue horizon and purple orchids, striped bromeliads, and gigantic ferns abound. Cozy in my bright world, I devoured tales of cloudy marshland skies where shrouded ghosts swept through layers of fog on clammy northern dikes. Rudolf nourished my soul as it longed for the elegiac tones and shades of a deeply European nostalgia.

My Family in the Pfalz

I was passing by Vati's room one afternoon; we still called it Vati's room although he had died over a year ago. Two upholstered chairs and a small round table with a reading lamp took the corner space where his bed had been. Mutti was sitting at the massive mahogany desk that remained as it had, facing the garden. "What do you think of this poem Mohrle?" I heard her call to me. I entered the room and took the paper from her hand. The date on the top left corner read October 1952. She was sixty-four then, I twelve.

"It's beautiful Mutti, honestly," I said after reading the words, and felt she must have been a little sad, for her writing conveyed a deep nostalgia for the hills, valleys, and chatty brooks of the Pfalz, the countryside of her youth. "I didn't know you wrote poems," I said pulling a chair over to sit next to her desk. "Please tell me again about the Pfalz. Tell me again about Germany," I begged. And so began another of those afternoons when my mother offered me glimpses of her youth.

"The Pfalz, long ago Mohrle," she smiled mildly, "was part of the Holy Roman Empire."

"Roman? Like Julius Caesar, Roman?"

"Yes," and I could tell her sadness was gone. "The Romans made themselves comfortable on the banks of the Rhine and began to cultivate grapes. Those people loved their wine," she raised her hand like taking an imaginary sip. I had seen pictures in the National Geographic of terraced land along the Rhine.

In melodic mellow tones, Mutti brought back the beauty of the fields and streams where she had wandered in her youth; and I learned about geography and history, about the Romanesque, Gothic, and Baroque cathedrals and castles that dotted the landscape. As Mutti talked about princes, electors, and archdukes, my mind filled the spaces with pictures of armor-clad knights singing to golden-haired princesses in towers, like in the drawings of Andersen's fairy tales. "When you finish high school I'll take you to my beloved Pfalz, and we'll stroll over the cobblestoned streets and you can run in the fields and skip on pebbles in the chatty brooks as I did," she promised. And so, the Pfalz became more and more a part of me. So much so that I never questioned it could not be, not even in the farthest recesses of my mind.

Most people spoke French and German because the Pfalz was a buffer state between France and the German principalities. "The simpler people made up pretentious words. For instance," Mutti laughed at the recollection, "regular soap is 'Seife,' as you know, but when the soap came from France, the simpletons called it 'savon-seif' – soap-soap," and she contorted her face to make it look really boorish. We burst out laughing, and together chanted "Saffon-seif, saffon-seif!" and I squinched my face like she did, and we continued to laugh and laugh.

What I loved most were her colorful descriptions of the food; the clear white wine she said was "the nectar of gods and a gift to the educated palate." Liverwursts and bratwursts seasoned with aromatic herbs were served on a bed of Sauerkraut that had been cured in champagne and sweetened with apples and grapes; and the crusty, grainy dark bread with a slab of fresh butter must have been divine, because Mutti had not given up trying to get the maids to replicate it.

I wanted so much to be a little like Mutti, or at least a little like the people in the Pfalz. I knew the answer, so did not ask why my nose was small when she said the Pfaelzer, like the French and the Italians, have large noses. Mutti's eyes were not Nordic blue like Vati's but hazel, and before years left silver strands, her hair was chestnut with auburn highlights. Ruth was also a brunette, had a large nose, and chocolate-colored eyes. They all looked alike: Tante Gustl, who was four years older than Mutti, and Tante Lisl, who was two years her senior. The former lived in Güntherstal, deep in the Black Forest, the latter in Saarbrücken on the border with France. Sight unseen, I loved everyone in that family and I dreamed of meeting my aunts and uncles, my many cousins and everybody else I was hearing about.

"Little Mohrle," Mutti continued, becoming pensive and perhaps wondering whether what she was about to share was appropriate considering my young age. "Things weren't easy when I was young. Not that life is ever meant to be uncomplicated, I guess," she mused looking into the distance. "But in those days, when diseases that today are cured without a problem... Well, then, in those years, people just died." She shrugged and slowly shook her head. "My father died when I was six, so I don't remember him at all. When Gustl caught typhoid fever in an epidemic, our mother never left her side and exhausted herself nursing her. I heard people say that she withered away caring for her beautiful daughter. Gustl was very beautiful, indeed... I was twelve when the angels carried my mother away," Mutti whispered. I saw her sadness and remember thinking it amazing that one could still grieve for someone who had died ever so long ago. "They buried her under an oak tree on a hill overlooking the vineyards. Everyday I walked the miles to her grave and after praying Our Father Who art in Heaven, I lay down on the grass and wept until I fell asleep." The tears that had gathered in my eyes ran slowly down my cheeks. "Don't cry, little one," Mutti said, wiping my face with her hand. I placed my arms around her neck and sobbed anyway. The idea of a lonely little orphan weeping for hours on her mother's grave became ingrained in my soul as the single most mournful image.

At seventeen, Mutti set sail for New York in the hope of studying medicine. Instead, she married the ship's captain and soon found herself pregnant. Although she must have known how the baby got inside her, she knew little else. She was alone in the apartment at the time of her delivery and during a long, desperate night gave birth. She dragged herself on the floor to the dresser looking for scissors to cut the umbilical cord. When the contracted midwife made her rounds in the morning, she found Mutti near death, holding a dead baby boy in her arms. I distinctly remember the words of her straightforward, distant and matter of fact report. The concept of a despondent and lonely young woman losing the life she had carried beneath her heart for months filled me with another wave of unspeakable grief. And so, Mutti's sadness and anguish also became mine.

After that misfortune, she was relocated to Hamburg where, under the care and attention of her in-laws, she had a little girl and named her Ruth.

"Can you believe what a terrible mother I was," Mutti joked as she tried to lighten my gloomy mood. "Ruth only wore trousers until she was six and had to go to school!"

"Why didn't she wear dresses? I wear them."

"At the time pants for girls were unheard of," Mutti chuckled mischievously. "And aren't pants more practical for all children?" She nodded. "They can move around better in them, right?"

"You probably wanted her to be a boy," I said with the seriousness of one who knows so much.

"I probably did," she chuckled indifferently.

"What happened to Ruth's father?"

"I left him."

"You left him? Just like that? Left him? Why?"

"I missed him terribly, of course; and he was a dear, honest man. But he was always at sea, Mohrle, and I was lonely. I didn't like those judgmental Hamburgers. Then I met Vati, who fell madly in love with me. I just couldn't help myself falling in love with him."

"And I bet Vati was handsomer, too," I added.

"Oh yes. His magnetic blue eyes made me weak in the knees," she giggled like a girl, "and his colorful stories of the tropics and the jungle... well, they were enough to unsettle the most virtuous heart." Then Mutti laughed out loud at her own funny words.

"I, too, would have left anybody for Vati, just as you did," I leaned over and whispered in her ear.

Like an oasis in the desert that attracts all water within its reach, I thirsted for Mutti's stories. With each one, I became more and more her child; her family was my family, her history my history. I had ancestry that dated all the way back to Julius Caesar; I had a family in Germany; I had aunts, uncles, cousins. In my subconscious I knew better, but I adopted them all as my own and they became an integral part of the framework that offered me security. The contentment of belonging to such a fine group of people and having such a wonderful history left no room to squeeze a serious thought about my own background. I didn't think to ask about Rosa and her community; I wanted only to know about Mutti's world.

Adolescence: A Rollercoaster Ride

Geez, my eyes almost popped out of their sockets. I quickly took off my panties and I put them to my nose to take a whiff of the mysterious dark smear that had showed up from nowhere. Thank heavens it's not poop, I thought. That would have been a shock. But what is it? I called Mutti and handed her my underwear; she then called Ruth. Together they examined the stain and concluded right there in the bathroom that "it's got to be it." Ruth produced a belt, pads, and proceeded to explain how to fasten the contraption. And so, at eleven, I learned that no woman in the world, "not even the Queen of England," was spared a situation that would continue for a few days and recur with regularity every month. "You might as well refer to it as your 'happy days,' or 'the curse.' Time will tell," they added, referring to the appropriateness of the term. And so, my 'happy days' would not be addressed again for a decade. The mysteries of creation, conception, and birth remained well outside my earshot. Issues about sex and making love never figured among my youthful reveries, because I never saw, not between Vati and Mutti, or Ruth and Rudolf, a charged erotic look that could have made me blush at accidentally witnessing it.

Perhaps it was because they were so much older, that I did

not notice how Mutti and Ruth actually had the attributes of sensuous women. Neither left her room in the morning without first placing a dab of perfume behind her ears. They had talcum powder, cologne, and perfume in delicate scents that were as distinct as their signature. The toiletries held in crystal vials and silver boxes on Mutti's dresser, caught the morning sun, projecting rainbows on the walls filling her bedroom with enchantment. They did not wear the bright colors of flowers or floral prints, and favored the shades of the earth and the blues of the sky and the sea. Lace, chiffon, and shantung were not for them; they wore linen, cotton, and silk.

Vati was no more; Ruth had moved away, so Mutti and I rearranged our spaces in Catalina. My bedroom became a small living room, a salita of sorts where Mutti could sit and visit with a friend or two who might drop by for cocktails before dinner. I graduated into Ruth's room, with its minimalist built-in furniture and Scandinavian aesthetic. The years at Lehnsen School were over and I entered the preppy American School. Ruth, much to everyone's delight, became pregnant at age 42. I was twelve in the fall of 1952 when Thomas, the first of two sons, was born. A year and a half later, Andreas joined the family.

Ruth was beside herself with joy that so late in life she had been gifted with her own children, and anything that made her happy made me happy, too. Was I jealous, I wonder? Just a little bit? No, certainly not consciously. As we were both Mutti's daughters and I no longer referred to Ruth as my Mama but as "my sister Ruth," I became an aunt of sorts to her children.

It was in those years, curiously enough - although as far as I was concerned they did not count - that I also became an older sister. Rosa gave birth to two little girls. I only remember seeing them when they were six and eight years old. The good thing about Rosa having her new children was that her tedious visits became less frequent. But she still showed up, still too often for my liking, and seeing her still disturbed me... with ever-greater intensity.

The American School was more like an exclusive club than a school. I entered the English language section, which I considered a mark of distinction. It underlined what I already knew: that language defined people. I was the only Black kid in the school, and one of a handful of students with a strong command of three languages. I easily made new friends with mainstream White children whose parents worked in the US diplomatic corps. My nickname, Mohrle, lasted less than a week. A girl named Anne asked me why, if my name was Catana, everyone said Molly to me. "It means 'darkie' in German," I explained innocently, whereupon all Americans called me by my formal name, finalizing the transition to Catana.

As an unencumbered "American" I joined the Girl Scouts which meant camping by the shores of lakes, sleeping in the shadow of volcanoes, and singing "America the Beautiful" and "She'll be Coming Around the Mountain" by the flickering light of campfires. We roasted Hamburgers that had nothing to do with Hamburg. The ground meat was not seasoned like ours in Catalina when Frikadellen or Swedish meatballs were made, and the sausages were quite different and eaten in a bun with an array of condiments referred to as 'the works'; marshmallows roasted on a stick over the fire became a favorite delicacy. Halloween meant costume parties and bobbing for apples; on Valentine's Day, I sent and received "I love you" notes from everyone in class; on St. Patrick's Day I painted green clovers on my glasses; and Thanksgiving in November, I came to understand, was a sacrosanct American feast that highlighted roast turkey and cranberry sauce.

I also enjoyed being in the kitchen on Sundays when the maids were out and I could try my hand at making pastries. On one occasion I decided to share my chocolate fudge with the class. Lo and behold, the very cute blue-eyed Mike, on whom I had developed a serious crush - he happened to look like the husband of my dreams - moved closer to me and helped himself to a piece of fudge. "This is really great," he said smiling shyly at me, "thank you." That did it. Henceforth my little basket with a red and white plaid napkin held my Monday morning culinary bait.

"I love you lots, I love you mighty," Mike wrote at the end of the year in my album, "I wish my pajamas were next to your nighty. Now don't get excited, now don't get red, I meant on the clothesline and not in the bed." Proving once again that love indeed goes through the stomach.

"Don't be offended," he said apologetically, "but I do love your fudge." I couldn't answer and must have blushed all shades of crimson, if I could have. Mike spoke to me! But by the start of the next school year Mike's family had returned to the States.

From the way I was accepted and received in their homes, I would never, ever have believed - had anyone told me - that my American friends came from, and would soon return to a society of angry segregation and bitter racial intolerance.

In 1954 Shakespeare's Julius Caesar was chosen for our literature class. The previous year the film was released in the States and would eventually make its way to Guatemala. I had not seen more than five or six films in my life, none of which were memorable. But Louis Calhern, the well-known Hollywood character actor, played Julius Caesar. He was Mutti's cousin once removed. Mutti sat next to me in the theatre as the actors spun their magic and changed my life. I saw her cousin but fell in love with James Mason as Brutus. The play became the watershed. Pre-Caesar I was a child, post-Caesar, well, a teenager enamored with a movie star and harboring serious theatrical ambitions.

Mutti could forget further efforts to get me to improve my grades so I could study medicine. I was on the way to becoming an actress, a famous one, at that. From one day to the next I became a loud teenager who raced home after school, and from the roof of the house - much to the chagrin of neighbors and to the amusement of passers-by - delivered by memory and imitation, in the loudest cracking voice, Brutus' and Mark Anthony's speeches to the Romans. Not far into Mark Anthony's "Friends, Romans,

Countrymen," Marta would run out to the garden calling for me to shut up and get down. That not working, she'd come up and pull me off the ledge, threatening all the while to find a way to stuff my mouth for good. The spectacle lasted until the rainy season washed out my performances. But by then, I'd been to the movie house more often, and I saw myself as Grace Kelly or perhaps Jean Simmons; I even had a name to suit my Hollywood persona: Drene Harvey.

One afternoon as I sat on the porch reading a Photoplay magazine my friend Putzi had leant me, Mutti came out with her knitting wanting to chat with me.

"When I was young," she started what would become another of her once-upon-a-time-in-her-life tales, "much younger than you are now, Mohrle, I wanted to become a performer."

That got my attention. I looked up at her bemused.

"Yes," she continued, smiling, "I wanted to join the circus." Her knitting needles clickety-clicked away. "The village circuses of my youth were but a group of performers traveling from village to village in horse-drawn wagons; nothing fancy, mind you. They showed up in summer around carnival time when the air was filled with the scent of fried sausages and sauerkraut. If they came in the fall, we'd get roasted chestnuts wrapped in paper cone bags to accompany the show. Roasted chestnuts, ummm." Mutti rolled her eyes at the thought of warm chestnuts.

There I sat, lured again into her childhood when I really wanted to read about Ava Gardner's indiscretions. But... Mutti and circus? Really?

"I loved the brightly colored, shiny costumes the performers wore," she continued. "They were loud insolent people who always seemed to have a lot of fun. The dancers swung their arms and legs around," she mimicked with her shoulders, "as they whirled to the grinding sound of a barrel organ. Once I saw a white tiger that had been tamed. Oh yes... I wanted to tame lions and tigers, too! Imagine me," she laughed at the recollection and threw her head back with glee, "loving the idea of taming wild animals and traveling along the countryside making people ooh and ah!" I kept looking at her all the time she was talking, and started to giggle. It was hilarious that anyone as old and sturdy as she would ever have thought of being a glamorous performer. There was no way I could picture Mutti as a young person, anyway, much less one wearing gaudy colors and swinging her hips. "That's why I absolutely understand you wanting a career in acting. It's just about every young girl's dream to be a glamorous entertainer," she said, her eyes glued to mine, "but other than slaves or servants there are no parts for dark people, Mohrle."

"So?" I snapped, feeling she had stabbed me in the heart. "Why should that matter? They'll create parts for me," I glared at her.

"Now Mohrle," I could tell by her voice she was becoming impatient at my lack of understanding, "just make sure you keep your mind on your studies," she offered dispassionately. "It hurts me to say this, but please take it to heart: there just are no parts for Black people." With empathy and concern, she added: "And as far as I can see darling, none will ever be created."

That hurt. In a secret, numb place, the words offended me. How could Mutti, after all her effort in raising me as a European, in the end only see a mere Black person when she looked at me? I felt so bad I could've burst out crying, right then and there and in front of her. But I wouldn't show her how deeply she had wounded me. Instead I said, "Okay," got up and went into the house whistling "Yankee Doodle Dandy" as I skipped and hopped to my room. The numb feeling in my gut began to hurt. I didn't know what to think. How could I think when my mind had gone blank? I closed the door behind me, and started to hate my appearance. How I looked to others, including Mutti, was so different to how I saw myself and what I thought of me. I would never be able to escape my Black skin. It probably would have helped to cry a little, but crying was something I wouldn't do, period. Imagine, someone seeing me with red eyes!

⤙

Mutti was right, for in the Hollywood of the times, other than servants and slaves, there were no regular parts that featured

Blacks. But had my relationship with her been a healthier one, I would have rebelled against her and, just for the sake of expressing myself, would have yelled a few choice things at her. My rebellion, however, imploded, turned against me. I was the brunt of my own inward rage. I was not, as other teens were, ashamed of their parents; I was ashamed of me. I took me everywhere I went, I couldn't even cross the street when I saw me coming as some of my friends did with their parents. Everyone could see the obvious: I was a mere dark-skinned person who everyone knew as a carefree jokester. No one would have believed that, at the core of my being, I was a lonely teen-aged girl who acted out her alienation by laughing and being funny, and making sure everyone else laughed, too.

And despite perfect attendance in school, the grades began to slide again. Not only the grades were seriously problematic, but also my negative thoughts and attitudes. Mutti, with all her love and concern for my wellbeing, had in no way anticipated the dilemma she now faced. She didn't know how to handle the situation. She also didn't know she could have trusted the knowledge and wisdom of Rosa. The opportunities to cement a tie to the woman who gave me life had long passed anyway, so no one ever as much as considered including the obvious.

Rudolf suggested I be sent to a place where I'd have to associate with Black people and the idea of shipping me off to a boarding school was born. That would be the best way to deal with the pesky situation.

I figured I'd be joining friends who were also preparing to finish high school in New England or Canada. But in those days, airplanes touching down in Guatemala were puddle jumpers called Viscounts. The flight from Guatemala to anywhere in the north of the United States would have taken me first to Mérida in Mexico, then to New Orleans, where I'd have to spend the night before continuing north the following day. It meant separating from my friends in Louisiana: they would go to a hotel for Whites, while I would have been welcomed in one for colored people. Mutti wasn't going to subject me to the indignity of racial segregation.

At the time Jamaica was still British, and the boarding school

Mutti chose was affiliated with Cambridge University. If I pulled myself together and worked at my studies, my diploma would allow me to pursue advanced studies in Europe. Jamaica, Mutti said to me, was the next best thing to having a European education, without the distance and expense of actually going there. She didn't mention that the students would mostly be dark-skinned. Most important for the family was that I would meet sophisticated educated people who were dark.

The last time I saw her

It was my fifteenth birthday, one day before my scheduled departure. I was in the garden playing with Ruth's boys when I froze: Rosa with two little Black girls was coming across the lawn toward me. My birth mother had come to say good-bye to me and introduce me to my sisters, Judith and Adela. I can still see them. They looked like little dolls in starched and crisply ironed immaculate white dresses. I don't remember anything else my mother ever said to me, but I will never forget the words she directed to me on that day.

"Hija mía," (my child) she said, and she looked as if she was mustering every ounce of courage stored in her small body, "you have been very fortunate to have gone to good schools and are now continuing your studies. Please remember one day, to do good things for other people." She stood before me like one addressing royalty, but all I did was glare at her. Who does she think she is to be giving me advice, I thought bitterly, but remained silent. Marta offered them chilled sweetened hibiscus tea and after emptying their glasses, Rosa said good-bye and left with her two perfect little daughters, as she had come: through the servant's entrance.

Why did she always have to ruin my day? I don't know why she comes at all, I thought. My wishes were then, as they had always been before, that she stayed away.

My wish came true, for I would not see Rosa again.

⁀⁀

Making the Best in a Bad Situation

Early in the morning on the day of my departure, I found an oval box in my shoe. In it was a silver and navy blue Parker fountain pen. It was a gift that would mark my passage from mischief-maker to serious student. Mutti and I boarded a busy two-propeller Viscount and lifted into a cool Guatemala sky, heading northeastward. Two hours later, hopping and skipping like an albatross trying to avoid scorching its feet, the plane landed on the sizzling strip in Belize. The door flung open and hot air flooded the cabin. Outside, I could barely breathe in the stinging mid-morning heat. Belize smelled of salt, bananas, and tar.

I was told the place had Black people; I just didn't reckon they'd be everywhere. I became painfully self-conscious. Was something wrong with my beige suit? My hair? My speaking German? I stayed close to Mutti, clutching her arm, even squeezing it when someone came too close for my liking. "Stell' Dich nicht so an!" (Pull yourself together) she'd hiss at me while smiling sweetly and shaking me off. I noticed how she asked for information, arranged for the luggage to follow us, and when and how she handed out tips. I should have noticed, but didn't, that she was not scared of anyone and no one meant us any harm.

Of the two days in Belize I only remember writing to Putzi that it was a frightening place. "Everyone is Black, from the street sweeper to the hotel manager. You'd be scared too."

In Kingston we stayed the first three days in a hotel that exemplified gracious British colonial living. At first I thought we were driving through a park, but the road led us to a white building that was more impressive than the presidential palace in Guatemala. Flamingos and peacocks paraded freely on the manicured lawns in a landscape of palms, giant ferns and waterfalls. There was a swimming pool and several in and outdoor restaurants. The breakfast room was an airy buttercup-yellow environment where golden canaries chirped in white rattan cages, while we scooped balls of chilled buttery papaya from Wedgewood bowls. I was quite aware of being the only dark guest in the hotel where the management was White, and the help came in assorted shades of brown to ebony.

The day prior to our departure for Hampton, we moved to a more modest lodging run by two Scottish sisters who were just about the sweetest old women I'd ever encountered. They and their staff chaperoned the girls while in Kingston. Mutti made sure to befriend the sisters, thus reassuring herself that I was in good hands while away from the school. She's fabulous, I often thought of Mutti; the way she talked to people, the way she got everything she wanted, the way people who had never set eyes on her instantly liked her. "How you shout into the forest," was one of her favorite sayings, "the forest responds to you in kind." She treated everyone with courtesy and humility, and the response was warm, friendly, and respectful.

In the afternoon, while sipping tea and nibbling cucumber sandwiches on the porch, we watched as the overseas girls began to arrive. By dinner the place was alive with laughter and gaggles of French, Dutch, and Spanish. We introduced ourselves to some and I right away liked Sandra from Maracaibo in Venezuela, who was also new that term. The next morning, with boxed lunches in hand, we set off for the St. Elizabeth Mountains on a relic from the early days of railroad travel. The locomotive, emitting billowing clouds of grey smoke and chugging laboriously, pulled the train along the countryside. Boring landscape, I thought, no colorful trees or bushes like we have in Guatemala. Here and there a beleaguered donkey needed a poke in the ribs from its ganja-smoking owner. Women with large baskets on their heads quaffed on corn pipes as they lumbered along. Cloudy afternoon skies greeted us at our destination.

Established in 1858 and perched on a wide hilly expanse, the school was a dominating U-shaped two-story construction. I don't know what I was expecting, but the minute I saw it, I hated it. Several smaller houses dotted the grounds. I later learned they were science labs, and music houses for lessons and practice. On a small hill facing the main building stood a limestone chapel next to a solitary poplar.

A blond, blue eyed, freckle-faced girl came bounding up to us. "Hi, my name is Sally," she said with exuberant energy. She handed Mutti a note that invited us to the headmistress's office once I was settled in the dorm. "I'm your prefect. Welcome to Hampton," and she handed me a green enameled pin explaining it was for my uniform. It was the color of the house to which I was assigned: Saint Hilda's. Henceforth, I'd eat and sleep among Saint Hilda's girls; for all competitive events, those in the other three houses (red, blue and yellow) would be my rivals.

Sally helped me carry my suitcases to the dorm, a long room with six beds. Curtains separating the cubicles were only to be drawn for privacy when washing or dressing. On one side of the bed stood a night table with a lamp and a decanter with drinking water, on the other, a stand with a large white pitcher in a basin. I had a dresser and a closet. On the bed reserved for me lay the ordered eight cobalt blue pinafores and bloomers, and white blouses. Sally's cubicle, with walls and a door, was at the end. Prefects were seniors, and a perk for that was being allowed to study into the night. Sally, who was Scottish and lived in Kingston, introduced me to the other girls. Peggy Chin was Chinese and lived in Mandeville, which was in Jamaica. Shirley Johns was English and flew in from Trinidad; Janette LeFoire was French from Martinique, Hatti Haaring, Dutch, came from Curacao; Antoinette Marsoobian, of Armenian origin, was Jamaican and lived in Montego Bay. I was the only new one and, I noticed, the darkest. (Years later I learned Mutti had made such a request.) I unpacked, and Mutti put my clothes away to make sure everything was neatly stacked. Then the dinner bell rang.

Mutti was escorted to the headmistress' private quarters; I joined the Saint Hilda's line in front of the dining room. My place was in the middle of a long table, at the head of which throned Sally. At the other end sat Denise, a sub-prefect - she was from Haiti. There were two tables per house, which meant that each house had two prefects and two sub-prefects.

A procession of slender, ebony-colored women balancing wooden trays on their heads entered the hall. They fanned out and placed steaming platters of food on stands. Someone said grace, and boiled beef was passed around. Then followed a bowl of vegetables and one of rice and peas. I helped myself sparingly to the funny-smelling wilted things. I knew I wouldn't bring myself to swallow them. Sally admonished me, as Joyce removed my untouched plate, that in future I would eat all the food I'd served myself. She had been friendly before; now her words carried the iciness of authority. I was not accustomed to someone so close to me in age telling me, in such uncertain terms, what I could and couldn't do.

After dinner, all I could think of was finding Mutti. The minute I saw her, I ran over and began my bombardment: "I hate this place! For heaven's sake, don't leave me here!"

Mutti looked sad, preoccupied, but I didn't care.

"Dinner was ugly grey meat! The carrots and string beans were cooked so long they were mushy," I gagged with disgust, "and the rice had peas in it and tasted like coconut! Muuuutti, the food here is repugnant! Uagh," I gagged again for good measure.

I knew she empathized with me but she only looked sad and, touching my cheek, said: "Food in boarding schools is not high cuisine, Mohrle. And the English are not known for their kitchen." She hooked her hand into my arm as we walked to a bench. "I understand it's going to be difficult," she said sitting down, "because you have to get accustomed to the ways of another country. Dear, dear child," she sighed, and sighing again, kissed me on the cheek.

The bell rang. "Bells, bells, bells. This is nerve-wracking," I moaned. This time we had to get in line and march to chapel for evening prayers. Mutti had no sentiment for church rituals. This was not a wedding, baptism, or funeral, so she climbed into the waiting car that would drive her to wherever she was spending the night.

When she returned the following morning, I was waiting and ready. I ran to her, awash in tears: "This place is hell!" I cried. "That pitcher with water in the cubicle? It's to take care of the morning shower. These people are filthy! They told me we shower every other day, and when there's a drought, which means there's no rain, we can easily go for a whole week without bathing. The bathroom should be called 'Egypt', Mutti; it's so far away. And Mutti," I sobbed, breathless and distressed, "they served sardines in oil for breakfast... I haven't eaten since the boxed lunch on the train," I wimpered.

Silently she took me in her arms. I was sure she was going to tell me to go pack my stuff at once and we were going home. But she only said, "Be brave, Mohrle. It's for the best that you learn to adjust to all sorts of conditions."

"There's no way I can adjust to this! I want to go home with you. You can't leave me here," I said clutching her arm. I began to cry, right there in the open. I didn't care who saw me. I wasn't staying anyway.

The bell rang. What did that mean now? Chapel? Again? Was I expected to troop to chapel twice a day? "Oh no!" I screamed, "This whole thing is getting out of hand!" Sally was suddenly next to me, and taking my arm, led me to the line. This can't be happening to me, I thought, despairing. Mutti smiled and in German suggested I pray not to be given sardines for breakfast again. More seriously, she added: "I'll see you later," and waved to me as I followed the line of girls.

I didn't see Mutti later. Not after lunch, nor after the afternoon rest period. Then I received a message from the headmistress inviting me to her office for tea.

Miss Wesleygammon, the headmistress, was a stern-looking woman with black, well-groomed short hair, expressive, thick black eyebrows, and a rather wide, thin-lipped mouth that covered a set of crooked alabaster teeth. She was dressed in a lime green linen dress with hand-embroidered dahlias on the collar. Her very black eyes were friendly, and her voice was rather sweet. I remember thinking it odd that such a sweet voice could come from so stern a face.

"Thank you for having tea with me, Catana," she said smiling, and gestured for me to sit in one of her caned Chippendale chairs. The mahogany-paneled office was dark. Etchings of flowers and tropical birds - the sort one finds in better art dealerships - graced the walls. Behind her large, solid ebony desk hung her diplomas.

"I hope you'll feel comfortable in this school and find that everything is to your liking once you've been with us for a few days," she said, smiling.

What was she talking about? Just wait 'till I get to my mother, I thought. I've spent one night here, but she'll let you know that she's blasting me out today. Not wanting to seem ungracious, I said in a polite soft voice: "I've never been away from home, and everything here is different from the way I'm accustomed."

"Care for tea?" Miss Wesleygammon offered.

"No, thank you." I was not in the mood; I was waiting for Mutti. I wanted the green light to pack my stuff.

"Catana," her voice was soft, her look piercingly direct and her smile had a slight edge of triumph... "Your mother left for Guatemala this morning."

"That's impossible," I choked, aghast.

"I suggested to her," Miss Wesleygammon continued, disregarding my shock, "that the best thing would be for you to stay here. You need the learning this environment and this school will give you." She sat upright, her back straight as if someone had shoved a walking cane up her butt. Gesturing, so as to make me understand that everything, but absolutely everything the school provided, including only one pitcher of water for the daily toilet, the sardines for breakfast, the rice that tasted of coconut, and boiled green bananas, was something I needed to learn about.

"She can't have left," I said breathless. My heart beat so loudly I hardly heard my voice. "She didn't say good-bye to me; she told me she'd see me later. Now is later. She's staying three days. Where is she?" My voice was meek, my mouth dry and somewhere in a dark, deep place I knew the devastating truth.

"Your mother left at nine, on the morning train to Kingston. I drove her to the station."

The weight of my body filled my brown leather shoes as the cool air of the fan, circling overhead touched my skin. I wasn't going to cry in front of this woman. But I couldn't fathom how Mutti would simply leave me, just like that go away without me. I hadn't finished... Heck, I hadn't even started complaining and she was already out of earshot in Kingston. How could she have done that to me?

Miss Wesleygammon stood up, and so did I. She took two steps toward me and gently placed her perfumed arm around my shoulder. Walking me to the door she said, "Your mother left because if she had not done so when she did, she would have taken you with her. She was very conflicted but knows how important it is for you, in the long run, to be here. She also knows that you are very unhappy staying now." She placed both hands on my shoulders and turned me to face her. "Your mother loves you very, very much, Catana. Things will be better in a few days," she looked at me kindly. "Please know that my door is always open to you; you can call upon me about anything, anytime. I am here for you."

With that, I was out of her office and on the way to my dorm. My dorm... that unfamiliar place I shared with other girls, where even what had my name on it was alien to me. I took my doll and hugged her to me as I fell onto my bed, heartbroken. Indescribable grief slowly seeped into the marrow of my bones. "What have I done that this should be happening to me," I thought as I cried every tear out of my body. In my fifteen years I had never felt so abandoned. I thought I had tough nerves; not so... now my heart felt like a fragile rosebud. When evening came, Sally sat down on the edge on my bed and gently informed me the dinner bell had rung. I said nothing as I picked up the pitcher, poured water in the basin, splashed my face and walked down the stairs across to the dining room on the other side, and got in line, swollen face, red eyes and all. I ate a little of the rice and tried salted, oily cod. I took a pea-sized portion of something yellow called ackee and swallowed it without chewing. No more special baby. Desert was tapioca pudding with coconut. I passed. I would eat what I had served myself, like it or not, just like everyone else.

A letter Mutti composed in Kingston arrived three days later. She had to leave suddenly, she wrote, and had no time to write me a message. "I love you, my darling child," she said at the end, and signed, "Be brave. Your Mother."

By the time I read the words she was already in Guatemala. There were no telephonic communications between Jamaica and home, and it took six to ten days for letters to arrive at their destination. News was always old by the time it reached me. In the remote Jamaican hills of St. Elizabeth, nothing could be rushed and I learned why patience is a virtue.

There were a hundred girls attending the school, ranging in age from ten to nineteen. More than a third came from overseas. There were Dutch from the ABC islands, Aruba, Bonaire, Curaçao; French from Guadeloupe and Martinique; Italians who lived in Venezuela; Spanish from Colombia; Lebanese Trinidadians; Chinese Jamaicans; British Belizeans. Add to that the local island mélange, and Hampton was the ultimate international microcosm with British faculty, chaperones of mixed ancestry, and Black servants.

First and foremost, Hampton was a place of learning where order and honor ruled supreme. There was no monkeying around as there had been in the American School. Fifteen minutes into the first study hour, the supervising prefect stood at the desk and declared, "All right girls, you are on your honor." Then she headed out the door. I, of course, thought it time to chat and let loose a little and looked around for someone with similar intentions. Everyone's nose was in their books except Nieves Sotelo's in the back row. She also had an expectant roving eye. We gawked at each other and grasped immediately what "on your honor" had meant. Believe me, it was a major cultural shock.

With little else to do, I had to adjust, buckle down and begin to study.

⁊

As water finds its level, I found mine and made friends with the overseas newcomers first: we were foreigners who spoke European languages and the language or dialect of the country in which we lived, such as Spanish, Papiamento or Creole, in addition to English. Jamaican girls as British subjects, were better in the local language than us overseas folks and went home during half-term breaks or for Easter vacations when the rest of us stayed, not at the school, but on the island.

In the first week at Hampton, Ana Maria, Sandra, and I were sitting on the steps of the chapel telling stories, when Ana Maria traumatized us by talking about adult intimacies.

"You girls ever been kissed?" she asked with a bright mischievous glint in her jet black eyes. "I mean on the mouth," she clarified, "the way a man does it with a woman?"

"No... Duh... How?" We answered.

"He puts his tongue into her mouth," Ana Maria said and began to savor our disgust.

"Ugh," Sandra and I gasped nauseated. "Ugh, ugh, ugh, you filthy pig!" we shouted, and spat on the steps.

"They do that for a while," Ana Maria continued unperturbed. It must have been too much fun to see our wild-eyed, blanched expressions as she relished our aversion to her every word. "And then, guess what?" Her eyes darkened even more as they filled with added evil pleasure knowing full well she was about to knock our socks off. "His thing gets hard and he has to get between the woman's legs and stick it into her vagina."

"That's ridiculous, you are such an idiot!" I gasped thoroughly repulsed, my scalp prickling and the hairs on my arms standing on end.

"How would you know that, anyway? How can anyone come up with such disgusting ideas," Sandra shouted.

But Ana Maria knew about adult mysteries because she had already kissed a boy that way, and he had allowed her to touch his hardened penis. "Did he get between your legs?" Sandra's eyes widened with bewilderment.

"No, but he taught me what to do to release his tension."

"Pig, pig, filthy pig!" Sandra and I yelled reeling from such disclosure. We got up and left Ana Maria on the steps of the chapel groaning with humor and wiping away tears of laughter.

Sickened at the revolting thought, I spent weeks traumatized and wondering if in fact people could get so close to each other. The singularly disgusting thought filled me with repulsion and slight curiosity.

I soon learned that not only Whites had the inalienable sense of entitlement of those who inherit, for all the dark people I was associating with had been born with silver spoons in their mouths.

BY MID-TERM, WHICH WAS AFTER six weeks, I had made friends with the ten girls in my class. My first Jamaican friend was Milva, in spite of, or maybe because I found her a little freaky with her blue-green eyes peering out of a brown face. Blue eyes in a brown face were out of place as far as I was concerned. Antoinette pulled her jet-black hair into a tight bun in the back of her neck. She claimed the fiery spark in her eyes was proof of her ancient Romany ancestry. I learned about gypsies from her. Lorna, who was as dark as a moonless night, fascinated me most. Once at night in a dark room, all I saw was the white of her eyes. She was soft spoken and words cuddled in her mouth like soft candy. A gifted storyteller, Lorna filled my head with stories of the Land of Look Behind, that mountainous limestone country in Jamaica where ganja smoking Rastafarians practiced esoteric rituals in the black of night. Uninvited witnesses to the powerful mysteries, she assured me, were struck dead on the spot, or disappeared in a sinkhole while fleeing on the jagged porous land. There were times when I lay in bed at night with thoughts and ears pinned to an imagined tom-tom-tom of distant drums.

Our spare time was not spent on our appearance. We had to be tidy, clean, and odorless. Even as I admired the great variety of ways one could braid hair like mine, I never stepped out of the style I had learned at home. I discovered, however, that my hair could be straightened. I desperately wanted straight hair. The first opportunity came my way during mid-term vacations as I stayed with other overseas girls in a hotel in Montego Bay.

The chambermaid gave me a hairdresser's address in a district of low, colorful houses, where grass grew between the cracks in the uneven pavement. Not quite trusting the neighborhood, I told the taxi driver to wait for me until I was done. The faded blue house had a grey door and didn't look like a hair salon. I knocked and a thin woman, whose angular movements reminded me of a praying mantis, opened the door.

"Wha' me kian do fo' yo, young liady?" she asked.

"Can I get my hair straightened here?" I responded.

"Uhu huh," she said and gestured for me to come in. I entered the dark, sparsely furnished room with significant apprehension. A sink was to the right, and next to it a chair and a table with metal gadgets and a jar with something blue in it. "Sit hiar, young liady," she gestured impassively. I obliged.

The woman put a thin towel around my neck and proceeded to run her fingers through my hair to feel its consistency.

"De hiar i clean, me na fe goin' wash it," she said, and without further commentary, began to plaster the blue, thick as peanut butter, greasy gook on my head. I had an evil sense that something horrible was about to happen to me. Then she took a heated metal comb and proceeded to put it to my hair. Sizzle... Instantly, my nostrils filled with the odor of hot grease on hair.

I distrusted everything about the place, but it was too late to get out.

"Young liady," the angular woman said, "how you want de hiar?"

"Straight. Just plain straight," I said rolling my eyes at her.

"Young liady, me mean de style," she added, sucking her teeth.

"Just straight," I offered her a fake smile. After all, what was she thinking? I'd style it the way I wanted once it was silky, straight, and bouncy.

After the hot comb she proceeded with hot rounded prongs. In the end she handed me a mirror to look at a head that was a mass of ridiculous greasy curls! Oh, my God. How disgusting! I wanted to style my hair like Liz Taylor or Grace Kelly; there was no way I could remotely achieve it with this ghastly mess!

I handed her the money and ran to the waiting taxi and told the driver to get me back to the hotel, and fast! Once there, I took the stairs three at a time to the third floor, hoping no one, particularly none of my friends would see me. In the bathroom I looked in the mirror: the hair was straight, yes, but so thick with grease I couldn't bring myself to touch it, not even with the tips of my fingers. I turned the hot water on in the sink and stuck my whole head under the faucet. I soaked the floor looking for shampoo and finding it, right then and there, began to wash the grease and straightening out. Then I took a shower and repeated the process. Still, the hair had grease.

"Yeah, look at her," my friends joked at dinner, "she chickened out," they laughed.

"I'll never tell you anything again," I said, annoyed. "It could not have been worse had I fallen into a vat of goose fat. Had to shampoo eight times, before I could recognize myself. I looked worse than Joyce on Sundays," I added. By then everyone was howling with laughter for Joyce happened to be the meanest, grumpiest, most unfriendly, and oogliest maid we had in school.

At seventeen, I still had no boyfriend, which was not surprising in Hampton, where the only males we saw were the old chaplain and the gardeners. One of my Guatemalan friends had already married, which may have been young, but not particularly unusual. Some of the Jamaican girls seemed to have someone who wrote sweet words to them, but most of the European ones were like me, we had no one who cared enough to write to us.

In her letters, Mutti had mentioned a young man who occasionally visited at cocktail hour and sometimes stayed for dinner. Werner stood next to her at the airport in Guatemala when I arrived for Christmas vacations. He was sent from Hamburg to assist Rudolf who, a year or so back, had joined a partnership representing the interests of German trading and shipping companies. Ruth and Rudolf had moved back to the city and lived in a house a few blocks from Catalina.

I thought he was cute, blue eyes, sandy hair and all, and welcomed his invitations to accompany him when he drove to San Jose, a port on the Pacific coast. I liked his intuitive nature and as he came from the North Sea, I felt he understood my nineteenth century, Caspar David Friedrich and Theodor Storm Romantic sensitivities. The fact that Mutti enjoyed his company accounted for his visiting us regularly after working hours when she'd engage him in all sorts of discussions, political, religious, and otherwise. Both kept abreast of world affairs and enjoyed their intellectual banter. When I returned to Jamaica, I was surprised to receive a letter from Werner. He wrote about missing me and looking forward to my return in the summer. I had a boyfriend! And what's more, one with sandy blond hair and clear blue eyes.

In time I became a St. Hilda's prefect and developed a reputation for order, reliability, and fairness. That was something the administration liked. No buttons were missing on St. Hilda's uniforms, all shoes were shiny in the morning, and no St. Hilda's girl slouched against the wall when waiting to enter the dining room. I hated to see people holding up walls. Not everyone liked my bossiness, but they had to comply. An advocate for the girls, I also related well with faculty. Thus, successfully navigating the tricky waters of opposing interests, I was chosen in my last year to be Hampton School's Head Girl. It was the ultimate honor. I was no longer part of the dormitory experience but had a room to myself with a view overlooking Miss Wesleygammon's manicured English country garden.

After sixth form, at the end of four years, I took the advanced level Cambridge Overseas School Examination. It was sent to Cambridge University for evaluation. Four months later a cablegram reached me in Guatemala congratulating me for successfully concluding my studies.

I was nineteen, and about to begin a life that would make me forget how well I had adjusted to being among people of my own race in the Jamaican environment.

Intruder

A serious family conflict, that would for years ruin my relationship with Ruth, began to brew while I was in Jamaica.

Rudolf disliked Werner's relationship with Mutti and figured he was trying to ensconce himself in the family. And Werner wasn't too clever either, for although he knew he had Mutti's total support, it was to his immediate boss that his attention should have been paid. What transpired in the conversations between Werner and Mutti? To what degree did Mutti voice her mistrust and dislike of Rudolf? Fact was: the family dynamics had polarized in such a way that there was constant icy friction between the two homes.

After one and a half years of letters and vacations at home I was sure I was in love with Werner, and Mutti approved of the relationship. It was December and my Hampton experience was over. Werner invited me to dinner in a restaurant where our table had been decorated with orchids. After desert he proposed marriage. Marriage? I joyfully accepted. Other than a peck on the cheek, we had never exchanged one of those kisses Ana Maria had grossed me out about during my first week at Hampton. But that night, when he dropped me off, Werner planted one of them on me. I hated it. Worse, I was overcome by a sensation that pulsated throughout my body. It was electric, unexplainable, and resonated deep down in my belly. I had never felt anything like it before... Not knowing what was happening to me, I scrambled out of the car thinking bewildering thoughts as I ran to the house. Had I eaten something poisonous and was I now going to die? Werner rushed after me, grabbed me and kissed me again. Thankfully, the weird feeling didn't repeat. He held me at arm's length smiling at me. Although it was dark, I recognized an excited twinkle in his blue eyes. When I told a more experienced girlfriend about my first kiss, she laughed hard and long and said, "From a kiss you got that?" And she proceeded to explain what an orgasm was. "You're supposed to like it," she concluded giggling. Eventually, within the right context, I of course came to enjoy it.

We got engaged December 12th, 1959. Mutti gave us a heavy gold coin so her jeweler could make our rings. Germans wear wedding bands on the left hand when engaged, and on the right when married. There was no party and the fact that we were engaged was something only Mutti knew until we began to walk about with our shiny rings. Ruth and Rudolf were most displeased.

Although she wanted to see me married, Mutti insisted I finish my education. "There's no marrying until you have a profession," she underscored. "Not all marriages last and should anything happen to yours, a husband like Werner would just about leave you in penury. And anyway, lovers need to be apart to test their commitment; the separation will only strengthen your love for each other." Issue resolved, that was that. We had already discussed the language academy in Germany and Mutti wanted to show me her beloved Pfalz. I knew she made sense, although the prospect of a two-year separation from Werner was depressing.

In May we were set to leave for Germany. In March Werner received a letter from the home office in Hamburg saying that, thanks to his outstanding work in Guatemala, he had been promoted to head their new office on the coast of Colombia. Rudolf congratulated Werner for "having fallen up the ladder." Mutti immediately suspected Rudolf had seen to Werner's removal.

I was uniquely naive and disinterested in money and quite unaware that my legal situation would not entitle me to an inheritance. A young ambitious German would have looked after such things and would surely have taken charge to make appropriate corrections. I don't believe Werner was materialistic. He was a dreamer, a romantic, who wrote poetry and love letters and fantasized about having countless little brown babies with me. Rudolf would not have needed to worry about Werner.

My love left for the Colombian outpost two weeks after his notification. He landed nowhere or in hell: in a mosquito-infested no-place-on-the-map, with no potential for advancement. His letters were passionate and filled with frustrations. He had to see me, be with me; he would visit us as soon as he could.

Catana with Hannali, 1943

Catana's new tricycle, 1944

Catana with Ruth in hand painted skirts, 1949

PART TWO

The Next Fifteen Years
1960-1975

In Germany

On May 17, 1960, the Norddeutscher Lloyd vessel pulled out of Puerto Barrios with a handful of passengers en route to Port au Prince, Santo Domingo, and San Juan before sailing north to Europe. Thanks to the family's history with the company, Mutti and I enjoyed VIP status. Even merchant ships observed a social protocol, which in this case meant nothing more than being seated at the captain's table for meals. Wherever the ship stopped to unload and load cargo, Mutti and I took the opportunity to visit some of the cities landmarks. It was a leisurely farewell to the continent of my origin. Once the tropical bounty was secured, the ship headed out of the warm Caribbean into the cooler waters of the Atlantic. On the way, Mount Pico, a volcano on the Azores glimmered mysteriously in the distance. On June 17, I awoke to find that we had arrived in Antwerp and I was in Europe, at last!

I hurried on deck to see what Belgium looked like at 5 AM on a cloudy summer day. There were no mountains; what I saw was an ocean of cranes and ships and more cranes and more ships. Antwerp was a huge, tidy port that oozed industry, commerce, and trade. The smell of our breakfast bacon being prepared in the kitchen mingled with that of steel, iron, and oil. After scouring the distance, I looked down on the loading deck. What was going on there? What were those weird things moving around on the loading dock? I tried to get my eyes to focus and blinked several times; I rubbed them again and again, and still couldn't make out what the amorphous, mealy-looking objects were that moved about laboriously in the hold of the ship. What on earth could those over-sized, larvae-like things be? I held my breath as I saw one mealy larvae move two extensions. Unbelievably slowly, I recognized that the grayish grub-like lumps were barebacked White guys unloading cargo. So help me, but in my 19 years of life, I had never seen pale-skinned men doing physically strenuous work. It was an extraordinarily shocking discovery that Whites could actually labor under the sweat of their brow like the Indians in Guatemala or the Blacks in Jamaica; it took time before I could adjust to the fact that Europeans could be found doing labor-intensive, menial work.

Notwithstanding that detail, I began to feel at home in no time in the city. At home in Antwerp and Brussels, at home in Rotterdam and Bremerhaven, our final destination. The bricks, the houses, the cobblestone streets... all seemed familiar despite the different local languages. Sometimes I sensed what lay around the corner or lurked behind a heavy medieval carved door. It felt as if I'd lived there before in a mysterious, remote existence and was at last returning to what had once been my home.

From Bremerhaven we travelled first class on the express train to Hamburg. Mutti wanted me to experience the elegance and speed of modern European rail travel to compliment the folkloric images of the tediously chugging Jamaican locomotives emitting billowing clouds of steam.

In Hamburg we stayed in a comfortable family-owned hotel-pension, and Mutti bought me a new car, an unpretentious Opel Record. Surprising was the wealth of Mutti's acquaintances that included banking magnates and museum curators. Although her finances did not fit in with theirs, they clearly acted as if she was a favorite friend and looked forward to her visits.

It was just past noon as I pulled my powder blue car into a circular driveway bordered with white floribunda rosebushes. We were having lunch with one of Mutti's dearest friends, Tante Mary. She regularly spent time in Guatemala visiting her children and grandchildren, but otherwise lived in a patrician mansion on Hamburg's beautiful Alster. Tante Mary was a reserved, sophisticated woman whose subtle sense of humor I appreciated even as a little girl. More than anything, Tante Mary always commented on my lovely German and my flowing curtseys, which made me love her even more. When I was six she gave me a small porcelain horse, remarking that it was time to introduce me to fine china, and so began my small collection of porcelain figurines. Now we were leisurely sitting on her porch overlooking the Alster, sipping a dry Spanish sherry before being called to table. The housekeeper prepared a delicate meal of food I had not tasted before: deviled quail eggs on a bed of green sprouts, a delicately prepared smoked trout with horseradish whipped cream, and early fingerling potatoes. "Mohrle, just taste these potatoes," Tante Mary said. "There are no better in the world than spring potatoes in Hamburg." An aromatic dry white wine accompanied the meal, and after a fresh berry tart we enjoyed a cup of strong mocha and a shooter of Armagnac. It was, as all things in Tante Mary's presence, uniquely refined.

A friend of Mutti's I had only heard about but not met, was Harriet. She also lived on the Alster in a residence reminiscent of homes in Thomas Mann's novels. The house reeked of old wealth; had I not been with Mutti, who acted as if it could be hers, I might have been intimidated. As friendly and uncomplicated as Doña Harriet was, it was in her presence that I felt most observed.

Table manners were never a problem and I participated intelligently in conversations about all sorts of current affairs. Fortunately, my upbringing and the education in Hampton paid off, so that by the time we left Mutti's opulent Hamburg friends I knew I had passed with flying colors what must have been a Pygmalion test. Mutti was complimented again and again on my courteous, poised demeanor.

On a rainy day we drove out of Hamburg, heading south. We were on our way to Günterstal in the Black Forest, where Tante Gustl, Mutti's older sister lived. It was summer and the days were long, so Mutti had to declare it was cocktail time way before sunset. We turned in for the night at roadside pensions promising a sturdy local meal and good wine.

We visited Tante Gustl and her side of the family, Tante Lisl and her clan in Saarbruecken, Onkel Gustaf, Mutti's half brother in Wollmesheim and his children, Cousin Milli in Anweiler, and Milli's daughter and grandsons in Pirmasens. It was my family, spread out in states of Rheinland-Pfalz, Baden and Saarbruecken. We toured through cathedrals, fortresses, and palaces, and my early education about Romanesque, Gothic, and Baroque architecture finally fell into place. Except that everything was more splendid than any book could have presented. I saw the dark hair and the noses Mutti talked about long ago, and I joked and laughed with everyone. In the most natural way I was welcomed as one of their own. The dry, fruity Palatinate wine, the crusty, grainy homemade bread, the aromatic, spicy sausages were all as Mutti had promised: every single morsel a gift to the palate.

Summer 1960. Western Germany had transformed from wartime devastation to almost complete restoration and was being touted as the German economic miracle. The Nazi atrocities were regularly deplored on TV and in films, and the country was tired of centuries of hostilities with its neighbors. Konrad Adenauer and Charles DeGaulle formally ended the historical - become traditional - German/French feuding that for centuries had regularly flared up between their countries. Strides were undertaken to heal the wounds, and an open and new dialog for racial tolerance and mutual acceptance was the order of the day.

By the time we reached Munich in October, we'd lunched or dined with everyone Mutti knew in Germany, even her dear friend Bernhard in Berlin. He lived in Frohnau, a part of the city that bordered the Russian sector. One could look over a regular wire fence and wave to people in the Russian Sector. A few months later The Berlin Wall would go up and such friendly communication came to an end.

Had I known about careers in the world of art, I'm sure I'd have chosen a degree in art history. But no one mentioned such possibilities, not even Rudolf who'd most furthered my interest in art. With the broken down communication within the family, Mutti's suggestion was that I become an interpreter to make use of my gift for languages. Not having a clear sense of how I saw myself as an independent adult, such a study was the line of least resistance. Late October we settled into a comfortable furnished apartment on Wittelsbacher Strasse overlooking the gently flowing Isar, Munich's renowned green river.

My friends from Guatemala were in Europe without supervision, but Mutti stayed with me for the entire two years I attended the language academy. She wanted to make sure curious young men knew I had a chaperone and kept their distance. Her perception was simple: she gave me "the right frame." On one or two occasions she phrased it exactly that way and meant that in her presence I was seen in a more positive light. I said nothing about the awkward comment. What could I have said? I trusted her to know her own people and their perception of Blacks. I was at ease in my German environment and took the general respect with which I was treated as normal and deserving - whether she was with me or not. I accepted her comment without questioning its wisdom.

Somewhere deep in my psyche, however, it displeased me to still be found lacking, after all the invested effort to raise me German.

Names, Naming, and Rebranding

I entered Germany as Catana Reed. Reed in English is the same as Ried in German: meaning marshland vegetation. The pronunciation of the word is identical in both languages. Mutti didn't want me to be taken for a German war baby. Age wise, she said, I was too old to be one of 'those' children, as they were born after 1945. "You have decent parents, and I don't want anyone thinking your mother was one of these German girls who got involved with a Black soldier."

"Because I speak fluent German, I'll be thought of as German, won't I?"

"Exactly," Mutti underscored nodding emphatically. I had to understand that if I were taken for German, I'd be associated with a category of German Mutti disapproved of.

"It's very simple, you'll just attach Cayetano to your name. Reed Cayetano," she underscored. "That way your name is as exotic as you are."

But hadn't Mutti disdained Edmundo Cayetano, the man my mother Rosa had been in love with and ultimately married? Again I was not ready to question what Mutti had said; after all she always knew what she was doing and Germany was her turf. As her product, I did not question her line of thought; I also didn't necessarily like the name Cayetano.

There was something fluid in Mutti's approach to names and naming. A name seemed to be a disposable thing to her, like having the perfect dress for any given occasion. She came into this world as Emma Katharina. But Emma at the time was a name that ended up at the brunt of unsophisticated, boorish jokes. There is no way an adult Mutti would have accepted being an Emma. I don't know when she reinvented herself as Esther, but by the time she was twenty she had discarded any hint of a possibly unsophisticated rural origin. However, when we were in the Pfalz, she responded, albeit a tad uncomfortably, when someone from her youth occasionally said Emma.

And so, under Mutti's tutelage, I too, would change my name, several times. Rosa had named me Adriana, but upon seeing me Mutti claims to have said, "Ach, das ist aber garkein Mohrle" (Oh, this is no darkie at all), as I was lighter than what she had expected. Although Mohrle stuck as a nickname, officially, I was Catana. In Germany I first became Catana Reed Cayetano so that no one would think I had a Black soldier as a father... In years to come, my name would change a few more times for a variety of practical reasons.

On my 21st birthday Mutti placed in my hands a manila folder that had become brittle with time, and upon which Vati had long ago drawn with blue and red ink an ornamental "M" for Mohrle. In it were all the important papers pertaining to me. Emblazoned with a large, multicolored official seal, is a birth certificate of epic proportions that chronicles in flowery language my entrance into this world. "On this day, in the community of Barrio Barique, a brown female child was born at sunrise with the fourth call of the rooster..." (Well, maybe not the call of the rooster.) Several women helped deliver me and each of their lengthy names is recorded. The document declares that I am the daughter of Rosa Mateo Nery. My name appears three quarters down the page of decorous discourse: Adriana. A few years later when I needed the litany translated for the German authorities, it cost me quite a few Deutsche Mark to have it done. No one had ever seen such a detailed account of a simple birth, and bureaucrats and translator commented that the certificate and story itself was colorful enough to frame. No father's name is mentioned.

I missed my love Werner, but only to a degree. I had loved his deep blue eyes, but those were now a rather pedestrian sight. There actually were eyes so deeply blue they radiated purple, all the way to the pale blue of a pallid Magritte afternoon sky. My attention was being diverted by the new world before me. I was the center of attention everywhere, and I mean everywhere. Wherever I appeared, people just fussed over me. Poor self-esteem? No way! There were absolutely no issues regarding any lack of self-confidence.

As my letters to Werner became less frequent, his began to arrive in ever-greater numbers. After a year of outpost living and fearing losing me, he relinquished his job to join us in Munich. He found a fine position and settled down in an apartment across town, primarily because it was cheaper. I did not know my fiancé was the embodiment of insecurity. His jealousy, possessiveness, and his insistence we marry right away eventually got the best of a shaky relationship. I wasn't ready for marriage, but above all we had snuck behind Mutti's back to do something she surely condemned. 'The pill' was not available in those years. The whole thing wasn't worth it and weighed too heavily on my conscience; I began to see my first lover in a different light and, without regrets, ended our engagement.

Jazz

One day Theo, a student at the academy whom God had created to be rosy always, invited me to a Jazz concert. His deep crimson blushes happened so quickly they seemed electric. He stood at the door of the apartment, this very fair youth with eyes the color of water, in a burgundy suit, magenta shirt, orange tie and chartreuse socks. I had never seen a man in a parrot costume; and this one glowed in anticipation at the prospect of listening to American Jazz. He smiled and said nothing at my appearance, but I could tell from his expression that he wondered why my evening clothes were in drab, classically understated hues.

Theo had excellent seats: third row, center front. Thunderous applause welcomed a few Black men as they walked on stage and seated themselves at their instruments. After five minutes I asked, "How long is this going to last?"

"Hopefully hours," Theo answered, breaking into a delighted smile. "This is the greatest music I've ever heard," he beamed ecstatic.

The loudness, the pitch, the mix of rhythms all made me break out in perspiration and gave me a headache. At times I even felt outright nauseous. "I thought Jazz was music," I said during intermission.

"My God! It's Dizzy Gillespie and his band!" Theo turned to me with an astonished look on his face. "He's the greatest in the world." But he was in heaven, and soon returned to glowing. Having a dark girl at his side only highlighted his bliss, never mind that she was not impressed by the sounds.

"Guess I've heard the name Gillespie. But these types of

sound arrangements are new to me." I decided, for Theo's sake, to can my annoyance for the remaining performance.

We turned in for an "after the concert dinner" at a popular smoke-filled student dig called Mutti Braü. Theo's order showed how much the third-row center-stage tickets had depleted his budget: he ordered a bowl of goulash soup with two spoons, and a medium beer with an empty glass. A few spoonsfulls of the excellent soup and a couple gulps of cool draft beer were the evening's treat for me.

When Mutti asked what I thought of the concert, I told her it was awful and that Theo's colorful costume was nothing compared to what followed. "Jazz isn't music. It's wild screeching, cacophony. All a shock to my poor system! I have a miserable headache," I complained. "It was hot; the theater was packed. People were standing in the balconies applauding like demented zombies. Apparently it was a world famous group, but I had a terrible time. I need aspirins."

"I knew it was a very special concert," Mutti said calmly. "You don't appreciate Jazz?" She asked perplexed. "I thought you learned everything about Black culture in Jamaica," she said and stood there with the appalled expression of someone who'd just been mugged.

In the four years of school in Jamaica I covered a ton of subjects that included world geography and the mineral resources in the British Commonwealth of Nations. African culture and African history were not taught. African-Americans were certainly never addressed. I had not learned a single thing about the Black cultural Diaspora, so that the many different Black societies: African, British Caribbean, Spanish Caribbean, North American, Central and South American were not part of my international understanding. The music played at Hampton was of the popular classic sort, like what I heard at home. Calypsos were considered folklore, like Guatemalan marimbas. Jazz? I couldn't remember anyone in Jamaica listening to jazz or even speaking about it. Simply and clearly put, jazz was American music. And I knew little about American culture, Black or White.

What I learned from shy, young Theo was that Germans, by

and large, are avid and enthusiastic listeners of Jazz and Blues, and not only understand, but appreciate the rhythmic complexity and musicality of such pieces. I wonder if I disliked the music because it was that of Black people? Hmmm...

It was my son, who years later and in no uncertain terms, sat me down and told me it was time I expanded my musical horizon. He was a teenager then and knew the sort of sounds that disturbed me. He presented me with jazz I would not only tolerate, but make an effort to listen to. It was Miles Davis, lots of Miles Davis.

The Glimmer of a Different Future

Germans racists? Not with regard to me. I proceeded to become the darling exotic everyone saw me as. Reference to my skin tone was always complimentary: beautiful, exotic, a Black princess, a dark Grace Kelly. However, I was a lot hotter in the German imagination than in reality. Mutti's fears of me being courted by German men had been justified, but her worry I'd fall for their advances was unnecessary. I was not a passionate tropical kitten who spoke with an accent, but a cool well-chaperoned young woman in command of High German.

During my second year at the Academy, the Mexican delegation at the International Handicrafts Fair in Munich engaged me as the interpreter for English, Spanish, and German. The dark interpreter intrigued those who had come to admire Mexican handy crafts. On April 24, 1962, an image of me smiling next to an intricately crafted Mexican silver mirror appeared in the Süddeutsche Zeitung and included a few details about me. I was causing a slight sensation as the only Black at the fair, and my fluency in German became known to a larger audience. A photographer asked me to pose next to diverse items such as Chinese silks, Persian oil lamps, Swedish furniture, or Rhineland pottery. What made the greatest impression on me was that for a few hours before a camera, I was paid several times the salary I earned for the entire two weeks as interpreter at the Mexican stand. That was real money for very little effort.

With all the fuss they were making, could there be a future for me as a commercial model, I wondered? Perhaps even in fashion? At 5'7" I was not very tall. But why should my aspirations stop there? The dreams of a teen in Guatemala resurfaced with a vengeance. One thing I knew for sure: translating and interpreting... working in a cubicle passing boring political or whatever maneuvers, into another language had no charm. I caught an article about a modeling school several months later, and pointed it out to Mutti.

"This is what I want to do," I said to her, handing her the paper. "I want to take this six week course, so that I'll be able to find work as a fashion model." It was time I started to explore what it was to be me, or at least start making my own decisions.

Mutti's hazel eyes clouded over as a distraught look descended on her face. We had been here years ago, and now I wanted this sort of career again. With a worried expression she said, "That is out of the question, Mohrle. You need to have a serious profession. This leads you absolutely nowhere," she waved the paper away dismissively, "there will be no work for you. Can't you see? The world hasn't changed. You won't have a chance in such a career."

Was she stupid? Look at my reception in her home country. Did she fail to recognize how everyone appreciated my dark skin and appearance? I was not delusional. Suddenly, amazing even myself, I raised my voice at my mother: "I've had it!" I screeched, "I want you to leave me so I can pursue the life I want to lead, to have the career I want, the friends I want, MY friends, friends of MY choosing, friends with MY interests!" I could barely see her through the tears of fury that welled up in my eyes. Mutti stared at me, frozen to her seat, stunned by the explosive emotion. "No language academy, no boring interpreter job where I have to sit in some god-awful cubicle and translate boring stuff from one damn useless language into another! No! You have to see it my way. At least just try to, for a change!" I dashed the tears from my cheeks.

"Mohrle..." Mutti stood up and moved two steps toward me.

I stepped back. "Noooo, leeeeave me and go baaaack to Guatemala, where you belong! Or go anywhere, just leave me here." More rabid tears cascaded from my eyes as I continued hysterically, "I'm sick with frustration at having to follow your demands." My voice by then was deafeningly shrill.

"How are you going to take care of yourself?" Mutti said calmly. "What kind of life is that going to be? Mohrle, for heaven's sake," she said in a steady, concerned voice, "I didn't raise you to lead a superficial existence! This is ridiculous child; it's a passing, youthful fancy. You will soon come to your senses and see I'm right, that you are too good for a profession like that."

"I don't want to come to any of your senses," I sobbed. "I know what I want. I want you to go away! I'm fine just as I am. Aaa-iiih," I let out a shrill frustrated scream that frightened the pigeons off the windowsill. Mutti paled as she looked at me, aghast. She had never seen such behavior from me since the child in the potato box incident; and that had been nothing in comparison. "I don't need your money! I can earn my own!" I blinked several times to stem the flow of tears. "I have a good mind to go to law school and become a lawyer so that I'll know how to legally separate from you! I want to be totally and completely legally free from you." My body convulsed in sobs filled with desperate abandon while my mind was about to leave me. Rage blurred my vision, and all I could see was white: white fury.

My mother just looked at the spectacle I was creating and simply replied: "It's all well and good if you can finance your studies." There was an edge to her voice as she added, "How do you propose to do that?"

Now she's mocking me, I thought. Oh how I despise her! "I've thought about it," I lashed out while fighting to regain some sense of composure. "Believe it or not, I have already thought about it. Many times. I'll apply for a scholarship. That's how I'll do it."

"And how do you propose to meet your living expenses?"

I just glared at her through my drying tears and hated her even more. She was underlining my total dependence; that I was nobody without her. I turned on my heels and went to the bathroom to splash cold water on my eyes. My face was swelling up. Gotta clear my head I thought as I grabbed my jacket and without another word walked out of the apartment. I scrambled into my car and drove out to the country only to end up at a friend's summer home on lake Starnberg. I spent the balance of the afternoon laughing and sailing and forgetting about my first and only serious falling out with my mother. When I returned in the evening I found a distraught Mutti who had worried long hours, not knowing in what frame of mind I spent the afternoon.

"I'm sorry for the way I behaved," I said sincerely. "We now know I recover quickly after a fit. I'm so sorry you had to be concerned about me," I said, embracing her.

We made up easily, and Mutti gave me the greatest gift to date, "I've had time to think about what's right for you," she offered gently. "I'll return to Guatemala as soon as your studies are over. I had not intended to stay longer than necessary, anyway." She smiled at me and sighed. "I only wanted to make sure you finished this step of your education, and I wanted to properly introduce you to Germany, to give you the right presentation. I have done that." Her sincerity almost made me cry again.

"Thank you," I gulped, "from the bottom of my heart." I put my arms around her as my heart leaped with joy. "I'm ready to live my life, and I'll do only what I know is right. You can dismiss worrying about me Mutti, believe me, I'll be just fine." I knew I was right.

"As you embark on your adult life, Mohrle," Mutti murmured, "know that you had a very happy childhood. Regardless of what will befall you in the future, you have the memory of an unencumbered youth to reflect upon. That can never be taken away from you, from now to the rest of your life."

"I know, Mutti," I said, "I know."

A few months earlier, when she had been lonely because I left her alone quite a bit, she said introspectively, "You could show a little more gratitude, Mohrle."

"Why? What do you mean?" I answered, a bit too brusquely.

"I have done so much for you. You could show a little appreciation for all I've done for you."

Granted, she had hovered over my wellbeing like a fairy godmother with a magic wand clearing obstacles from my path. She had cared for me and done much more than what would be expected of a parent. At the time, however, she got a completely detached look from me. I was actually angry. "You want me to be grateful?" I blinked at her. "I've never asked for anything. It was your decision to keep me." Now suffer it, I thought.

"I am only saying, Mohrle, that you could show a little more affection. That is all," she said humbly.

"I don't like to hug and kiss as I did when I was little. Doesn't say I don't love you, I'm just not the affectionate type," I shrugged it off. I was actually a bit angry with her wanting demonstrative gratitude. Fact was: I loved her dearly. So I went over and kissed her on the cheek.

We shared a beer and liverwurst on rye, as we discussed alternative plans for her departure as well as financial arrangements for me. It was September; she'd leave by ship in November after my final exams. That way she'd arrive in Guatemala for Christmas preparations. In Bremerhaven I made sure she was comfortably installed in her cabin. I was 22. Mutti asked about the outcome of my final exams. I lied to her for the first and only time, when I said I had passed. I didn't care anymore. She would soon be at the other side of the Atlantic and I was free!

⌇

... But not so fast...

Every third or fourth day a letter from Mutti arrived. "My darling Child," they began, and ended "Your Mother." They were Mutti's testament of love: a consuming, possessive, oppressive love. I was not her child and she was not my mother, but no one would have known by the way I occupied her every thought. I was her breath, her pulse, her reason for living. She loved me and bonded me to her so fiercely that it would take two decades after her death, and years of therapy to understand how deeply

I was bound to her emotionally. My morals, even after I knew she had been less than perfect, were predicated by her early indoctrinations. I never trusted my instincts and instead followed her conventions, thus denying my better knowledge.

I couldn't separate from Mutti even though she was not present physically. Her significant network of friends and acquaintances kept watch over me and reported faithfully. Ultimately, however, the constant travel my profession required had me away when her people called.

And then, my lack of financial sophistication was shocking. Although I was working consistently, I never had money for the car insurance, gas and electric, or telephone. I was earning more than any of my friends, and still came up short when I had to pay for things I couldn't see. Until I figured that out, after some two years, Mutti always subsidized me. Why was it a mystery that I had absolutely no concept of finances? No one spoke to me about such issues as I was growing up. I was never given pocket money. Whatever I needed, until the day I left Mutti on the ship and walked into my future, always, but always had come to me without my asking for it. Limited funds? Budgets? Savings accounts? No notion of that! I grew up with everything, except money in my hands.

Learning to make ends meet became my most difficult challenge.

Success and Heart Ache; Loss and Love

By March 1963 I had concluded the modeling school, and my calendar was replete with bookings for spring fashion shows. It should not come as a surprise that I was lured to the limelight the minute lights and cameras focused on me. After all, had I not been Mutti's little star among the German children in Guatemala? Now I became the most photographed model in the shows, and articles accompanying the pictures invariably mentioned my fluency in the German language. It took no time for a theater director to show up offering me a part in a comedy. "Dark actresses only play slaves or servants," had been Mutti's words, and sure enough, my first role was that of a maid. I played a witty Ivory Coast student working as an au pair in Paris, who caused hilarious trouble for her employers. The humorous French situation comedy opened late August and was a success.

As fate would have it, in the final week before the play ended the strongest film agent in Germany came to the performance and at the end left a note saying she wanted to meet me! How could this be happening? It better not be a joke, I thought. The next morning I walked into the agency, and without sitting down was led straight to Elli Silman's office. Elli came toward me, embraced me, and then held me at arm's distance. "Yes," she said, looking me up and down, "you absolutely could play the part! Come to Berlin to the Film Festival next week, Catana, I'll introduce you to people who are casting a film. They have been looking for months for the right actress. I think they'll be pleased to see you." Then she added all business like, "I'll sign you up, if they cast you!"

Can't remember what I answered, but I floated out of Elli's office, giddy and barely believing my luck. I could be cast in a movie! A week later, with Elli at my side, I floated into Arthur Brauner's production company in Berlin. "This is our Eliza," someone said as we headed down the hall to the producer's office. One would think that meeting Mr. German Movie Mogul in person would have been a memorable encounter, but all I remember is that after the interview I was cast as Eliza in Onkel Tom's Hütte (Uncle Tom's Cabin), the most significant European co-production to date. Never mind that the part was that of an enslaved girl...

Before filming began, I took speech, diction, and acting lessons. I wanted to be in Strindberg and Ibsen plays, be Shaw's Cleopatra, play Goethe's Gretchen. I could even see myself as Brunhilde, Isolde, Lorelei... and when I was old, I wanted to be Berthold Brecht's Mother Courage. It was not a publicity ploy, but German papers wrote about me as the Mohrle who dreamt of playing Gretchen. Because of youth and naiveté the notion was cute but not realistic. The reality was that I had a major film on the horizon and was signed by a prominent agent. It was time I rebranded myself. So, I dropped the Reed and would henceforth be Catana Cayetano, the model and actress.

Onkel Tom filmed on location in Yugoslavia for nine months, mainly in Belgrade. Leading English, French, Italian, and German actors were my colleagues. The director, Geza von Radvany, was a multilingual Hungarian whose heavy Magyar accent permeated all languages. Actors spoke their language of preference, and the whole film was later dubbed into as many languages as needed.

How was I to portray an American enslaved woman, when I only had a vague idea of modern slavery? I had no Black heroes; there were no Black role models in my pantheon of historical characters, male or female. My role models, past and present, were powerful, wealthy, and White. As an actress, I was inexperienced but willing to learn my craft. As a person, the specter of my eventual lack of confidence and ensuing confusion regarding my identity was beginning to take shape, but would not break for many years. Fortunately, my portrayal of Eliza ultimately gained much praise and was even written about in Hollywood's trade paper Variety.

"More feeling, forget yourself, ride the emotion," was Ernst Fritz Führbringer's (the famous German stage actor who generously agreed to tutor me) repeated advice. "What are you protecting? You are a passionate girl! Go, ride the passion, let me see it!" he'd exclaim. He couldn't believe that the spirited, joyful individual who bounded up three stairs at a time into his studio was blocked at showing unrehearsed emotions. The elements that defined my essence were not accessible to me. I didn't know I had the ability to openly express emotions. I rehearsed my parts so long that I was able to fool everyone, for although my work was cerebral, it was also convincing enough to be received well.

Much, much later, I learned that most people who have access to their emotions also have a clear sense of who they are. But in those years, when I had the upwind wherever I went and could have soared like a condor, I didn't know I could fly. For that I would have needed to know who I was. Decades later, after life taught me what unrehearsed emotion and 'riding the passion' meant... I was no longer an actress.

Shortly after the conclusion of Onkel Tom, I met Mish, a happy-go-lucky character pursuing a master's in business administration at the university in Vienna. One year older than me, blond, blue-eyed, athletic, and cute, I succumbed to his charms and we became impassioned lovers. Mish taught me most of what I needed to know about the more practical and mundane ways of survival, such as Vodka being easier on the system than Gin, and taking two aspirins after drinking and before going to sleep, avoids a hangover in the morning. With regard to my career, he was quite astute as well. When my agent arranged dinner dates for me with directors or produces, his advice was simple: "Send those senile geezers packing, Catana," his baby blue eyes blazed, "I'll guarantee that you going out with them will only encourage your agent to fix you up with more horny old men who only intend to take you to bed. If the old guys really have a part for you," he said exuding confidence, "you'll get it whether you have dinner with them or not. What are they going to do? Paint Elke Sommer black? White girls have to prostitute themselves for a part, you don't need to do that." I followed his advice and landed parts while simultaneously gaining the reputation of being aloof and an outright snob.

Offers for work in dramatic pieces, comedies, even two musicals came my way. If the parts called for an American woman, I was offered the role. Americans have an image of themselves as a nation of blond and blue-eyed people. Europeans, however, easily see them as dark. I portrayed young educated American women who happened to be Black. It was a direct and uncomplicated association for producers: she's Black; she's the perfect American... No more was necessary, not even having the character chew gum. I worked in theater, television, and films; roles were either there or they were created for me. Just as I told Mutti years ago it would happen.

But there was something that was not good: I could not carry a tune. András Fricsay was casting a musical for the Vienna stage. I told him quite clearly that I was not right for the part, but he simply shut me up by saying: "That's ridiculous, there's no Black person in the world who can't sing!" I took the part and proved him wrong, and my songs went to other performers.

The crowning part in my acting repertoire came in Cardillac, a Nouvelle Vague film directed and produced by the young German renegade Edgar Reitz. I played the female lead in a movie that received multiple international awards and commendations.

Mutti was beside herself with joy that things were going well in my career. However, reading the magazines and paper clippings I sent wasn't enough, she had to come visit, and did so for a few months in 1965. Although she knew I had not disgraced myself in any way, she was concerned that at 25 my prime years were slipping away and I had done nothing to secure a suitable husband. I had a small circle of friends, but her concern was (even though she never said it) that I might drink too much like my father Gil, and might sleep around like Gil, and then end up pregnant before marriage, like Rosa. She never said anything negative about my mother, but I had somewhere internalized the stereotypical view of Blacks as sex driven beings with little shame and no morals. I don't know how I got to have that perception, when I had no frame of reference to go by. Those I saw drink in excess, sleep around, and have shotgun marriages were my White friends and acquaintances. In fact, had I dared to go around with the same abandon with which some of my best friends behaved, I would have been branded, tarred and feathered as an insatiable nymphomaniac town whore. My friends, however, were merely amusing and delightful 'free spirits.'

While the attention I received from men flattered me, I rejected anyone who alluded to my physical attributes or to feeling seduced by me. Seductive was something I did not want to be. I had no intentions of attracting anyone physically. At the time the Twist was the rage, a dance I refused to participate in because it required shaking the body. When Mish and I went to discotheques we sat at the bar sipping vodka tonics and chain smoking.

Maternal Confessions

One afternoon while drinking coffee and munching on Viennese pastries, and knowing I was intimate with Mish, out of the blue Mutti found it necessary to give me some adult advice. "You've reached womanhood, and it's normal for you to want to be with the man you love. So it falls upon me, as your mother, to tell you some things you need to know." She smiled sighing and seemed unusually bashful. Oh, my God, I thought, while she looked at me steadily, making sure I was paying attention. "After being with a man, I mean being in bed with him... Sleeping with him... It's imperative that you get up right away and douche him out. Otherwise, Mohrle, you'll get pregnant." I stared at her and said nothing, certainly feeling uneasy. "Promise me child, no matter how happy, or how tired, or in love you may feel... promise me that you will not fall asleep without douching him out every time," she stressed.

"Yes, sure," I managed to say. How embarrassing was that? "Is it how you avoided having more children?" I asked after a few seconds.

"Yes. And you see, it worked."

"Why didn't you want a child with Vati? He adored you."

"Didn't feel like going through the ordeal, and I didn't trust giving birth in the tropics. Douching did the trick. And after all, the passion goes out of a marriage sooner than you'd imagine." I didn't want to continue such a conversation with her, so I said nothing. The silence was awkward. "Now promise me you'll never breathe a word of what I'm going to confide in you," her lips drew into a crooked, slightly mischievous smile. "Certainly never tell Ruth for she is unaware of this and it would be a terrible shock to her."

"Absolutely, Mutti," I said hurriedly, my interest now piqued with curiosity. "Rest assured, I will never breathe a single word about this to another soul."

"All right then," she sighed and reclined into the cushions. "There have been several men I've been in love with. They were brief passionate relationships that had to be dealt in with utmost delicacy."

Wow! Mutti! While I was fascinated by what she just said, I was also bothered at the way she drew me into her confidence. She did not then, nor in any of the pictures when she was young, look to me like a woman capable of succumbing to seduction and infidelity. This woman, who for me had only figured as a mother, was also a woman of secrets; I had underestimated her completely. On that day I also recognized that she was someone who was well in control of her passions. But why was she confiding in me and not in Ruth?

"Do I know them?" I dared ask.

"All have died, except Bernhard."

"Bernhard?" I laughed. "That ugly old man?"

"He was never a beauty," Mutti said bemused at my shameless laughter, "but we were young once, and he had great charm."

Mutti and I had flown to Berlin to see Bernhard shortly after our arrival in Germany in 1960. He and his wife lived in a two-story house in the American Sector of the city. Bernhard! What a cantankerous, funny old man. At the time I could not have known the context of Mutti and Bernhard's dialogue when she asked him for the ingredients of his champagne cocktail. He told her that every time he made it, she asked for the recipe.

"Bern," Mutti insisted, "I keep asking because you never give it to me; and you know it! You either add an ingredient, or say you include one when you don't. All I'm hoping is that before either of us dies, I get hold of the recipe for this yummy concoction. After 45 years," she smiled sweetly at him, "isn't it time you come clear?"

"You've had it all along Esther, it never changed," he winked at her. "What I include is a good portion of love... You probably fail to add the love, my dear," he grinned. With that, the conversation moved to another subject. Bernhard's wife just laughed. She had heard the silly dialog many times before. Hmmm, Bernhard!

Mutti reached for her handbag and took out her small golden compact case. Handing it to me she asked if I liked it.

"Absolutely, I've always loved it. It's exquisite, inside and out," I opened it and smelled the delicate scent.

"I want you to have it when I no longer need it," she nodded smiling. "Bernhard gave it to me as a souvenir on a trip we made together long ago," she repeated, "long ago," as if it belonged to another lifetime.

No one ever knew that every time she held it, which was perhaps several times a day, she might have thought of Bernhard.

ALTHOUGH MISH AND I HAD REPEATEDLY declared our love for each other and spoken of marriage on several occasions, we planned to wait until he finished his studies. Unfortunately, the time came when he said "I need to see you without your mother." But it was not so easy to get Mutti out of the way. "Tonight, we need to be alone. Tonight," he repeated. "I have to see you tonight. It is urgent."

He looked distraught as he opened the door. He began to pace up and down in his apartment. I had never seen him so desolate, so at a loss for words, and knew that whatever he had to tell me was going to be bad. Without offering me a drink, he took me in his arms and held me tight. "I am so sorry, sweetheart," he said in a breaking voice, "this is going to be a terrible shock, but I got someone pregnant in Vienna and have to get married."

How could I believe this? Who could it be? When? "Well, then have her get an abortion," I gasped in shock at the devastating development.

"Too late for that," he said quietly. "The baby is due in four months. I only found out a few weeks ago."

"Why didn't you tell me sooner?" I pushed away from him. I was not ready to feel so betrayed, to see my world shattered into a million pieces. I couldn't think, couldn't breathe, everything spun as dizziness engulfed me. I rushed to the bathroom where I vomited repeatedly a green, bilious, mass into the toilet. I sank to the ground as wave upon wave of heart-wrenching grief poured over me. What a monumental wake-up call!

Mish sat down next to me on the bathroom floor and handed me a glass of warm water. "Drink this," he instructed. "It will make you throw up again, but your stomach will feel better," he said. How can he be so clinical at a moment like this, I thought and drank the water only to throw up again.

"I just don't understand, Mish, what about us, what about us?" I whimpered.

"Please don't hate me," his voice was calm as he asked for my forgiveness. "I love you more than I love anyone and can't bear the thought of having screwed up our future. But I'll fix it," he said, a somber expression clouding his deepening blue eyes. "I plan to divorce as soon as the baby is born. You'll see, I promise," he whispered.

The next morning he took the train to Vienna, and two days later he was a married man.

While it was horrible to have Mutti witness my heartbroken state, it was soothing to have her at my side when I needed comforting most. How many times had she told me to put on my "moral corset" (meaning keep a stiff upper lip) when I was set to react out of sorts in a given situation. Now she could be proud at the way I handled my desolate heart. The show went on, just like it did when Vati died: no one noticed I was wreathing in pain.

A few days after the wedding, Mish was back all set to resume our affair; and we did. The only difference was that we knew he was a married man and would be a father in four and a half months.

"Don't give up on him," Mutti insisted. "I have seen you two together and know he means it when he says he loves you. And also, pay attention: he didn't go on a honeymoon..." In spite of the huge betrayal, she still wanted me to marry Mish. What she really liked was his very well-situated family. Mutti and I were both delusional. How could we trust such a proven unreliable guy? No matter how much he claimed he loved me, he had been unfaithful enough times to get someone pregnant. Coming back to me, in spite of being married, was a clear indicator of his potential for chronic infidelity. What was it with Mutti that she had such a warped perception of love and loyalty? Was it part of what she also wanted me to understand, that a bad marriage was better than none at all? Those were low standards when you had choices, and I saw myself as having those, although, with Mish buzzing around, they didn't come calling.

"Whom ever you marry," Mutti said pointedly, "remember, this bit of wisdom: in a relationship one of the two must be more in love than the other. See to it dear child, that it is not you, for otherwise you will suffer."

"That's just cynical," I said, saddened at her approach to being in love.

I learned a painful lesson through Mish who shattered the myth I tenaciously held onto, of Germanische Treue (Germanic trustworthiness) that speaks of the undivided, eternal devotion and fidelity that can only be shared with a German partner. I began to pay attention to what went on in some of my friend's relationships and discovered that promiscuity was alive and rampant. No better or worse than in the rest of the world.

Never to be the Same Again

When Mutti returned to Guatemala in the fall, she took residence in one of the six houses in the gated community Ruth had been building on the property immediately behind Catalina. Ruth and family had moved into Catalina. My new home is lovely, Mutti wrote delighted. Her back wall was covered with tall ever-blooming bougainvillea bushes giving her enclosed yard a cheerful look.

After years of reneging, I finally agreed in 1967 to visit Mutti in Guatemala during the summer months when my work was slow. My intention was to fly over immediately after a fashion shoot in Tenerife on the Canary Islands. On the return flight I stopped in Madrid for a few days to visit Gaga, Tante Gustl's daughter, thus a cousin of mine, of sorts, who was married to a Spanish gentleman. They looked worried as they picked me up at the airport and the mood in the car as we drove to the city was solemn. What odd people, I thought. Once at home, Gaga showed me a telegram from Ruth. Mutti had suffered a devastating stroke. I felt lost at reading the words. I'd have to postpone my trip to Guatemala until further notice. Of the three days in Madrid I only remember walking around in a bewildering fog.

I cancelled my Fall bookings and flew to Guatemala. Ruth was at the airport, her face ashen from stress and lack of sleep. "Brace yourself, Mohrle," she said, "Mutti is paralyzed on the right side and cannot speak."

Stiff with apprehension, I entered Mutti's living room.

My mother sat in a wheelchair. Her once lovely clothes looked like drapes around her diminished frame. With her healthy left hand she cradled the limp right one; in a few short weeks, the once sturdy body had become a frail shadow of its former self. Tears fell from her eyes upon seeing me, and her delicate body shook with unimaginable grief. I could feel her profound disappointment that after all her joyful preparations for my arrival I should find her like this. I fought hard to keep my tears at bay as I put my arms around her. "You look much, much better than I had expected, Mutti," I said, in a voice and demeanor that brought forth outstanding acting ability. Through her tears she gave me a crooked smile, and the glint in her eyes told me she was thinking I was a dreadful liar.

I settled into "my" room and the customary household routine continued uninterrupted. A full-time nurse tended to Mutti's personal needs and a physical therapist came by to work with her every day. She was well taken care of and maintained her regal presence as she sat, hunched over, in a wheelchair.

Who could say whether it was her mind or her heart that allowed Mutti to submit with immeasurable grace and composure to the limitations imposed by that paralyzing stroke. But with stoic resignation she endured immobility, silence, and loneliness at the end of a life that had been painted with broad strokes in the colors of humor, travel, and adventure. Mentally sharp, her eyes still hazel and keenly focused and observant, she would frustrate at being able to say only two words: "Ay," as a form of lament, and "Stuhl," chair, in German.

Each morning her pair of long-legged red-footed ducks waddled through the French doors into her bedroom to greet her. They stayed until she'd acknowledge them, smiling and murmuring, "stuhl, stuhl." Then they'd waddle back out to the garden. After her therapy exercises we'd sit in her garden in the shade and I'd tell her about my work, which always interested her. There was my recent trip to Tenerife and the visit with Gaga in Madrid, the two weeks I was in Moscow in the spring and the fortnight I spent in Malindi and Mombasa in Kenya for a bathing suit company. As far as my acting was concerned, I related the plot of the two television shows I had been in. She understood everything because I had written to her about all that, but now I needed to fill in other details such as the new sort of foods I savored and who my colleagues had been on the trips. And when friends came by, I had to repeat the stories without leaving a single detail out.

But the atmosphere continued tense between Ruth and Mutti's houses. Ruth, but particularly Rudolf, rarely came over to see her. It should not have surprised me when Mutti began to insist, and became adamant that I take the smaller items she had specified for me in a Will she had completed days before the stroke. She knew her daughter would not have the document opened, and that if I would not take the objects, I would never see them.

When I left Mutti after Christmas, her condition had improved slightly, but due to her advanced age and the placement of the clot in her brain, a significant recovery could not be expected. It was a sad visit; so very different from how we had planned. But Mutti was alive, and I promised to return as soon as my schedule allowed.

The Phantom Reappears

Sometime at the end of January 1968, a few weeks after my return from Guatemala, the phone rang and my friend Gabi hollered excitedly through the receiver. "Hey Girl, listen. I'm in Milan on a photo shoot and just met this really nice American guy who wants to see Munich. I gave him your number 'cause I know you speak English. Go and have dinner with him if you're around. He's a lot of fun and ever so easy on the eyes!"

"Oh, sure Gabi, how nice. And I hope you're fine, too," I responded, irritated. "You may not know it, but I can't stand Americans!"

"Heeey! Hold on, I don't like them either, but this one's civilized. Trust me. He's from New York. Let me tell you something: you'll be sorry if you don't check him out," she laughed happily. "He's a dish!"

"Skip the crap Gabi. Tell him to lose my number!" How dare she want me to spend time with a stranger?

"He already left. Have some fun, you old bore and don't forget to thank me! By the way, his name is Fred," she said, and hung up.

Fuming, I threw the receiver into the cradle and decided there was no way I'd bother with the American.

He called a few days later as he was passing through Munich en route north to Amsterdam, Copenhagen, London, and Dublin. I was leaving in the morning for the Pret-a-Porter Salon in Paris, and happy to tell him that. I wasn't fond of Paris but liked the sound of saying I worked there.

"Okay," he said, and added with an easy American charm, "I'll call you on my way back to Rome in about four weeks."

I'd forgotten about Fred when he rang a month later. I was leaving for Berlin the next morning. But... My hair was freshly done, there was no date for the evening, nothing of interest was on TV, and then, well, he sounded pleasant enough, so I figured: dinner, why not? We agreed to meet in Schwabing in front of the Datcha, a trendy restaurant that specialized in southern Russian cuisine. It was the evening of February 28, 1968.

Fred, who first wanted to have a look at his blind date, stood several yards to the side. As I walked by him I felt it was he, but continued. Then, I heard my name.

"This isn't where we agreed to meet," I said turning. "How'd you know it was me?"

"Had a hunch it might be you," he answered. And I figured: sure, how many Black girls are there in Munich anyway?

As we followed the maitred', people stopped their conversations, looked at us and smiled approvingly. We were led to a booth with comfortable leather seats. Lit candles were on the table, and aging Russian folk paintings hung on the dark wood-paneled walls. After settling into our chairs and having a good look at each other, we smiled, liking what we saw. I had in front of me a fine-featured, dark haired man with beautiful eyebrows, whose gray-green eyes smiled at me seductively. His classic looks seemed comfortingly familiar. Anywhere, absolutely anywhere in the world, this man would be seen as gorgeously handsome. Our waiter brought the customary bottle of Russian Vodka, filled our double shooters, and placed it on the table in a bucket of ice. We studied the menu and began to compose a meal we'd remember with pleasure for the rest of our lives: a selection of fishy appetizers, followed by Tamalan, an always flawlessly prepared filet mignon, next to a mound of white rice with a raw egg yolk in the middle, sprinkled with sumac, the dark, lemon flavored Middle Eastern condiment. Dessert would be an ambrosial crème brulé with Grand Marnier.

I was twenty-seven years old, Fred thirty-six. He was an actor and commercial TV announcer who had just finished shooting a series of TV ads in Italy for the American market. In my adult years I had avoided Americans. What I knew about the States I didn't like: a place where the last three summers had seen cities ablaze with rage and rebellion; where Blacks were on the streets demanding the most basic civil rights that had been denied them for centuries; a country whose foreign policy saw fit to keep corrupt rulers in power in third world societies like mine in Guatemala. But I didn't think of American social issues and foreign policy as I talked and laughed with the confident, charming Irish-American whose sort of wit and humor was completely new to me.

When I told him I was from Guatemala, for instance, he exclaimed grinning: "No wonder I like you! You're Irish! Who'd have thought I'd meet a girl from Glaghamora in Munich!"

In those days, I was a heavy smoker. Half way through the meal, as I lit yet another cigarette I noted, "You don't smoke."

"No, I don't," he answered.

"When did you give it up?"

"It didn't mix with sports, so I never started."

"Oh, oh," I said, already fully aware I was in love with the guy, "I guess I'll have to stop smoking."

"Please don't," he said right away. Leaning over and taking my hand, he looked deep into my eyes. "I'd rather take up smoking than change anything about you."

WHAT A LINE!

After dinner, we walked to a nearby disco and danced. I, who never danced, stood up and moved my body most shamelessly for Fred until the place closed.

It had begun to snow, and the white flakes fell gently on our shoulders as Fred walked me home. Under a street lantern he drew me to him and placed a full, tender, erotic kiss on my mouth. I gave him my key to the door of my apartment. We stepped over the threshold and became inseparable: unable to keep our hands off each other, ourselves from the other. There was nothing foreign or uncomfortable between us. We explored our bodies and already knew every atom: we had been there and were back. When we fell asleep, exhausted, we were like lovers of another time who had searched for centuries and finally found their way to each other again. As our bodies meshed and molded into each other's folds, it never occurred to us, even as we separated, that we came from different societies, belonged to different races, and were comfortable in different languages.

I cancelled my early flight to Berlin, booked for midday, and barely made the last plane in the evening. Fred came with me, and we spent our first month together in Berlin. He instantly began to work in commercials, even a German Karl May film, and didn't make it back to Rome until we moved there - one and a half years later.

Years later, revisiting our enraptured encounter, I asked Fred how Gabi had described me.

"Well," he ruffled his brow trying to remember, "I asked her whether you were light or dark. She mulled the question back and forth, and then said, 'dark'."

"Yeah, what else could it have been," I shrugged, smirking at him.

"I was expecting a German brunette," Fred grinned.

"Gabi never told you I was Black?"

"Nope."

We laughed hard and long and tears ran down our cheeks.

"Then how'd you know it was me when you called my name?"

"Just knew it was," he shrugged.

And I? I recognized Fred right away as the phantom of my childhood dreams. What was interesting is that in the years I dreamt him, he always was, as in reality, a decade older than me.

Fred, when we met in Munich, 1968

When I visited Mutti in the summer, I showed her his picture. "This is the guy I dreamt of as a child," I told her, "he is the one you suggested I paint on the wall."

"Stuhl," Mutti said without missing a beat. "Stuhl," she repeated emphatically several times. And I knew she meant I should make sure I married him. Her concern, as always, was that I have a partner so I would not grow old alone.

That was also the summer when Ruth accompanied Rudolf on his usual morning walk to the office; she gave him a peck on the cheek, said goodbye, and returned home. He hung his coat up, sat down at his desk and signed three letters. Then he must have slumped over and expired before anyone noticed. It was a horrific shock but another one of those simple deaths in the high altitudes of Guatemala City. Ironic, that Rudolf, who always seemed so healthy, would precede ailing Mutti in the race to the grave.

In time Mutti's friends, finding her so pitifully incapacitated, made less of an effort to visit, so that the highlights of her life were her grandsons and Ruth's very occasional afternoon visits. Mostly, however, she yearned for the eight weeks each summer when I'd fly in from Munich to be exclusively with her.

On the last day I would see Mutti alive, we had our customary afternoon tea in her living room. I poured milk in our cups, added the tea and a little honey, and placed a cup in Mutti's left hand. She took a sip and bending over, her hand trembling with its weight, replaced the cup in its saucer.

"Stuhl," she said, with a faint smile, and meant thank you. And we began another conversation with the only words that came out of her mouth.

"Stuhl... stuhl, stuhl! Ayayay." Her confinement irritated her. She stretched her left hand toward me: "stuhl!" she insisted looking directly at me. And again, "Ayayay, stuhl, stuhl."

I asked what was wrong with her hand.

"Stuhl," she said shaking her head. "Stuhl," she insisted,

putting her hand out again, moving it right to left. Her pupils zeroed in on me with an expression that said, "you MUST understand what I want."

Then she made a fist and tried to straighten her ring finger.

"The ring?" I asked her.

She smiled faintly and began to weep. How ridiculous to have only two stupid words available, when she wanted to say so much.

"Stuhl, stuhl, ayayay," Mutti began again and once more pointed at me.

"Want me to take your ring off?"

She nodded emphatically. Her look radiated determination. She kept her arm extended and was expecting me to remove the diamond.

"You want me to have it?"

Mutti had given me a copy of her Testament. I knew she had not bequeathed the diamond to me. I reached over and held her hand.

"You didn't write it in the Will. If I take the jewel now, Ruth will say I stole it."

She began to weep, her frail body shaking as she sobbed. "Stuhl, ay, stuhl, stuhl," her tone was adamant as she looked at me and sighed. Annoyed, she purposefully placed her healthy left hand under the withered one, staring at the crippled limb, willing strength into it so she could take care herself of what she wanted me to do. But I wasn't going to help. I couldn't bring myself to remove the stone and leave her hand without it. She had told me long ago that the three-carat, perfect blue diamond had been Vati's gift.

I took my mother's hand and touched the ring; it sparkled like a tiny chandelier.

"I caught its sparkle when you knitted my sweaters, served me food, and caressed my cheeks," I said to her. "These are the fingers I held on our afternoon walks; the diamond should stay here where I remember it best."

Again, tears welled up in her eyes. That was the way it would be. She understood, too, that it was enough for me to know she had wanted me to have it. The oil paintings she had specified as mine were in the room. In one, overcast skies hover over a loaded barge as it trudges along the Elbe, the old Hamburg warehouse, no longer extant, in the background. The other large work depicts a scene with Indians kneeling in prayer on the steps of Santo Thomás, the famous church in Chichicastenango.

"My favorite works of art in this house will grace my home one day, and will continue to surround my life with your love," I said as I bent over to kiss her cheek. "Thank you for remembering how much I like them." Her smile was faint and filled with the sadness of resignation.

She didn't drink her tea, but listened intently to my words. I could feel my entire being ache with love for the woman who had touched my life with so much magic. "Your love has left indelible marks in my heart," I said through the lump building in my throat. I caressed her cheek and moving closer to her, I put my arm around her frail shoulders and whispered in her ear: "I will carry your love with me from this lifetime to all beyond through eternity." Heavy tears fell from my eyes. "I have treasures from you, dear mother, that are eternal," I kissed her gently on the cheek. I had never opened myself to Mutti like this. She needed to know I loved her with every atom of my being. Mutti's sad eyes were focused intensely on me while I poured my heart out to her. Her lips curved into an indulgent, loving smile. Tears pricked my eyes as I held the invalid she had become, and together we wept through the silence that engulfed us.

As I was tending to Mutti's African violets one afternoon, the maid came in and announced that my sister had come to see me. My mother Rosa's network must have informed her about my presence in the country, so she sent Judith to pay me a visit. I was twenty-eight, Judith around twenty. My half-sister entered the room with exuberant joy. She conquered my heart with her buoyant disposition, her many smiles, her easy laughter. I looked at her face, saw a reflection of my own, recognized our kinship and joyfully embraced it. I was overcome with happiness at seeing her, but the unexpected visit must have perplexed me to such a degree that I left the encounter as a mere charming visit, and did not bother to continue a connection to my sister Judith.

⤚⤙

On the morning of my departure I delighted in telling a visibly nervous Ruth at the airport that Mutti had wanted me to have the diamond ring. Her eyes turned to ice. Her teeth clenched until the jaw squared; her entire demeanor hardened as she searched for words to lash at me. I observed the behavior for a few seconds, finding it humorous. With even greater pleasure I let Ruth know I had not taken anything. I saw relief warm the blood that had frozen in her veins.

⤚⤙

Two weeks later, I was working in Berlin when Mutti suffered a second, more devastating stroke. Death was expected imminently and given the local burial codes, Ruth assured me Mutti would be buried before I reached Guatemala. She suggested I stay in Germany and honor my contracts. But one day passed, then another, and yet another, and I wished I'd flown to be with my mother the minute I'd heard of her worsened condition. How was I to know that Mutti, as if wanting to give me time to reach her, would linger between worlds for nine days before allowing herself to glide into eternity? She passed away three years after the first stroke. It was the 24th of August. Three days after Vati's anniversary, and two days before my 31st birthday.

FRED STOOD IN THE LOBBY as I entered the hotel after the fashion show. He came toward me with a serious demeanor, attempting to smile but failing miserably. "You are here?" I asked, uncertain if I should be happy to see him. He embraced me, and I wrapped my arms around him enjoying his nearness.

"Ruth's telegram arrived in Munich this afternoon, and I

didn't want you to be alone tonight with the sad news. I hope you don't mind that I flew in to be here with you. I'm terribly sorry, darling," he whispered. Then he added, and I will never forget it: "Don't worry about a thing, sweetheart. From now on, I'll take care of you."

We spoke little at dinner and ate less and later fell asleep wrapped in each other's arms. There are always miracles in my life, I thought, for here I am in the arms of my love, grieving my beloved mother, and not feeling lost or alone.

But why had Fred thought he needed to take care of me? The protective feelings were familiar; they felt so much like Mutti's cloak to keep me from those who might set out to hurt me.

Fred had spent part of his childhood in China and had lived and worked in New York City and Paris, so he'd been exposed to people of different races since childhood. His concerns regarding me were similar to those Mutti had harbored: both saw me as naïve. Although I knew what was going on in the States during

Catana with Fred in Rome Italy, 1969

the hot summers of the 60s, I did not include myself as belonging to the race of the oppressed. I had never experienced the hatred some American Whites had for Blacks. But when Americans I did not know were around, I was grateful and felt protected by the mere presence of my White husband. By having "the right frame" Mutti had talked about years ago.

The sixties were years of frigid Cold War tactics. Radio Free Europe and Radio Liberty were American stations based in Munich that broadcast US propaganda into countries behind the Iron Curtain. Fred became friends with several individuals who were employed by the radios.

The compatriots Fred met and introduced to me were easygoing, uncomplicated, generous people. Tim Huston was fluent in German and several Eastern European languages. His wife Allie kept their home comfortable and bright and always open to friends. It's debatable whether her pleasure in preparing gourmet meals was greater than her acquaintances' delight in eating at her table. The Huston home had the uncluttered charm of people who had grown up in a vast expanse of country. I saw them as cultured in a fine American way. I could not have picked it up – and nobody felt it important enough to mention – but the melody in Tim and Allie's speech betrayed a Southern origin.

In 1969, Allie's mother arrived for Thanksgiving, and a festive, traditional meal was prepared to which Fred and I were invited. It was a formal dinner table, set for twelve people. I distinctly remember the creamed baby peas with parsley and julienned water chestnuts, for I had never experienced the delicious mix of such distinctive textures.

When I went to the kitchen to see if I could lend a hand with the preparations, I was introduced to Allie's mother, a woman in a cotton duster sitting at the worktable. I tried to engage her in a conversation about her trip, what she thought of Munich, of the Bavarian Alps, but received only monosyllabic answers.

Black Forest wine accompanied the dinner and flowed in abundance, sparking brisk conversations that were drowned in wave after wave of laughter. Allie's mother did not join the company and preferred to remain in the kitchen. I felt bad for her. Based on my understanding, I knew what had happened. I came from a society where servants were commonplace and class distinctions a fact of life. I had grown up being served my meals by those who had prepared them. And kitchen help did not sit at the family table. Allie's mother, as she had introduced herself to me, belonged to the servant class. I assumed she felt socially out of her league in Europe, that her table manners - probably more than her peculiar speech - would reveal her social shortcomings. Out of consideration, she had chosen not to embarrass her daughter.

In fact, everyone else knew why the woman had stayed away. But I had not placed within the geography of their country what I knew about its history, and was blissfully unaware that - because of me - the plight of the American North and South was being played out in Munich between a woman devoid of sophistication and her worldly daughter.

Fred and I had a wonderful time and said so, and upon leaving were asked to return the following day for leftovers. When we left in the early morning hours, Allie's mother was still sitting at the kitchen table, still stewing away in her flimsy cotton duster. By then, she was completely juiced on the moonshine she had made in Kentucky and brought from her blue grass country to share with her children on Thanksgiving in Munich.

WHEN INSULTING SITUATIONS HAPPENED, which was seldom, it took time before I realized what was going on; that is if I became aware it was directed at me in the first place. As was the case one early evening when Fred and I were vacationing in Florence. We had finished sipping espressos at a Café on the Piazza della Signora and were strolling arm in arm along a narrow medieval street. We noticed two American couples on the other side of the alley. They were looking in our direction and seemed to be talking about us. We were accustomed to people finding us interesting, and because of our professions we were sometimes recognized.

This time Fred was unusually aware of the foursome whose curiosity we had aroused. When one of the men crossed the street and came toward us, Fred left me and began to walk in his direction. Then I heard him say: "Mind your goddamn business, buster! This is Europe!" As if zapped by lightning, the man stopped in his sneakers. His chalky face, including his big ears, turned crimson. He spun around on his heels and quickly rejoined his companions. They exchanged a few huddled words and left in the opposite direction to where we were going.

"What, for heaven's sake, was that?" I demanded of Fred.

"I was aware of those Southerners eyeing us and commenting about us in the Café," Fred said seething under his breath. "They've been following us, and that particular jerk was up to no good."

"I don't think they meant anything," I said, shrugging.

"Nope," Fred countered, gently placing his arm around my shoulder. "I actually overheard those miserable redneck bastards!"

"Don't get all worked up about it," I looked at him and noticed how his eyes turned gray when he was angry.

"It's okay now," Fred said as we watched them walk away. We turned, and arm in arm resumed our stroll and our romantic evening. Years later I learned what redneck meant.

There was much laughter in our seemingly carefree view of the world, and have gathered a collection of stories we call 'remember whens.' Our many separations - a feature in the life of performers - kept us in the state of honeymooners when we were together.

Transitions

A letter from Ruth arrived with an enclosed telegram that was dated August 19, 1972. The telegram had been sent by Rosa's husband, Edmundo and communicated that Rosa had suddenly died of a cerebral aneurism. To her condolences, Ruth added a few words saying she had been a good mother.

Rosa passed away seven days before my 32nd birthday. Mutti left me a year earlier, almost to the day.

Fred and I married in our fifth, and Patrick joined us in our sixth year. It was 1973. We had not planned on having a child, not then, or ever. Our lives were unsettled, our schedules erratic, our lifestyle did not lend itself to raising a family. When we discovered we were expecting, however, we decided that a baby was exactly what we wanted. Radiant with joy, my pregnancy became without a doubt the highlight of my life, and I know for sure that for nine months I never stopped smiling, not even in my sleep.

I had conceived and was looking forward to becoming a mother, yet I never thought, not for a split second, of my own conception and birth. I never wondered how my mother felt as she carried me, if she listened to me living inside her the way I delighted at the slightest move my child made within me. It was as if there had been no precedent to my experience. But there had, of course, because I wanted a daughter. "Only one child, one little girl to love and spoil." When the doctor placed the baby in my arms he said, "Congratulations, young mother, meet your sweet son..."

"I'm too tired for jokes," I said half dazed.

"Ah, yes, but you'll grow to like being the mother of a boy."

Son? Boy? How ridiculous, I thought, that a grown man, a doctor at that, can't tell the difference between male and female. Then, I looked at my baby and never thought of a daughter again.

Fred came in the morning wearing his moss-green velvet blazer. He looked more handsome than I had ever seen him. In his arms were all the long-stemmed red roses of our florist's shop. After a while more and more roses arrived until my room was filled with big and little roses: white ones with pink rims, deep salmon ones, canary yellow, orange, little mauve moss roses, all with sprays of baby's breath. The nurse told me that every vase in the clinic was in my room. My husband was beside himself with joy: he had wanted a son but hadn't dared to say so. When the nurse brought our baby, it was the most natural thing for Fred to hold his child. Through tears, he named our baby, who looked like him, Patrick.

Patrick was as rosy as the other infants in the nursery. Each time I held the little pink bundle in my brown arms, or placed him at my brown breasts, I thought: how extraordinary that my child is so light.

"I can tell you right now, he's a smart one, Fred said jokingly. "With you as a mother, he knew enough to show up looking the way he does."

There was plenty of truth in that, for with the exception of the little African in the movie Onkel Tom's Hütte, I had never held a brown baby.

Fred & Baby Patrick, Munich, 1973

Catana as Eliza in German movie
Onkel Tom's Huette, 1968

Catana as model, Rome, Italy, 1969

Catana With Mutti in Hor Zu
article, 1966

Catana on the cover of CHIC fashion
magazine, Sept. 1970

Studio Hado Prützmann, Munich 1970

Studio Hado Pruetmann, Munich, 1975

PART THREE

Things Start to Unravel
1975-1989

Coming to America

As much as I loved Fred, there was no way I would follow him to the States where he spent a few months each year building up his retirement portfolio. Once we had a child, however, and wanting to keep the family from lengthy separations, I agreed to move to California.

We arrived in Los Angeles on Patrick's second birthday, in July 1975. Two weeks later I met with Walter Kohner a film agent who handled primarily European actors.

"I am curious to know, Catana," Walter said the minute I sat down for the interview, "why you left a successful career in Europe to come to the States?"

"Family reasons," I shrugged. "Just wanted to keep my son closer to his dad."

"You are aware that it won't be easy for someone like you to gain a solid foothold in American show business..." he looked at me over the rim of his glasses offering me a weak smile. I nodded, but said nothing. "You're new in Hollywood only once," Walter admonished, "thus, you must make the best of any situation that presents itself. We will certainly support you as best we can, as long as you understand how things are here. The parts will be few and far between, and you will need to be patient." Ten days later I had my first audition: a nineteenth century Caribbean harlot, James Earl Jones' concubine in a swashbuckling movie. "Dress the part, wear something sexy," Walter suggested over the phone, and added, "Good luck!"

I entered Universal Tower wearing a beige silk halter-top and black silk trousers. In my opinion it was an alluring outfit in an understated, elegant way. I was led to a large waiting room filled with actresses who had obviously "dressed the part." Tiny skirts, lots of legs, blouses that revealed everything... they all seemed to sport 'Hollywood boobs', those round, immobile, and hard as a rock breasts. I couldn't believe the wild hairstyles and vulgar make up. I had never been in one, but this could well have been a steaming brothel all right. If I had to look anywhere close to that, I had no chance; my acting ability just wouldn't stretch that far.

Fortunately, my agency had pull and after signing in, I was lead straight to the casting office. There were four people in the room; Mr. Goldstone stood up and shaking my hand, introduced himself as the director.

"So, you are here from Europe! Welcome to Hollywood," he said smiling in a delightfully friendly way. "Tell us about yourself," he added as he relaxed into a chair.

I let them know about my acting work and added that I spoke several languages.

"Wow, several languages!" Goldstone exclaimed impressed and suggested I give them a sample.

I put a few sentences together in my mind, and began, "Seit fünf Wochen bin Ich in Los Angeles, y hace dos semanas compré un condominio muy bonito en Sherman Oaks. Nostre cose dall' Europa non sono arivate ancora, mais je suis certain qu'ils arriveront cette semaine. (I've been in Los Angeles five weeks and two weeks ago we bought a very nice condominium in Sherman Oaks. Our things have not yet arrived from Europe, but I am sure they will get here this week.) Then I'll have everything here and will be settled, finally."

"Gee! Fantastic!" Mr. Goldstone exclaimed. "I want her screen-tested," he shouted to his assistant. "Take her information and make arrangements with the studio." Turning to me he added, "You're not right for the character you came in for. But let's see some test results; I have an interesting idea." With a beam that covered his entire face, he came over to shake my hand and walk me to the door. "Hope to see you soon," he smiled broadly. That was it.

"She jumped right off the screen," was the report an insider gave Fred after the screen test. Six weeks after arriving in Hollywood I signed my first film contract. A cameo was being written for me into a major movie starring, among other luminaries, James Earl Jones, Robert Shaw, Geoffrey Holder, and Peter Boyle. I was the girlfriend of a Polish pirate played by Avery Schreiber, who spoke every language except Polish. My costume was quite lovely: lacey, frilly, and decent; and the three solid scenes were hilariously funny.

Fred and I attended the screening at the Motion Picture Academy. I knew exactly where my scenes were supposed to be in the story. I waited, and waited... and waited... and then the movie was over. What? What happened to my part? I had seen the rushes, my scenes were funny, convincing and good, but my part was cut out. Entirely. In fact, Jones' concubine, the role I had initially presented myself for, also ended on the cutting room floor; as did all lesser characters played by actors of color. I waited for the credits and, lo and behold, all our names were meticulously recorded. It was incomprehensible that Black actors had been extensively auditioned and hired, and would receive residuals for their work, only to ultimately, regardless of the quality of their performance, be eliminated from the film.

Same thing when it came to being cast in commercials. It was the blonde who had all the knowledge and answers and promoted products. Brunettes received the wisdom imparted by the blonde. Blacks? Blacks were nowhere to be seen on commercials. I also auditioned for such, and even had a few callbacks. One young woman who I'd seen on a few auditions said to me as we waited to be called in for a Clairol product: "They won't cast any of us. They waste our time calling us in, but they don't cast us."

I frowned unbelieving, and asked, "Why's that?"

"It's the law now, they have to give us a chance. So they call us in but in the end they'll claim we are not right, or we don't get it... They comply with the law, but find a way to keep us invisible and out of work." There was disappointment in her gentle, reluctant smile.

"If you know that, then why do you bother to come?" I asked, honestly perplexed.

"Well, it might just be the one time they'll actually cast a dark person."

What indignity, I thought. That's where American society was the mid nineteen seventies.

At least the people at Universal had recognized my distinctive quality and had made an honest effort.

IN PART, IT WAS THE GENERAL social environment that scared me; in part it was how I began to feel about myself that I could not convert the early excellent situation into a lasting one. How could I portray an African American woman in America? It was not as it had been in Europe where my complexion had been enough. I knew nothing about African American culture, where being Black was infinitely more complex than simply being dark.

To add to my general sense of displacement and confusion, a few weeks after arriving I was anxious to have my hair straightened. Friends had found a salon in Beverly Hills that catered specifically to the needs of a Black clientele, an exclusive Black clientele. It was not only expensive, but too 'Hollywood' for my conservative taste. There was a lot of hoopla, gaiety, jokes; everyone giggled and laughed and half the time I didn't understand what the people were saying, to me or to each other. It was like being in a foreign country. But worst was that at the end of the ordeal, I did not like how my hair looked. Particularly not for the kind of money I had paid.

A Panamanian neighbor gave me an address in Watts. It was a small and clean establishment, and the woman in charge was friendly and jovial. She left me with straightened wavy hair. It was the first time that when I ran my fingers through it, my hair felt naturally straight and dreamily soft. When I needed a touch-up a few months later, I took Patrick with me. He could not have been much older than three, and was with me when Fred wasn't home. Accustomed to being with a caring parent, our son was always very well behaved.

The woman was not as friendly as before and while washing my hair poured water over my face and soaked my dress.

"You're very rough today," I said. "Look at my dress, I'm soaking wet."

"Umph!" came the grumpy response.

As I was sitting under the dryer, I heard her address Patrick in a tone I had never heard anyone use with a child.

"How are you speaking to my son? How dare you talk to my little boy like that!" I glared at her.

"Ah saw him thrashing mah magazines 'round,'" came her boldfaced lie.

"Don't lie to me," I said to her quietly, "he was only looking at a magazine."

Not knowing what he'd done wrong, Patrick came over and I helped him scramble onto my lap.

I didn't appreciate the woman's ugly expression and wondered whether I should fear her or not. I certainly wasn't going to let her out of my eyes. When my hair was dry, I took the curlers out, put the exact cash on the counter and left without combing my hair out. She came to the door, her eyes flashing angry daggers at us. I placed Patrick in the car and climbed in and fled the scary neighborhood. Once we were out of what I felt was danger, I secured Patrick in his car seat. We had done nothing, said nothing that could have justified such animosity. It was the first overtly racist treatment I had ever experienced in my entire life. I had never lived through anything quite as frightening before. My innocent little boy was attacked because he obviously had a White father and I, because I had a White husband.

Eventually, I identified a male stylist on Pico, not quite as marginal as the last, but still... Ruth's oldest son, Thomas, was visiting at the time and drove me to the beautician. He waited for me in the car and as the session lasted longer than anticipated, came in to reassure himself that all was OK.

I had not learned at that time that it's perfectly fine to tell inquisitive people to mind their damn business. After seeing Thomas, the hairdresser had all kinds of questions.

"Who dat fella?"

Like a dummy, I responded that he was my nephew, visiting from home.

"Aha," said the man, "where you home?"

"Central America," I said, not even wondering why I was answering.

"Wha's dat?"

"South of Mexico."

"Uh, huh, den how come you na speak Spanish?"

That much he'd caught on. Like an idiot, I explained that I had a German family.

"You husban' Jaman?" He persisted.

I took the chance to simplify matters and said yes.

"Now why would a beautiful sistah like yousef not marry a brother?"

Oh, dear, here it was: 'sistah,' a term to which I was severely allergic.

"There are none in Europe," I snapped.

"Tha's still no reason to marry White," and everybody in the establishment opened their mouths wide and laughed with gusto.

"Don't tell me you can't have your hair done somewhere else," Thomas said as we drove off. "That's a horrible place. I kept looking in to make sure you were all right."

"I hate California," I lowered my head. "I don't understand Americans. Not the Black ones, and sometimes not the White ones either."

"Go to the sort of place where you deal with people of your own class," Thomas offered unconditionally.

So, I returned to the pretentious salon where the meaning of words, gestures, looks... were all strange and often intimidating. I was intimidated because I felt that as a Black I had to understand what they were saying. I also thought they felt I understood what was going on, when I didn't. Even my accent, slightly European and slightly West Indian, did not justify my not understanding African American culture. The actress Leslie Uggams was once there. She was enchanting and talked a little with me. Billie Dee Williams and Ben Vereen tried to flirt with me on another occasion. NOW I know it was flirting, then I thought they were intrusive and rude.

To simplify matters I decided to forget straight hair and keep my own natural and short. That way I didn't have to go to anyone in particular. The bonus was that I looked twenty years younger than my actual age.

Through my hair I learned that at the time, a certain segment of the African American population could be dangerously racist toward people like me who were Black and cosmopolitan. I had not anticipated that. I also learned that regardless of the environment, I didn't understand the codes of behavior, the language or the culture. The business of 'sistahs' and 'brathas' was alien to me. To this day, I am still horrified when I hear African American children being barked at, particularly when they're doing no wrong. I never saw anyone bark at a child in Guatemala or Jamaica. And no one ever barked at me. It would never have occurred to me to bark at my son. The only person who dared to mistreat my child in my presence was a Black woman in Los Angeles.

After two seasons on Villa Alegre, an educational T.V. show where I played a bilingual Latina physician, my lack of self-confidence began to consistently cripple me. I knew I was not a Chicana, which actually did not matter, but I became so critical of myself, that I didn't think I was Hispanic enough. No one in the cast knew I felt this way because of my fluency in Spanish. But by the end of the second season my workdays began with a vomiting session. Increasingly paralyzed and incapable of adjusting, I decided I was too old for an acting career and put show business behind me for good.

In the United States, the magic carpet Mutti had so carefully woven for me began to deteriorate into a mangy rug that could easily be pulled from under my feet.

Nightmare in 1977

In the fall of 1977, I accepted Ruth's invitation to spend the month around Christmas in Guatemala. Ruth's son Andreas was in Germany studying architecture. Thomas was a medical student in Guatemala. By then both Mutti and Rosa had died, as had Ruth's husband Rudolf.

Ruth made a schedule for our visit and suggested that four-year-old Patrick stay with her in the city, while Fred and I joined a group of tourists on a three-day trip to the Mayan sites of Copán and Quiriguá, the colonial Fortress San Felipe, and from there sail by yacht down the Río Dulce to Livingston. In my 37 years, no one had ever mentioned I could or should visit my birthplace. Now Ruth wanted me to go there, and with my husband, of all people!

The bitch, I thought of Ruth, as old rivalries began to surge. She wants Fred to see the dump of a village where I was born! Surely, she knew how deeply my origins pained me, and I felt this was a way for her to get even with me for having consumed all her mother's fascination.

Fred, as always, was ready at the drop of a hat to go on an adventurous exotic excursion and I couldn't disappoint him. So, concealing my extreme reluctance, we headed for the jungle in a spacious bus with every comfort for such an expedition. Crawling on Mayan digs brought the usual thrills of encounters with scorpions, curious snakes, and playful monkeys. My laughter and carefree demeanor masked the weight I felt as we headed toward my lowly birthplace in the company of gregarious, albeit pretentious, socialites.

When time came to travel to Livingston, we boarded an elegant three-deck yacht captained by a friendly young Black man with brilliant green eyes. I had seen such dazzling eyes on a man who visited us when I was little and Vati was alive. He was the one I associated with colors: his skin was brown, his eyes were green, his name was white - Blanco. As a child I feared Mr. Blanco.

Curious to know if there was a relationship, I asked the young man if his name was by chance Blanco. A bit surprised at my question, he responded affirmatively. "I knew your father," I said to him. "When I was little, a gentleman from Livingston occasionally visited my parents bringing freshly frozen fish in a block of ice. His eyes were just as green as yours, and his name was Blanco."

"My father has brown eyes," the young man answered smiling

broadly. "The one you knew was my grandfather. He had green eyes, like mine." Then he looked at me intently as if trying to see if he knew me. "You are Mohrle," he said with glee at having made the connection, "you are the girl don Pablo stole!"

STOLE! STOLE!! I had never heard that term applied in reference to me. "Stole?" I said, but he continued:

"Everyone knows about you. You are an actress in Germany and a fashion model." He smiled and nodded... "We saw pictures of you in the newspaper with a long article about your success. So..." he said approvingly, "You have come back to visit Livingston! Welcome!" His smile was broad, and bright, and beautiful.

I just grinned. "Wait," I said, as if he were going anywhere, "I have to tell my husband." I turned and ran down the stairs to the lower deck. I could hear roaring belly laughs, and knew Fred was nearby telling one of his tall tales.

"Hey Fred, guess what," I said pulling him aside and lowering my voice. "You have to hear this. That young captain is from Livingston and he knows about me!" It was awkwardly thrilling to find someone at the periphery of the world who years ago had read an article in the Guatemalan newspaper, and remembered it well enough to recognize me.

"Stole?" Fred asked after he heard the young captain's term.

"It's the village talking, not worth the mention," I shrugged it off. We returned to the pilot's deck, and talked to the man with the green knowing eyes. He told us about his children and his life on the river and on the sea, and I decided to dismiss but not forget the term he had used.

The sun was high in the heavens by the time we reached the beginning of the estuary where the sweet river waters become one with the salty Atlantic. Beyond a wide bend in the river, like a mirage, our destination floated into view. Pelicans skimmed along the waves searching for unwary fish. Closer to the pier, a horde of skinny, long-legged dark kids laughed and shouted as they skipped and jumped along the water. The only still and serious one stood on a boulder pissing intently into the wider stream.

Livingston. What a decrepit village at the far end of nowhere. In 1977 I hated it, hated the way it embarrassed me. Later, I'd understand that no one cared whether I had been born there or not. Fred, better than I was able to grasp, had no problem with Livingston. In fact, it delighted him. He had met and married me in sophisticated Munich. For years, he had looked at me and always seen the same dark face and obviously didn't mind. He knew I was one thing for sure: and that was dark. He had committed himself to me at a time when interracial unions were nearly unheard of, certainly not a popular feature. He also knew my story as I had told it to him, and was fascinated finally to set foot in the jungle and the remote village.

Blanco's grandson showed us how to reach the Casa Grande, and Fred and I retraced the path my parents - my Black ones and my White ones - had known so well.

The wooden house with a large verandah didn't look anything like the pictures I had seen of the beautiful mansion my parents had to leave behind. In serious disrepair and filthy, the house looked like a forlorn lover, haunted by memories of a generous past. The once manicured lawn was brown with patches of dirt. Mutti's lovely home was now an army barracks, a run-down and dirty one at that. A heavy-set woman labored up the hill. When she reached us, Fred asked her if that was indeed Don Pablo's house. She caught her breath and nodded, and without taking her eyes off me, smiled knowingly and said: "Usted es la Mohrle."

Casa Grande living room, Livingston, 1940

Catana in front of what remained
of Casa Grande, 1977

"Everyone here remembers you!" Fred exclaimed excited. Soon he would be telling people that a throng of children had followed us chanting and pointing: "She is Mohrle, the child the Germans grabbed," his actor's imagination giving way to fantasy. Truth is, no one followed us, and I was glad to get back on the yacht and head away from the wretched place. Thank heavens for Mutti!

Had they in fact stolen me? Had Mutti kept me against my birth mother's will? How could they have done that? One mother takes me, the other lets me go? I could never have given up my child. Concerned that everything be right for Patrick every minute day or night, I didn't even entrust him to a babysitter. If he wasn't with me, he was with Fred; and when he started kindergarten, I drove miles to drop him off and pick him up. I didn't at first trust the school bus either.

Ruth and Thomas created a spectacular Christmas Eve for Patrick. Thomas recruited his best friend to be Santa Claus. In typical Latin American fashion, Santa was delayed in traffic. Patrick ran out to meet him in the garden. Santa held onto the child's hand and began to recount his trials and tribulations in trying to find him. "Patrick, thank heavens I finally found you," he said harrumphing in a Spanish accented English. "Please excuse my lateness but I looked for you all over Germany, no one knew where you were," he stopped to catch his breath. "I was desperate, until finally someone told me you were in California. Then your house in California was empty! Thank heavens for your neighbor Selma who pointed me to Guatemala. Who knew, Patrick, that you would be all the way here in Catalina? Oh Patrick, I am so happy I have finally found you," he exclaimed and plunked down in the nearest chair, claiming exhaustion and releasing the large sack he was carrying. A multitude of presents spilled all over the floor. The child had never seen such an abundance of gifts, and all were for him. Patrick was almost in his teens before he finally grasped that Santa was not real. Not even the one who had so convincingly searched all over Germany and America only to find him in Guatemala.

BUT THE TRIP REMAINED FILLED with overt and subliminal tensions between Ruth and me. Even Catalina felt oppressive, constricting. I thought I remembered more and better rugs, more paintings, and a more sophisticated decor. And then Ruth's insistence I visit Livingston with Fred, and my visceral feelings of humiliation.

On the last evening of our visit, black clouds covered the sky and the wind whistled ominously through the chimney as Ruth, Fred and I sat down to dinner. We had not begun dessert when, after royally pushing each other's buttons, things between Ruth and me turned toxic.

I no longer remember what the exact reason for it was, I only know that Ruth burst out with, "You always played to Mother's love and never considered how her doting on you and only you must have hurt me. No one else ever counted for her but you," she said in a state of emotion that was uncommon for her.

"I can't help it that she loved me," I responded screeching. "You did things that were dishonest. Mutti told me about them. About what you were capable of doing and, as far as I could see, she was right." Ruth knew exactly what I was alluding to, for it had to do with finances.

"How dare you bring that up? None of it was true," Ruth screamed wild-eyed, her voice cracking. I had never witnessed such passion in her. "Mother made up stories to justify having neglected me." Ruth's eyes filled, and tears ran down her cheeks. "I've never been able to deal with the pain... of not having been loved... by my mother."

"How could I be responsible for Mutti's feelings?" I yelled, too rabid to feel sorry for her. "I could not possibly have helped you." Still I added, "She loved you, Ruth. But she also knew you; and as I understand things now, you proved your mother right. She told me so." I was so enraged my chest hurt. I sobbed and heaved and wiped away fiery tears that had lain dormant for decades.

Fred looked on in dismay, his eyes flying from Ruth to me, and back again. In his family, feelings and emotions exploded at the drop of a word, but he had never witnessed a more caustic combustion. He watched in disbelief how two usually composed people lost themselves in a long-overdue passionate outpouring of emotion.

"As far as I'm concerned, Ruth," I hissed, rubbing salt in the wound, "I have Mutti's love, for all eternity. No mortal can change that reality. It cannot be taken away from me, ever! What are you complaining about? You have everything here; that should comfort you and make you feel warm and fuzzy. I covet none of it and I guarantee and promise you, I never will."

We were awash in tears, including my sentimental Fred. Enraged, I left the table and went to my bedroom without a further word.

"And why were you crying?" I demanded furiously of Fred as he followed me.

He took me in his arms and pressed my head to his shoulder. "My heart goes out to Ruth, sweetheart. You are heartless. Why are you so hard-hearted, so blinded, that you miss the tenderness in Ruth's love for you? Ruth has always shown it; I've been aware of it everyday."

"Mutti's love for me will always fuel Ruth's jealousy. It's our history," I said bitterly.

I felt the pressure surging in my throat. My eyes welled up again and overflowed. Overwhelmed by the situation, and not knowing what to do with all the misery, I just let my husband hold me while I dissolved in sobs. "She loves you, Catana. Ruth, too, loves you so much, and you love her, believe me," he whispered as he cradled my gently. I knew Ruth had loved me, once... before Rudolf. But after the mess with Werner, I just couldn't see that she still did.

Ruth and I embraced the next morning at the airport when we said goodbye. But, stubborn as I was, stubborn as a mule, I took off for the States without apologizing.

Resettling and Settling

Patrick was five when he began kindergarten in a Waldorf School in Northridge, then a White neighborhood deep in the San Fernando Valley. It was 1978, and we'd been in California three years. I often drove him to school or picked him up in the afternoon. Occasionally, I stopped at a small market for groceries. Each time I was asked to show identification when I bought wine. The first time the woman at the register apologized, seeing that I was twice as old as 18. We even joked about my youthful appearance. After being a regular customer for half a year, I still had to show an ID when paying with a check. I noticed that other customers, White customers, didn't need to do that. That's when the coin fell: I was being singled out and in an insidious way, humiliated.

Most racist insults bounced off me. I am sure some still do, and I wonder whether an insult is in fact one, when the person at whom it's directed doesn't understand it.

I became increasingly confused and unhappy in Los Angeles. I couldn't fathom the place; I felt it lacked culture, that people had painfully superficial values. But mostly there was too much about me I didn't grasp. I had not cared that Blacks viewed me with skepticism, but when Whites' attitudes began to be encoded as negative, I had nowhere to turn. It would have been counterproductive to confide in my friends for as far as they were concerned, I had the best of all worlds.

Of all the places I'd lived in, I felt most at ease in Munich. I gladly accepted a friend's invitation to visit in the spring of 1979. When I returned to Sherman Oaks after three weeks, I let Fred and Patrick know I bought an apartment and we'd be moving back to Germany. Aware of my unhappiness in California and unable to help me in that regard, Fred agreed to return to Europe. We sold our house, and three months later, we were in Munich. With the help of an influential friend of bygone years, I obtained working papers and a steady job.

Every morning Patrick fed the seagulls on the Isar as Fred walked him to school. Fred was a popular dad who never refused a teacher's invitation to play an English-speaking clown for the class.

But I felt Munich had changed. Although I saw my friends of previous years, my day-to-day colleagues were humorless bureaucrats who made it known through snide insinuations that they knew someone at the top had pulled strings for me. I landed the job through connections, not merit, and as interesting as the company was, I disliked my work.

On our first vacation we visited friends in San Miguel de Allende, Mexico. We not only fell in love with the quaint village, we decided to move there. I'd take up painting, I reasoned, while Fred worked in the US and came to visit every month and a half or so. Patrick took the uprooting and settling and resettling in stride: it was a family affair. Together we packed our things, together we traveled, together we unpacked and rearranged everything in a new home, elsewhere. Patrick spoke English and German; now he needed to learn to say everything in Spanish, and he did. I enjoyed living among artists again, mainly because in San Miguel it was an international European group.

After a year and a half - Patrick was in second grade - he

began to ask the sort of questions that would not have occurred to me as a child.

"Am I German, Mommy?"

"No, sweetheart," I answered, "but you were born in Germany."

"Are you German?"

"No, Patrick, I'm Guatemalan."

"Am I Guatemalan, then?"

"No, you are American, like your dad." That sufficed for the afternoon and lasted for about two weeks. Then I received a note from his teacher informing me that my son refused to sing the Mexican anthem.

"What's the matter with the Mexican anthem?" I asked him.

"It calls for Mexicans to go to war. I'm not Mexican. It does not apply to me."

"Do you know which war it was?"

"Sure," he said. "The war when the States invaded Mexico." He looked at me intently, then added, "Mexico lost that war..."

"Mexico lost more than just the war; Mexico lost half its territory," I said.

"Who won the First World War, Mommy?" Patrick followed up.

"The Allies."

"Was the States the Allies?"

"Part of them."

"And who won the Second World War?"

"The United States and the Allies," I answered, wondering where he had learned about the wars and why he was so intent on knowing who won what. After all, he was only in second grade.

"What am I doing here? I'm American, I should be in the States," the child concluded.

As I spent hours painting, Patrick was also inspired to put on paper what he concocted in his imagination. His works detailed battlefields between Indians and Spaniards, or Mexicans and Americans. My son was learning the history of a mixed-race peoples who commemorate October 12th - the date of Columbus' arrival - as El Día de la Raza and celebrate the dawning of a new, a mixed race in the Americas. The celebration acknowledges the painful birth of a nation whose inhabitants must honor their blended ancestry in order to triumph.

I wonder how much having lived in Mexico and learning about its proud, painful history brought Patrick to grapple with his own sense of self. How did he see himself? With a White and a Black parent, the blood of conqueror and conquered pulsating in his veins, it must have crossed his mind to think, 'Who am I? The one who won, or the one who lost?'

Our son needed a family that looked like him, one he could identify with. He had met Fred's sister Jeanne in California, and it was extraordinary how much he resembled her. In 1981 we put our intentions into action, and flew to upstate New York for Thanksgiving week. Patrick met his grandmother and Fred's other sister Jackie, and dozens of cousins (I'm not exaggerating.) Everyone thought he was fantastic because he said "I beg your pardon?" or "Pardon?" when he didn't understand something, and at table asked for a serviette, not a napkin. It seemed uncanny to all of us, how perfectly the child fit into his father's clan.

On the flight back to Mexico, Patrick sat next to me in the airplane, sobbing. "I want to live in New York, Mommy. That's where our family is, that's where my daddy is." And I knew then and there that our time in Mexico was over. At the end of his school year - a week before his ninth birthday - we moved to Upstate New York. It was summer 1982.

The Northeast is a far cry from Los Angeles, of course. Geographically and weather-wise it reminded me of Europe. For Patrick's sake, I decided not to move for awhile.

My intention had been to continue painting, but beautiful as the area was, it offered little inspiration. Not having finished my formal education, I found no work commensurate to my knowledge. So, at forty-two, I hunkered down in Delmar, NY and began to complete a college education. Fred had a pied-à-terre in New York City where he worked during the week. The family was together on weekends. Patrick interacted with his cousins, started piano and trumpet lessons and became one of the cornerstones of the music program in his school. We were on a comfortable and predictable track; the years of flitting around were over, the Tully's became grounded in the State of New York.

During my accelerated Bachelor's degree, I had to fill out innumerable forms and each time had to identify racially or ethnically. Was I a citizen? Was I Black? Was I Hispanic? What was my identity? I d e n t i t y... It was as if I was hearing the term identity for the first time. Slowly, very slowly, I grasped, much to my horror (what friends already knew) that I had a problem with self-definition. Never before had I needed to clarify who I was. Others did it for me: I was different. Period. Now I had to say what I was, or what others expected to see precisely in the definition. Which box should I mark when I didn't see me fitting comfortably into any. There was no box marked "Exotic." Whatever I chose, I felt I'd end up falling into a stereotypical category to be judged, catalogued, and shelved.

The very first courses I selected focused on African American literature. I literally devoured books by Toni Morrison, Maya Angelou, Alice Walker, Zorah Neal Hurston, Ralph Ellison, Richard Wright, Frederick Douglas... I specify these writers not only because their works touched me deeply but because they addressed an understanding of racial and cultural identity I ignored. My studies covered the history of modern slavery and the painful African American experience after Emancipation and during Reconstruction. And, finally, the Civil Rights Movement, during which I had already been a young adult living in Munich, but had chosen to ignore. Through books I managed to get a fat dose of what African American anger was about, how deeply Black history had, for centuries, been mired in injustice. With chills running up and down my spine, I began to comprehend why being Black in the USA was always a political issue way before it became personal. And why White Fred, from White upstate New York, had been so unconventional and brave in choosing me as his wife at the time he did.

~

While concluding my doctoral internship in 1988, I received, out of the blue, a call from Guatemala. "Hi, Catana, it's Ruth," she said rapidly. "I'm calling to tell you that I've just given Gil your address." I almost dropped the receiver; I didn't know the man was still alive. Ruth was fluttering at the other end like an agitated bird. "He was here, n' called n' asked about you," she continued hurriedly. "I told him you're in upstate New York. He's retired now and he and his wife travel all over the States by car." She paused to clear her throat, then continued hastily as if not wanting me to say anything. "He said they might pay you a visit, so I'm calling you right away; I don't want you to be shocked senseless should they suddenly appear at your doorstep." She paused to catch her breath.

Oh dear... my father Gil might look me up. What the...? "Thanks for letting me know," my voice was flat, distant. What was there to say? Maybe he was already at my curb! Cripes! "Where does he live?" I managed to say through anxiety.

"He said in Brooklyn. Listen, Catana," - now that she had dropped the bomb, Ruth was calm - "Don't be alarmed. I had to give him your address. After all, he is your father and he's no one to be ashamed of. He stayed at the very best hotel in town, and he has a fine sense of humor, you'll like him, wait and see."

"Don't worry, I can handle it; after all I've nothing to be ashamed of either," I said, and thanked her for alerting me.

I was not interested in meeting Gil, far from it, but I guess I was curious because a few days after Ruth's call, feeling somewhat mischievous, I called the Brooklyn directory for his number. I toyed with the idea of hearing what his voice sounded like. I wouldn't identify myself, of course, for that I'd need a lot more nerve.

"Hellou?" A woman answered.

"May I please speak with Josephine?" Josephine? Where'd that come from?

"There's no one here by that name," came an icy reply.

"Oh dear, I was given this number for Josephine Hernandez. It must be the wrong one. I'm sorry," I hung up. The wife, I figured, and redialed hoping to hear a different voice. But it was she again. I concluded that he'd have answered if he were home. So I waited until evening.

Bingo! I had Gil on the phone! "May I speak with Josephine, please?" I said, in a carefree manner that belied the acute attention I was paying.

"Oh, Josephine..." he mused. "She's not here. What a pity, you just missed her!"

I realized right away that he'd been told about my earlier calls. "I called this morning," I said trying to keep him on the phone. "At least this is the right number. When do you expect her back?"

"That's never easy to say, because she's out fishing and you know how the currents are... It may well be days before she returns."

"Oh well, thank you." I hung up, and bent over and burst out laughing like a teenager after mischief. That geezer was wicked! And the tropics were branded on his soul and psyche. After living in Brooklyn some 50 years, he still connected to canoes and going fishing on the high seas!

He didn't call and didn't come by either.

Energies set in Motion

When energies are released into the ether, the Universe responds with miracles.

I was at my desk reading papers when the phone rang. "Hola Bicho, sorpresa!" (Hey kid, surprise!) It was Putzi, my dearest childhood friend. She was in Miami en route to her home in Paris. We had not spoken to each other for what seemed ages. After catching up a bit, I told her that Patrick thought he wasn't growing as fast as his friends, and feared not being tall. Fred, at 5'10" was the tallest in his family, and I had no viable frame of reference for my side.

"Tell him not to worry, he still has years of growth ahead of him," Putzi said. "And anyways, your dad was at least six foot tall, remember?"

"How would you know that?"

"Because my father was six foot, and like mine, yours also had to duck when going through the arch in the hall. Not too many did that."

"Are you sure? Six foot? Patrick will love it. But I don't remember seeing my father at all. When did you see him?"

"Only once, and how could I ever forget, bichito, (endearing term we used for each other when we were kids) you were terrified of him!"

This is the weirdest thing, I thought. How come I don't remember meeting my father? "And I was what? Terrified you say?"

"He was on his way to the States and came to say good-bye. At one point he grabbed you and said: 'I'm taking you with me!' He was joking of course, but you sure didn't think it was funny." I said nothing. "Ay, bichito loco, come on! You must remember! You were in a state of panic! You stood there like a tin soldier, only nodding when he tried to get you to say something. When he left, someone had to push you toward him to shake his hand and say good-bye." Putzi began to giggle. "Don't worry, I didn't get too close to him either... And it's a good thing he had a solid sense of humor, for a lesser man would've been devastated by the rejection." We burst out laughing just as we did as kids decades ago. I wiped away tears of hilarity. My stomach ached and I heard Putzi in Miami whimpering, "Ayayay..." We hadn't changed in all the years: when we laughed, we did so until it hurt.

Finally, between gasps, I moaned, "Do you remember approximately how old we were?"

Putzi collected herself. "Pablo was still alive, that's about as close to an age as I can get. Probably around 7, maybe older."

"What was he like?"

"He was tall for sure and I think he was quite handsome. I remember being impressed. I also remember, quite distinctly, that you didn't talk about his visit, and it took at least a week before you were back to normal again. Do you know if he's still alive?"

"Yes. Ruth called not long ago telling me he lived in Brooklyn. I was curious to hear his voice and called him, but did not identify myself," I giggled again.

"You chicken!" Putzi scolded, but I could see her grinning. "If I were you, I'd get in touch with him. After all, he is as close to you as Patrick. Bichito, be a grown-up and connect with your dad." She paused, and before I could say anything added: "Better still, go see him! If I had time I'd strengthen your backbone and go to Brooklyn with you."

"You are a crazy girl," I said, not at all humored. "I am chicken, you are right." What was she thinking? Me go to Brooklyn and chase him down?

"I'll call you in a month to check on you and have you tell me how your dad is," her tone was serious, as if she meant it.

"You do that," I snapped. "At least it won't be twenty years before we chat again." After our good-byes I shrugged, and knew she'd forget to call.

Without deliberate intention, I opened the bottom drawer where I kept the brittle manila folder Mutti had handed to me on my 21st birthday. It was the same folder on which Vati had carefully drawn an "M" with blue and red ink, and wherein I still kept all official documents regarding Mohrle. From my birth certificate to my various vaccinations, to report cards... all was in that folder.

I removed the colorful official Guatemalan papers and began to read them again. There was the original birth certificate of 1940 and two other formal documents both dated 1944. In one, Gilbert E. Reed declares his paternity, stating that I was to carry his name and enjoy all the privileges and rights of a legitimate child. In the other, a shorter one also dated 1944, my name is officially changed from Adriana without a surname, to Catana with the surname Reed. In another delicate envelope was a small photograph of my father. Putzi said she remembered him as good-looking, and Mutti and Ruth on occasions when they referred to Gil, described him as attractive. As a child, when I pouted, they also said I looked like him. I did not cry; I pouted. "Look at that lip sticking out!" Mutti or Ruth said laughingly, "Looks like the rim of the birdbath! Pull it in, Mohrle," they teased, "or a bluebird will fly down and land on it." And they'd add: "She looks just like Gil." I had checked my upset face in the mirror and thought I looked ugly. So, to me, Gil had to be ugly.

I had seen the photograph before but never bothered to really look at it. How old was Gil when he wrote 'Best Wishes, GEReed, 1945'? He's slightly chubby, I thought to myself, but far from being fat. On his lips (his lower one protrudes a bit, like mine) lies the trace of a smile, a rather smug one and not the sort of expression I like. Really, what could they have found appealing? What could my mother Rosa have liked about this man?

Putzi indeed forgot to call, at least not as she had threatened in a month. She called three years later.

At fifteen, Patrick was a perfect blend of his parents. He had fine features and dark, serious eyes that could stare you down with impunity. The curls in his hair were kept short so he always looked well put together and his hands, delicate like those of a violinist commanded with power his chosen instrument, the piano. He tanned quickly in summer and just as quickly lost his color in the fall. He was deeply involved in the school district's music program and received private music lessons for piano and trumpet. When he was approached with a significant scholarship to enter high school at the Interlochen Arts Academy in Michigan, Fred and I did not interfere with his decision to accept. He had spent the two previous summers at the music camp that accompanies the academy so he knew the place well. After all, I was 15 when I ended up in Jamaica.

At the end of his sophomore year, Patrick decided to give up his primary instrument, the trumpet, and change entirely to piano. Although the academy accepted his wishes, Fred and I decided it was time he come home and finish the last two years of high school in Delmar. He had a brilliant piano teacher in Albany, someone who had all along mentored him in music. Having been an athlete in his youth, Fred was aware of Patrick's athleticism and welcomed the more rounded education the public school would offer. Our son only agreed to stay home after I bribed him with a car. It was 1989; he was 17.

"Sweetie," Fred said with a dubious expression on his face, "I am quite sure you are unaware of being a monster of a control freak."

Controlling? Me? I only wanted what was best for our son, and best for him now was being at home as he finished high school.

Catana and Patrick 1978 in
Sherman Oaks, CA

PART FOUR

Confronting Confusion
1989-1992

I stand motionless atop a rugged cliff, scanning a landscape where a cloudless sky spans the horizon. The jasmine-scented breeze touches the tassel hanging from my cap and dances in the folds of my gown... Yes, my gown, my newly acquired heavy black silk academic regalia. Three velvet stripes on the sleeves honor the doctoral degree, and the blue, gold, and white striped hood lying on my shoulders represents the School of Humanities. "Here they are," I hear the breeze whisper in my ear, "time for you to try them on." I turn my head to the right, and from the corner of my eye see a majestic wing, the sort a renaissance artist would have pinned on the Archangel Gabriel. "There's one on the other side as well," the breeze adds jokingly. I would hope so, I think to myself, and smile. "They are light but powerful, Catana; it's time for you to use them." I hesitate. "Go ahead, go now." Tentatively, I hunch my shoulders forward, then upward; I spread first one, then the other wing. I look again to the right, then to the left and carefully move the pair of magnificent extensions. "They're perfect," the breeze murmurs, "now fly..." Obediently, I flap my wings once, twice, and the wind lifts me up. "Courage," the breeze calls, sensing my fears. "By the way, you look like a natural at this. Good luck," I hear as the wind carries me onward and upward, and I soar like an eagle. Like an eagle I dip and glide weightlessly, but purposefully in the air. I survey the immensity of what lays before, below, beside me. Mountains, hills, valleys, I glide through canyons and ravines, skim over streams and lakes, over sandy coastlines, and up again to hover above snow-capped mountains: inhaling the breathtaking splendor that surrounds me. Suddenly, unexpectedly and uncalled for, the glorious wings collapse spectacularly and I spiral downward from the heavens, out of control, like a dejected angel.

I awake frightened, disoriented, and bathed in cold sweat.

AFTER SIX YEARS OF FOCUSED ACADEMIC WORK, I completed my doctorate in Humanistic Studies in 1989. Following my advisor's suggestion I applied for an academic position at a college nearby.

The dean was duly impressed by my credentials and after the interview called his assistant requesting she make the necessary arrangements for me to meet the team of interviewing faculty.

A friendly Black woman with kind eyes and a relaxing, motherly quality escorted me to her office where she offered me a seat in a chair across from her desk. She picked up my résumé, read it with interest and studying me, said: "Nowhere in this Vita do I get the sense that I am reading about a Black person." I was stunned by her comment and explained that my degree was in the Humanities, broadly speaking. Instantly, I began to worry that she had discovered something important the dean had missed.

"It's all very interesting and interdisciplinary, of course," she said in an easy manner, "but you don't show studies that deal with Black issues."

"I'm Hispanic," I answered too rapidly for my liking, "and my high-school education took place in Jamaica; I have a British high-school diploma, and have studied and worked in Europe for many years." A nasty sense of discomfort began to engulf me. Why was I explaining anything at all to this assistant? What business of hers was it anyway? She was Black and I already knew what she was about to do. She, like all Black people, was not going to accept me as one of her own, and in spite of her friendly demeanor, she intended to put me down.

"Why don't you join a Black professional organization?" she suggested. "That would make it clear to everyone that you are Black... on paper as well as off."

I sighed with relief and thanked her for the suggestion. She was right, the obvious should be reflected in my Vita: as an educated older woman, Hispanic, of African descent, I was a valuable multiple minority, the sort colleges were desirous to employ. The woman had only been helpful and friendly, when I was ready to assume the worst. I had hoped to land a job before I was fifty, and I succeeded, for I was forty-nine years and eight months old when I signed the contract. That was early 1990. I would turn 50 in August.

What had happened? What had the panic in the assistant's office been about? Why had I been riddled with insecurities? Again? No matter how much I'd been commended for my work, I still worried I'd do or say something asinine and blow it. What was it that caused such inner turmoil, such a debilitating feeling of inadequacy? I had not only done well, I had done great! After all my hard work, I should be at a place of inner peace and comfort. I had been a successful actress; had landed parts when they were few and far between for people like me. Same thing with my career as a model; I worked almost all the time. In Mexico, where I taught myself to paint behind glass, my paintings sold the day I left them at the gallery. And now, after very few years, I completed an academic career I was deservedly proud of. That should be enough reassurance, right? This should not have happened again.

But it did. What a let down! And I can't tell any of my friends about these debilitating circumstances for, as always, as far as they're concerned, I've lived my entire life in the best of all worlds.

Vivaldi played softly in the tan and white waiting room where prints of tulips and roses graced the walls. There was a touch of cinnamon in the air; it was peaceful. I sank into a seasoned leather chair and closing my eyes, tried to relax while the music filled the room. Mozart followed Vivaldi, and as if on cue, a slender woman in pale blue linen opened the door to the office. Shoulder-length, thick, shiny hair the color of rich chocolate framed an unadorned, rather beautiful face. Her hazel eyes looked at me calmly, steadily like her name, Constance. I would call her Connie, and she would become my psychological counselor. Her expertise lay in valuing women, men, and children equally, and in understanding the intricacies and complexities of female relationships.

We sat in her office in comfortable chairs facing each other.

"Congratulations, on your doctoral degree, and at a point in life when others start slowing down, it is indeed quite an accomplishment," she smiled and I could see a sincere expression of admiration in her eyes. "Where did you grow up? Tell me a bit about yourself." Her voice was soft and melodic.

"I grew up in Guatemala, attended high school in Jamaica, and an interpreter's academy in Germany. Rather than pursue languages, I became an actress and fashion model in Europe where I met and married my American husband. We have a 17-year-old son. Now, I'm sitting in your office trying to figure out why I suffer from deep-seeded anxiety." I proceeded to tell her about having been raised by Mutti, Ruth, and Vati, and that thanks to them my life can only be said to have been charmed. "I am quite sure the issues plaguing me and I am trying to deal with now, stem from a remote existence, one far removed from this lifetime. I hope," I concluded smiling mildly, "that you can help me shed some light on what torments me."

When she finished taking notes, Connie wanted to know more about my German family.

"There was Mutti, which is a term for mommy in German, her daughter Ruth, who was thirty and unmarried at my birth. Ruth played a significant role and I used to call her Mama until I was ten. And there was Vati, a German term for daddy. He was slightly older than Mutti."

Connie thought about the selection and then said, "Please tell me about Mutti."

My answer came quickly, confidently. "She was an admirable woman. Her life's endeavor, it seemed, focused on doing everything she could that was right for me. I lacked nothing and don't remember ever asking for something. Everything was always provided as if sent and delivered by angels."

"Do you think she could possibly have controlled you?"

"Not me," I grinned and raised my eyebrows. "But she controlled Ruth. Everyone in town knew it. Once, decades after Mutti's death, Ruth admitted to me that it had taken her years to realize how much her mother had controlled and overshadowed her. Connie," I interrupted the flow, "I don't think this whole thing has anything to do with my mother. Nor does it have to do with control, for that matter." I didn't want to waste my time here. Remembering Fred's comment, I laughed. "My husband recently called me a wicked control freak, though," I added grinning.

What does that mean anyway? And why would Fred have said such a thing? Had that really been controlling? When I look backed at the way I was with Patrick when he was little... He never had a babysitter. When friends invited us for dinner he came along and slept on a bed while we were there. He was always with either Fred or me: always under supervision. How had Mutti been? I clearly remember one of our maids being around when I played at a neighbor's house, and how I was also never left alone. Then an image of Rosa peeking at me through bushes surfaces... Had that been a figment of my imagination? No two ways about it, Mutti made sure no harm came my way. Heavens, she even came to Germany with me for two years, and I was already an adult! Mutti control me? My scalp prickled. Oh what horror! Could she have? Did she?

"We tend to replicate our mother's habits, we become the mother she was. She's the one we learn our mothering skills from," Connie said calmly. "I notice that you have become introspective for a moment; you seem bothered. What's the matter?" She added gently.

"Nothing, I guess. It's just that I'm realizing Mutti actually controlled not only Ruth, but me as well. And that is a shock I'll need time to recover from," I offered her a bashful smile.

Even though I had said my issues were not related to my present lifetime, Connie asked me to tell her more about my childhood. So I told her about having grown up very much a German child in Latin America, that I was deeply steeped in German culture and was, early on, fluent in three languages. "I have always preferred to identify as European, and prefer to be among them," I said seriously. "I find it hard to have to categorize myself in the States."

"I can understand the European aspect, but why do you have an issue here in the States?"

"Here, everyone has to be something: some race or ethnicity

or color... Everyone has to mark a little box saying what they are. Before coming to this country I had a nationality. I know I have dark skin, of course, but I'm not African or African American, and Black culture is alien to me. Wow!" I burst out laughing, "How did I get to this?" and I laughed some more.

Connie said simply, "The issue is probably foremost on your mind." Her lips smiled but the expression did not quite reach her eyes. "By the way," she added, "what is your opinion of Blacks?"

"Honestly?" I looked at her pale complexion, those pale eyes, and wondered if this White, middle-class American woman could possibly understand me and my complex background. Would a Black counselor understand? I don't think so. "They tend to rattle me, Connie," I answered.

"Could you say in which way you feel they rattle you?"

Where do I start? "Well... for instance... there are so many negative images in the media. It's as if every murder, rape, violent act is done by a Black. I know it's not the case, but it feels like that to me." My eyes clouded as I added, "I fear and mistrust them. I know they sense there's something inherently wrong with me, and they mock me because I don't understand them."

"Do you think you see yourself as being part of a negative generalization, not as an individual?" I nodded, and Connie said softly, "What do you know of your birth parents?"

"Not much," and I proceeded to tell her what I knew about Rosa and Gil, and having seen Rosa several times.

"Then you knew them," Connie glanced up.

"Yes, but they're unimportant," I gave her an irritated stare.

She leaned toward me as if sharing a secret. "Birth parents are never unimportant," she said evenly. "They gave you life. You carry their genes and many of their characteristics." Her voice was as clear as her message direct. "What can you tell me about your German father?"

I shrugged and filled her in with lots of details I knew about Vati, that his father had been a cobbler in Hamburg, that he was 19 when he arrived in Guatemala in 1905, that he was on his first vacation in Germany when WWI broke out and had to go to war, that he was helping out in his father's shop when he met

Mutti and that he pursued her like the devil pursues the penitent soul until she left her husband to marry him, that he was the German honorary consul in Livingston, that he ended up in an internment camp in Texas, and that, when he returned home in 1945, he was physically incapacitated. I had to admit my surprise at the many details I still remembered about Vati's life.

"What you need to do now," Connie said quietly and bending over toward me, "is search for your own history so that you know it as well as you know that of your German family."

"I know all there is to know about me. Mutti told me all there is to know." My tone was sharper than I intended.

"You need to know your history, Catana. Not the story Mutti wanted to you to believe."

"My German parents were stellar examples of what parents should be," I continued protesting. "I have always trusted their judgment, their ideals... implicitly. There is absolutely no reason to question my upbringing." My heart was racing. Did Connie mean that the people who nurtured and raised me with so much care and love, are supposed to share the same platform as two beings that mean nothing to me? Was she betraying my trust by not listening to me and wanting me to shed light on my birthparents? How am I supposed to do that? This woman's not that bright, I thought, annoyed.

"You need to know who, and what, gave shape to your world view and your sense of identity," she added with a gentle, yet impassive expression, "and that would be, I imagine, the German environment."

A lump began to build in my throat. I stared at her. "There's nothing wrong with the way I grew up," I repeated, and began to feel constricted in her tidy, delicately scented office. I had to get away from those pale, steady eyes as they focused on my soul.

"Catana," Connie's voice was low and gentle, as if talking to an upset child, "consider how they fit into your life; not you into theirs. You will need to think about that. It does not have to be today, but be open to explore the past. You have done much good work this afternoon, but please consider what I have said." She was not dismissing me, but I took it as a good point for departure.

"Thanks." I said, standing up. Everything on and about me felt tight. I rushed down the wooden stairs and out the door. Outside, I took a few deep breaths of cool, stabilizing evening air, and decided then and there not to see Connie again. What was it about this mild-tempered woman with her gentle eyes? Was she too American, too middle class? And what would be wrong with that anyway? Nothing. I looked at the wispy pearl grey clouds of the waning day and shuddered although I was not cold. Don't be scared, I tried to reassure myself, just because you've started down a particular road, doesn't mean you have to stay on it. You're a free woman, after all, I thought as I got in my car. Free woman or not, I felt desolate as I sat at the wheel feeling miserable. I couldn't drive. My mind went blank as tears filled my eyes and spilled down my face. Oh, Mutti, Mutti, Mutti, help me, I thought and allowed myself to weep.

⌒

The night I finished reading Jamaica Kincaid's *Annie John*, the wind blowing outside my window ushered messages into my dreams.

I was Annie John, and had just turned three. The Black mother and I stood hand in hand on an elevation next to our Caribbean home. I was wearing the white dress she made for me and felt the warm, jasmine scented breeze blow gently through the gauze, caressing my body. My hair was woven into four braids, as I used to wear it when I was young. I was barefoot and my toenails looked like luminous little shells left on the sand by receding tides. We observed a fisherman in his canoe on the turquoise sea while macaws with bright ruby breasts perched on branches of water-logged trees on the sand below. We walked behind the house, past the laundry drying on the line between bushes of mauve hibiscus. We passed my mother's orchard filled with cassava, breadfruit and bean stalks, we passed the coop where chickens were laying blue and pink eggs. She moved carefully with me, past tall cedars, ever deeper into the cool of the forest, until we reached the pond whose waters it was said turned to silver on moonless nights, when spirits came to drink. I was happy with that mother, comforted simply by her presence, her hand firmly holding mine. In the silence that surrounded us, her love flowed from her heart through her hand, to my hand, to my heart. Without a single word, our love claimed each other's soul.

What a mother that one must have been, I thought upon waking in my sunlit room, all tingly after the delicious dream. Such an enviable sense of security, of total trust and comfort... But by the time I sat up in bed, I felt wretched and ungrateful and my face was covered with tears. My heart, my soul was leaden, and I knew why: Mutti.

Mutti had, like all loving mothers, taught me with so much care and devotion everything she felt I needed to know to function in the world in which she expected me to live. Even when little, I knew I spoke German better than the other children. I had excellent, polite manners, was always cleaner - immaculately clean - and my curtsies still flowed with grace long after other girls had stopped doing theirs. I knew I did things better than the lot of blond, blue-eyed kids and I thoroughly internalized my superiority.

Later, looking gravely at the seemingly unburdened teenager I had become, and worried about my nonchalant approach to life and school, Mutti would say: "Mohrle, please keep in mind that you must always be better than the White ones, for even then, you will at best be considered equal." If I heard it once, I must have heard it a thousand times. She raised me to feel superior to everyone around me - and those around me were White. But by then, I saw myself as whiter than even my palest friends.

The woman who carried me under her heart, whose placenta had fed me for months on end, and who had opened her body for me to emerge, never had a chance to convey what she thought important, important for me, her child, to know. As polished a little girl as I was, Rosa, my Black mother, could not have been proud of the disdain I harbored for her.

After more than half a century, on a sunny morning following a windy night, I thought with empathy about Rosa. I think she died when I was thirty; I no longer know for sure.

It was uncanny, but just as I was considering Rosa I had to deal with painful, pressing issues that presented themselves at a high school in the Adirondacks. I had the time after graduation and before starting my engagement at the college, so I accepted an offer to teach a weekly class in cultural diversity... And I had to face Myrna every Friday for six weeks. What a singular nightmare!

The minute Myrna saw me enter the school she shot out to greet me in an effusive way offering me her assistance. I knew where my classroom, my office, and the faculty lounge were. "Thanks, Myrna," I tried for a friendly approach, "I'll let you know should something come up." But she still lingered around until I entered my office or the classroom. What was it with her?

Myrna was what I had long ago come to perceive as physically and culturally flawed, and not necessarily because of her color. In my opinion, her use of words and her accent defined her as belonging to a socially and educationally deprived segment of the population. To me her language and demeanor was that of unrefined people. Her laughter was loud, coarse, outright vulgar, and she always looked like a circus horse on parade: everything was too tight, too bright, too short for her round butt and crooked legs. And her workplace! What a mess! It embarrassed me on a very personal level. Why should I have felt that way? It was her messy space, not mine.

How had that woman managed to secure her position? What's more, how could she possibly keep it? She was the only Black employed full time at the school, and I could only assume she intimidated everyone by throwing that fact in their faces. She made derogatory, inappropriate comments about my colleagues; I didn't say anything, figuring that perhaps it was a Black way of showing one's solidarity. She said she was glad to see me there; but I figured all she wanted was to get me into her sphere of influence so I would support whatever political objectives she might have. I just didn't know what to make of it all.

Once Myrna asked me if I had children, and I showed her a picture of Patrick. She instantly deduced that my husband was White. At the very next opportunity she came out with another of her comments: "Whaat Folk? Man, them stupid! Ah'd nevah' have nothin' doin' wit' a whaat man. Dem too much work," she sucked her teeth and grinned disdainfully. Sensing I didn't understand what being Black was about; the woman also knew she could upset me through my ignorance of African American culture. I loved reading the literature, but in real life I had to face the likes of Myrna. She probably thinks I got the job because in her eyes I was "White." Truth to tell, while Americans after meeting me might think I'm a bit different from the African Americans they know, there's no way they'd see me as White. And how could I stand in front of students addressing cultural diversity in its many forms, and then be unable to include that simple, loud-mouthed, coarse secretary in my personal collection of diversity? I was like those anthropologists who revere the artifacts created in antiquity by an indigenous people, only to disdain the contemporary descendants.

Whatever this woman had over me was in my mind, and it was driving me crazy. I felt obliged to identify with her not by culture nor by class, but by race. And she was the incarnate stereotype of what I hated about Black people. Worst of all, because of my own Blackness, I felt that people meeting me at that very White school thought as negatively of me as I thought of her. I agonized at the thought that they might see us as being the same.

Myrna was putting me through hell, or was it I who was doing it?

I was at home at my desk correcting student papers, and her image constantly popped into my mind. I put my elbows on the desk and held my head, confused. What am I to do? How am I to handle this? I better find a way soon before someone at the school discovers my conflicted attitudes regarding that awful Myrna. She can't help her appearance and probably not the way she is, but it just kills me that she takes liberties with me. She acts as if she's entitled to my things because we are both Black. Aargh... Why can't I put her in her place when I have the opportunity? Why can't I tell her in Technicolor to mind her damn business, better still, go straight to hell? I know I'd have done that long ago if she were White... It's because she's Black! Geez, the class-conscious snob is resurfacing. After all my experiences, am I still a snob? That was when I was much younger, but no more. What's the matter with these people, I agonize. Why do they torment me so? Is it all Blacks? How would I react in a room full of them? I sit, elbows on the table, holding my head, hoping my racing, anguished mind will settle down.

Connie had said that when I found myself in a confounding social dilemma, I had to look at my childhood environment. What had I heard or seen, what sort of subliminal messages might I have received from Mutti or from others around me? It's torturous to have to go there. Mutti, how could there be anything wrong with what Mutti perceived? She had lived in Livingston for two decades, for chrissakes, she knew Rosa, she knew Black people... I remember her in Belize and Kingston and know she treated everyone the same, regardless of color or class.

If it's only Myrna pushing me off the deep end, what might Mutti have said about someone like that grotesque being?

Like the day she came into my office. She stood there, just looking at me, loudly sucking a grapefruit, asking for an article I used in class. How would she even have known what the article was about? She came in and said, "Jus' show me where you keep dem articles, so I don' have to look fa 'em," and continued dealing with the fruit, spitting a seed into her hand that bounced off and fell to the floor. Think she picked it up? NO. What nasty habits... I'd lend her my articles if she weren't so messy. I could just see her sticky fingers going through my papers. Mutti would be as disgusted as I was. And then that Myrna called me 'sistah!' 'Oh, sistah,' she said to me! Well... I'm nobody's 'sistah,' much less hers.

"You'll have to sign for them," I said to her and locked my closet when I left. She won't ask again.

I can't get over Myrna just eating anywhere. Why does she walk around eating... at any time... and always with her fingers, licking and sucking them as if it was a ritual, as if there's a right and a wrong way of doing it? Have I seen White Americans eat with their fingers? I don't think so. It's so aggravating that I can't get her out of my mind; more than that, it's confusing that her repulsive behavior and crude mannerisms are beginning to fascinate me as much as they repulse me.

What would Mutti have said at such lack of decorum? Probably that the behavior is upsetting in anyone. How did Mutti really feel about Blacks? What I observed (if one can call it that) in Belize and Jamaica she was fine with everyone. What did she say about the Black people who brought the fish from Livingston? I don't remember. All I know is that in those days there were no Blacks in Guatemala City, so I couldn't have observed her even if I had been paying attention.

Fortunately, my days of driving to the Adirondacks would come to an end soon, and anyway, I was looking forward to having Patrick home from boarding school.

While in Michigan, my son perfected a habit of going for walks. Occasionally he asked me to join him, which I gladly accepted for, although he was friendly, he was also a tight-lipped, introspective teenager. On walks I could get him to talk to me. One afternoon, as we were strolling under the leafy canopy of the town park's forest, I brought up the situation at the high school. I told him how Myrna, when I asked her a question to which she felt I should know the answer, had said: "Aah haid to explain that self same thang to a whaat woman," and on one occasion when I wore my Scottish kilt, she commented that only a White woman would wear such ugliness. "Whatever I do," I said to Patrick, "whatever I wear, however my hair looks... for Myrna, it's never right. I don't want to even talk to her, because I know she'll take any opportunity to put me down and make me feel inferior."

"Don't act like Myrna's the first Black person you've ever dealt with, Mom," Patrick said after listening attentively. "No matter what she says and what you think now, you don't have a problem with Black people at all. It's only that particular one that bugs you."

"Not really. I've always had a problem with Black people. I think I scrutinize them like White people do, perhaps even in a mistrusting way." I held my head down as if paying attention to where I placed my feet.

"That may be so, Mom, but Myrna is disrespectful," Patrick

responded evenly; "that's what's annoying about her."

"And she's disrespectful because she knows I don't get the likes of her. I probably behave like an animal that lies on its back and surrenders to the stronger one." I stopped and looked at Patrick, and laughed. "That's a great insight," I said, pleased.

"Sure is, Mom," my son grinned. "I don't think she is in any way stronger than you. Just get that out of your mind. Here, for you," he said, handing me an acorn and giving he a hug. "Mom, I've been with you all of my life, and I want to say that you're completely impartial. Except in sports, of course, when you always want the Black athletes to win!" He burst out laughing with joy. "I also know you read a lot of books by Black writers." He raised his arms and stretched, twisting at the waist. "Writers from the Caribbean, Africa, the USA, all sorts of Black writers. If there were Black writers in Alaska, you'd have read their works, too."

I laughed at that. It should not have surprised me that Patrick watched my every move: only children don't have siblings to distract them from observing their parents.

"Think of the educated Blacks you know, Mom... No grief with them, right? And the Black folks when you were growing up... they were cool, too, weren't they?"

It had been a long time since I'd heard so many words coming out of this boy at one time, and it was embarrassing to have been caught making a sweeping generalization. I admitted that I understood it was only this particular person I was stuck with, and added for clarification, "There were no Black people in Guatemala City, at least not as I was growing up."

"Jamaica then. You knew some in Jamaica..." He was sure of himself, and he was right. "Hey, Mom, we should have a Jamaican vacation! You know I love Bob Marley's music. Why haven't we gone there?" We said nothing while I was lost in thoughts about my early contact with Black people. Patrick couldn't know it, but he had a way of making me re-think my theories. Was he an old soul, or was it his youth that forced me now to recover forgotten incidents of my younger years?

"I remember a family Mutti had met in Kingston," I began my recollection. "Sometimes at the end of the school term I stayed with them for a few days before my flight to Belize. The father, Dr. Dezon, was a medical doctor and a professor at the university. They had two daughters, Daphne and Phoebe, who were a little younger than me. It was a very formal family that adhered to the manners of fine English upbringing. Daphne once wrote to me describing their vacation by the sea. On two occasions, she reported, they'd been so relaxed they hadn't bothered to change for dinner," I chuckled at the memory.

"How sweet!" Patrick laughed.

"They were the only Jamaican family I got to know. They spoke British English and their home was very dignified, indeed."

"Formal is fine, Mom. It's cool. No Blacks at all in Guate. City, are you sure?" he looked at me intently.

"You're forcing my mind, Patrick," I said, as elusive images began to taunt from the edges of my memory. "She was an artist," I murmured, and Mutti had her paint a portrait of me. I was about seven or eight. Mme. Goudere was her name, and I think her husband was the Haitian ambassador in Guatemala. They were distinguished people for sure and spoke French."

"Aaah," Patrick grinned sheepishly, "you didn't consider them as Blacks, because they were cultured... Right?"

I didn't answer, as he was not necessarily right with that assumption. Truth was, I had interacted, probably reluctantly, with a handful of educated Black people. Come to think of it, I never thought I was racist until Myrna showed me differently. If I had any role models at all, Mutti provided me with Ralph Bunche whom she admired tremendously, and Marian Anderson who Mutti said sang German Lieder better than anyone, ever.

IN THE EVENING AFTER PATRICK retired I looked for my Marian Anderson record, a relic from my childhood that without being looked at or listened to in decades, had wandered with me over borders, through countries and continents. I lit the candles on the table, poured myself a glass of wine, and relaxed into the cushions of the sofa as the diva began her rendition of Schubert's Lieder.

With the music, memories of childhood returned, of cool,

rainy afternoons, when at teatime we sat in the living room listening to music while resin cracked in the fireplace. How old was I then? Was Vati still alive? I think so. I must have been older than eight, younger than eleven. I still remembered every word of the poems written by Goethe, Heine, Chamisso, put to music by Franz Schubert: Nineteenth century German Romantic poetry interpreted by a magnificent, Black American singer. My mood grew melancholic, as I felt surrounded by ghosts of the past. Then, of all people, Madame Goudere again reappeared, like a barely audible, long forgotten tune.

I was seven when Mutti told me the wife of the Haitian ambassador had invited us for afternoon tea. Like everyone in Haiti, Mutti explained, the Gouderes spoke French. They lived on Sixth Avenue, a short walk from our house. I was surprised to see the ambassador's wife. Her skin tone was lighter than mine but darker than the servants. I guess Mutti had seen no need to tell me the Haitians were dark. I didn't quite know what to make of an elegantly dressed dark person, and couldn't keep from staring at Madame because I thought she was beautiful. It had not occurred to me that people her coloring could be good-looking. She saw the world through large, slightly slanted dark cocoa colored eyes and wore her curly raven hair gathered into a loose chignon in the nape of her neck. Her movements were naturally relaxed, and it seemed to my young mind that she slinked when she moved; she slinked like a slender Abyssinian cat. I can still feel how that embarrassed me. She was sophisticated and friendly in a reserved way. What she did not do was fuss over me when she met me. I was accustomed to hearing people compliment Mutti on my looks, my curtsies, my poise. So, right away I considered Mme. Goudere stuck up and didn't quite like her.

The Gouderes fired everyone's imagination, including mine, and I came to think of Haiti as a legendary, fairy tale place where pomegranates, persimmons, and kumquats abounded - not that I necessarily knew what they were. Nothing anyone said in our house or elsewhere about the French-speaking Caribbeans escaped me: How Mme's French couture dresses must have cost the ambassador a pretty penny; how beautiful their dark twin babies looked in their perfectly ironed white batiste and lace clothes; how funny it was to see the roles reversed: European nanny for Black children. And then, the Parisian high-wheeled double baby carriage... No one had one like that because parading babies around was not what people did. Babies remained in the gardens behind the high walls that hid the houses.

I don't remember meeting Monsieur Goudere, but I saw Madame every fortnight for three months when I sat for the portrait Mutti had commissioned. At the last session Madame asked me to take my dress off. To choose a background color, she wrapped several scarves around me, finally selecting the tone of a pink carnation. Then she draped a yellow chiffon scarf over my hair. I appreciated the feel of her soft, colorful silks and satins on my skin, but most of all I loved her elegant perfume. When she finished dressing me, she nodded and said "Très, très joli" (very, very pretty).

I had that portrait. Somewhere. Even before Marian Anderson's recording ended, I began to look for it and found it tucked away in the wardrobe behind the winter coats. It was still wrapped in the same paper and string, just as Ruth had handed it to me in 1977 when I was in Guatemala. I untied the knots, peeled away the wrappings and found a rendering of myself I had not seen in... could it be more than forty years?

Look at the face of that little brown girl with a big bright smile, showing off her new front teeth, I thought. It was as if I were seeing the picture for the first time. I didn't remember having looked that cute. Moreover, it was a beautifully executed rendering in pastels - the work of a skilled artist. But Mutti must not have liked it. Why did she commission the portrait - I sat still for Madame for hours - never to hang it up? My eyes followed the contours of the friendly smiling face, and the little round shoulders that are so cute in children. A bright yellow turban with pink polka dots covered my hair, and a string of turquoise beads lay around my neck. The background was held in soft tropical pinks, how the colors appealed to me... and, sure, that's how I had looked! Except... that in the painting my nose was a bit broader and my lips a bit thicker than in reality. I carried the painting to my bedroom, placed it upright on the dresser and bade the little seven-year old in the colorful turban good night. Tomorrow we're having you framed I promised her, pleased with the evening and my re-discovery.

I was about to doze off when I sat up with a jolt and reached for the light. "The turban!" I said out loud. Of course! Mutti must have hated the turban. Mme. Goudere had taken the liberty to portray me in her artistic vision. She had created a picture she thought beautiful, but she had not represented Mutti's German Mohrle. That's why the painting never graced our walls.

It occurred to me that perhaps Mme. Goudere resented the fact, or perhaps perceived it as humorous, that Mutti was raising a Black child with European mannerisms and refinement. But Madame was bringing her babies up that way, and she was not European. I don't believe she meant the turban as an insult, but if she had, it could not have been more successful, for the affront would have been handed down by none other than a class-conscious Black, not a White. By centering me on a pink background, undressed, my neatly combed hair covered with a yellow turban, Mme. Goudere had stripped me of all that was Mutti's.

As Mutti's child, I had been removed from the people with affinity for bright pinks, yellows and turquoise. As Mutti's child, my hair was not natty and unruly and didn't need to be covered by a turban. On the contrary, my hair was always neatly braided and held with thick silver clasps and crisply ironed ribbons. Mme. Goudere herself would never have outfitted her babies with a turban. By painting me as she did, the Haitian ambassador's wife brought Mutti her Black child and, in so doing, deeply offended my German mother.

Could it be? And I shuddered. Could it be that Mutti loved me, but not the me that was Negro?

I HAD TROUBLE STAYING ASLEEP. Childhood scenes danced in and out of my dreams. Shapes and colors: yellow, pink, turquoise. My thoughts wandered all night from Mutti to Mme. Goudere. I saw Mme. Goudere, her studio, her brown babies... I couldn't remember the Goudere's coming to our home. We didn't socialize with them. Perhaps there was a language barrier, our not speaking French, their not speaking German. I don't know, but I never saw her again.

On what became a turbulent night of remembrances, scenes surfaced to consciousness like vignettes on a merry-go-round. I remembered sitting on Mutti's lap, holding a typically colorful picture I made of the flowers in our garden.

"Mohrle, this is beautiful," she said happily and I glowed with pleasure at her delighted expression and praise. "It looks as if you used all the crayons in the box. It's truly enchanting," she said, studying every flower. "Tell, me little one, which is your favorite color?"

"This green, right here," I said earnestly, putting my finger on the brightest green in the grass.

"I see," Mutti said. "And which is your next favorite?"

"This one!" And I pointed to the bright yellow sun, happy at possibly playing a new game. Maybe it was called 'my favorite color.'

"Green and yellow," my mother laughed. "And after that, which one?"

"Pink," I said, showing her the bright pinkish-orange in a big, round dahlia.

"Oh, Mohrle," Mutti looked at me, making sure I was paying attention, "those are very bright colors. They are beautiful in paintings, like this one. But keep in mind, dear child: colors that look good in a painting are too bright for you to wear as clothes. After all," she caressed my cheek, "you don't want to look like the village people on Sundays." I felt secure in her embrace and sensed her love flowing through me. She had liked my picture! What is more, she taught me a valuable lesson, and I accepted without question that I was never to have happy colors on me. She was right. I didn't want to look like village people on Sundays. So, I refrained from wearing such tones, certainly not green, or yellow, or bright pink-orange.

I TWISTED IN MY SHEETS LIKE a fevered creature, as morning exercises came to mind. I saw me as a child pressing my back against the wall hoping that eventually there would be no space between it and my waist. How old was I? Four? Five? I didn't follow the program regularly, or for long anyway, but it made me aware that a pronounced buttock was not desirable, and I understood that beyond color, Black and White people had other differing physical characteristics, like most Blacks having longer legs and shorter upper bodies. And then, the buttocks and the nose. Some Blacks, like Asians, lack a bridge between the eyes. In any event, I grew up not having a "sway back," as Mutti called it. Occasionally, I would be reminded to massage the small elevation at the top of my nose. "There should be a bridge," Mutti said. For her, good-looking, classic noses had a bridge. Pretty feet had an arch, so my shoes had leather inlays: I also have arched feet.

When morning came, I had not slept. I was awake all night, remembering. I was so little when those direct and subliminal messages informed me things about my body needed adjusting. It had all taken place so long ago, so early in my life, I had forgotten.

THERE NEVER WAS, NOR WILL there ever be a question in my mind: I was an immaculately, well-taken-care-of, and much-loved child. My upbringing had been to my singular advantage. Not only in Europe, but everywhere I've been. As a child, I could not have considered such attention as unusual. After all, didn't all parents work with their children so they look good?

It appears, however, that in Mutti's regimen, I had not only to be German but also look German... My mother created a European Mohrle, a Mohrle for European eyes and pleasure. She tried to control what she felt my shape needed to be, and it's no wonder she was beside herself with pride when I became a successful fashion model and actress in Europe. I was her beautiful creation. But I never considered myself good looking, and didn't spend much time in front of mirrors. Not as a child, and not as an adult. I was fine, but as far as "real" good looks were concerned... well, I didn't have them. It's debatable whether my body conformed to Mutti's expectations, but I became extremely aware of physical configurations that are racially distinctive. Ultimately, I internalized since earliest memory, that for me to be perfect I needed to reject God's creation and correct it to fit the European ideal of beauty.

These days, the mere thought those messages from long ago had such a lasting impact, unravels me. How could it all have festered for decades in my subconscious, to surface now and make such an impact?

I was exhausted. Still, I slipped out of bed and into a dressing gown, and decided to relax on the terrace with a cup of tea. Juliette, my grey kitten jumped on my lap and made herself comfortable. In the exchange of breaths, Myrna had to come to mind. That Myrna, with her ghetto upbringing, didn't have my problems. I accepted, on a deeply painful level, how someone like her could well ignore European manners and decorum, just as she rejected European norms of beauty. "Black men like butt," she once said to me, proud of her large buttocks and surely referring to mine which were not very pronounced. Good, I thought then, you have enough for ten of them! I did not care what 'Black men' liked. But Myrna's mother, who must have looked like her, and her father, who also must have had a butt, told her she was beautiful. And she believed them. She resembled like the rest of her family and others in her community that surrounded and nurtured her. Those were the only opinions she would ever care for. Not what Whites thought. White folk, in her eyes, were ugly.

It was, as I said, a new day, one in which my vision appeared to have sharpened, like that of a hawk gliding above the earth. Overnight my perspective had broadened, allowing me to see and be willing to accept a wider landscape. The dewdrops on the grass reflected the mellow tones of a summer dawn. Juliette stirred on my lap and purred with pleasure. After a windy night when I opened to question for the first time what I was taught, the order in nature reflected a new and developing inner peace within me. I wanted all to be well in the yellow sunlight. I wanted to make room in my heart for every Myrna in the universe, and for me.

My next lecture for class at the university would be about

social aspects of colonialism and colonial mentality: about the internalized self-rejection in a colonized people. About Black and brown people who had lived autonomously prior to the European encounter and who, in the process of becoming colonized, started to reject their history and culture and started to see their traditions as inferior and insignificant. I would talk about how Europeans saw theirs as the only history worth studying; and how from the European perspective the history of peoples beyond the sea began when they faced the White Man. Columbus arrived in a part of the world unknown to him and proceeded to name the places where his caravels landed. He gave names to a geography that already had a name, given to it by the people living there for millennia. He named the inhabitants "Indians," although they had their own their tribal names.

Long before Columbus, in the original Paradise of the Old Testament, Adam had done the same by naming what he saw as he walked about: tree, hill, pomegranate, woman.

Mutti, it suddenly occurred to me, had behaved similarly when it came to me. I already had a name, but she renamed me after her understanding, maybe even after herself. She replaced Adriana with Catana.

It occurred to me that I hadn't changed my cat's name. The old man who handed me the six week-old kitten called him Rusty because of his reddish fur. The name stayed. And before, when we left Mexico, I gave our dog to our gardener. Patrick had chosen the name: Austin. Years later, on a visit, I saw the gardener and asked how the dog was. "Austin is fine," was the answer.

"Didn't give him a new name," I commented.

"He had a name," was the simple response.

"I, too, had a name!" I now said out loud.

My name was ADRIANA.

As surely as Columbus had planted the Spanish flag in the ground saying, "I name this land San Salvador," Mutti had branded me by giving me another name.

She colonized me! Came the sudden horrifying, realization. She colonized my brain. She raised me to be what I was not: exclusively European. She taught me her European history, her

European values. By so doing, she invalidated my indigenous culture, my people's history, my own history. She made me reject my heritage and thus, reject myself. I internalized my self-rejection just as colonized peoples are taught to internalize their sense of inferiority. I had grown up with a colonized mind!

As Adriana, I would always have reminded Mutti that I was Rosa's child. As Catana, I was hers.

As Adriana, I was born humble, but would have felt secure in Rosa's heritage. As Catana, I became Mutti's polished product, yet insecure and painfully dependent on approval.

I am both Adriana and Catana, of course, but which one do I crawl into when I need comfort? Which 'me' reassures, protects, offers consolation? Which 'me' makes me whole? Takes the confusion away? Which one is my essence? Who is my mother when I have both?

It was 1991 and I was in Connie's office, again discussing mother issues – when were we not? At times I was critical of Mutti, but I would not be so for long. After all, how could I quibble when she raised me with the best of her intentions and abilities? "She gave me everything in her power to give; only one thing she could not offer me: a White skin," I said softly.

"That's true," Connie agreed, and looking at me evenly added, "But she could have given you your Black one."

"Huh?"

"Had she allowed you to know Rosa, you would have become comfortable in the skin you were born with." Connie leaned back in her chair. "Maybe hard to deal with now, but it's that simple," she concluded gently.

We said nothing while I considered her words.

MUTTI'S GOOD INTENTIONS WERE never the issue with Connie. At issue in the session was Mutti's overpowering presence that eclipsed Rosa's ability to unfold in my life.

I had been re-reading letters Mutti wrote to me when I was

in Germany. She made a point of telling me about all her visitors. From the doctor making friendly house calls to the seamstress, the gardener, several maids who had once worked for us, and of course all her friends who would stop by in the evening for a cocktail or two before going home for dinner. The way she held court was indeed a testament to her popularity. Before I began to work with Connie, it did not occur to me that Mutti never mentioned Rosa. While I was in Jamaica I vaguely remember hearing that Rosa had inquired about me but I did not care whether she had or not. Now, however, I was being directed to pay attention to details in my relationship with Mutti. Had she intentionally avoided saying anything to me about Rosa? Connie was sensitizing me to the way I had received or had failed to receive news about my birth mother. Mutti was of course aware of my warped feelings. Did she not want to upset me when she withheld information? Reluctantly, I began to accept that, as Mutti detailed all her visitors, it would have been appropriate for her to also mention when Rosa came by. Regardless of how I may have felt at the time, if she had come to ask about me, Mutti should have said so in her letters. The ball would have been in my court, and it would have been my responsibility to respond... or not.

"You say your 'German' mother, Catana, when she wasn't your mother at all," Connie's voice was soft, the expression in her eyes gentle. I didn't like it when that happened; I knew by then that something serious would probably follow in the next sentence. "How do you feel about giving... What was her name again?" She asked knowing full well what it was.

"Esther. You know you know it," I said with slight apprehension.

"Yes," Connie shook her head reflectively. "How do you feel about giving Esther the place she should have?"

"What do you mean?" I asked knowing I was being lead into a minefield.

"Her name was Esther. How do you feel about addressing her by that name? Call her Esther." There was a definite edge in the low-key delivery. "We actually don't notice," Connie continued keeping me firmly in her gaze, "that we live in a pattern that doesn't fit us, and fool ourselves by believing it's the right structure, when it's not so. To gain some semblance of clarity, it's necessary to go back to the beginning and do some reprogramming. We need to assign each person or event the true place in our reality."

"And what is all that supposed to mean?" I sighed, furrowing my brow and not understanding her words.

"If you designate the right place for everyone in your life," my counselor proceeded gently, as if talking to a hurt child, "where would Esther be? Start at your conception. Then your birth..."

I let out a deep, heavy sigh. She had done it again; she had planted another bomb. Reprogram the positions my various mothers had in my life? That would mean displacing the only woman I considered my mother from her pinnacle. Mutti was not present at my conception or my birth. By calling her Esther I would escort her to her true, her real place in my life.

"Doing that will force you to become mindful of the actual relationship." Connie smiled and continued slowly, "In moving forward you need to see Esther's place in your life. Not you in her life." I looked at her and wondered what could be going through her mind when those pale eyes of hers just looked and looked so peacefully at me, observing me while I squirmed. "Esther can handle the truth," she whispered after a while. "It only seems to you that you're being disloyal to her. But you are at the threshold of wanting to be true to yourself. Keep in mind that Esther knew she didn't give birth to you. She might have wanted to with all her heart, but the reality is: she was not the one who gave you life." Sitting back, Connie concluded, "Just accept that Esther can handle hearing you say her name. I know she would want to help you find your peace and dissolve the many obstacles and doubts that confound and confuse you."

"So you want me to bring her down from the pedestal I have had her on?" I said, trying to absorb the enormity of what she asked me to do: Remove the mother I loved, and who considered me her child, from the shrine where I kept her.

"That's an excellent analogy," Connie responded softly, giving nothing away. "But in truth," and now a faint smile came over her lips, "what you would be doing is bringing her down from the pedestal upon which she helped you place her."

A shiver ran up my spine. Tears began to collect and I swallowed hard to dash them away. "I have to think about this, Connie," I said, as the constriction was building in my chest... I quickly embraced her and hurried out of the office as the tears rolled unbidden down my cheeks. Could I bring Mutti down? Would it hurt her feelings? It was the truth; we all knew it. But how could I go about changing what I called her, what I referred to her as?

Too confused to think further, I sat in the car, overwhelmed and weeping, again, after a meeting with Connie.

⌒

Before going to bed that night I lit a candle on my desk, and on my finest stationery began to write. As I put pen to paper, I found myself relaxing. The tension began to leave me.

> _Mutti, darling Mutti,_
>
> _I loved you always; I still love you, and forever will. But I will love you as Esther, the woman who gave me all the love she had to give. You were Esther and my Mutti. But you did not give birth to me. It feels like sacrilege, or heresy... But the truth is: it's neither. I need to know Rosa, and I need your help in restoring my mother to her rightful place. Her name was Rosa. When the maids announced her, they said: "Niña Mohrle, Doña Rosita is here to see you." You see Mutti, Doña Rosita was my mother; she gave me life._

⌒

As I lay awake on that clear, starlit night made for dreaming, I entered the split consciousness of a dream state as I whispered to my mother:

> _Rosa. I still find it difficult to call you mother, and yet you are the one who carried me carefully below your heart. I shared your body, I grew inside_

you listening to your sighs, hearing your silent desires, your secret wishes. I was there when Mutti assured you she would take care of your baby should it be a girl. I heard you begging me: "Be a girl, be a little girl, and you will be well provided for." You wanted me to be a girl. I heard your heart beat. Every single beat your heart made for nine months I heard it. I knew when you were tired, when you were happy, when you worried. I felt your joys and your pain, and when I was born we were both relieved that I was female. You smiled at me and held me, and as you kissed me I could smell your sweet delicate scent. Your lips were soft as they touched my forehead and then my cheek. You were so young, and I was happy to see who had carried and protected me all the months of my physical existence. You were gentle, pretty, and proud of your baby. I loved to look at you then: my young, radiant mother.

A tiny star appeared on the ceiling of my dark room and glowed into the luminous shape of my mother. Her look into my eyes was real, deep, all consuming.

No one could keep me from going to see you, Adriana. You needed to know who your mother was. I called you Mohrle, but your name is Adriana. I had no say in anything, so I said nothing. Bringing you my presence was the only way I could show my love for you, my only way of affirming you as my child. You are my blood. I came so you had to look at me; you had to look at me, to know you came from me. I am your life, your history, your memory. You had to look at ME to remember the truth. I brought it to you as long as I lived. Neither time nor distance will ever remove me from your knowledge.

"I am amazed at your perseverance... Rosa... at your fortitude," I respond to the image, my eyes fixed deeper on hers than ever before. "You were a woman with little recourse, yet you made the sacrifice only to endure countless humiliations, shed countless tears. And still, you came.

"Lately, in my sleepless nights, I sense you at my bed and your look, long ago engraved in my subconscious, rests gently on me as it did when I was young. You sit by me in silence feeling my anguish, sensing my desires, sharing my secrets. I should have taken the opportunity to know you in life, to recognize the strength in your humility, in your courage and dignity. I would have learned courage from knowing your perseverant heart.

"You died, too young, and never heard a kind word from me. I feel you,

*and I thank you for being with me as I prepare to accept myself as your child.
Good night, R....Mother?"*

*Adriana, I will always be with you. You were my first child. I had four
children: four. I always yearned for you most; I will never give you up and I
will never stop loving you.*

The star diminished, and slowly faded away.

After giving my mothers their rightful place in my existence,
the Universe responded with another miracle. In my case, the
Universe moves things through the phone lines. When I picked
up the receiver, my German artist friend Anita was on the line.
"I'm in Washington D.C. and I have to see you," she said in her
low, controlled voice. She was on her way to New York City
before returning to Munich for Christmas.

I met Anita in 1980, a few weeks before Fred, Patrick and I
moved to Mexico. During the years we lived in San Miguel de
Allende she came there to paint and stayed at a mutual friend's
home. After an intense creative day we'd sit by the fireplace after
dinner and enjoy a well-deserved glass of Rioja wine. It was during
those months that Anita became my most trusted friend. We
talked mostly about art, but also about our lives: her childhood in
war-torn Germany, mine with my German family in Guatemala.
Once in a while, one would catch grave words the other was
unaware she was sharing.

Anita has the enduring quality of a favorite childhood melody.
Her appearance is predictable: a classic dark blue suit over a white
or pale blue blouse. In her youth she appeared older than her
years but with time, as she grew into her features, she seemed not
to age at all.

Now she stood at the train's door holding what looked like
a roll of white paper. Before descending on the painfully narrow
steps she said, referring to the parcel, "Take this, and don't crush
it, for it's more important than I."

What she was guarding with her life was a watercolor of

the Rio Dulce she painted the previous year, when she was in Guatemala. Knowing my history, she made the effort of visiting Livingston. "I was relieved this hadn't sold in the Washington gallery," she said, "for suddenly, I had an unbridled urge to pick it up and bring it to you. I want you, and no one else, to own it."

It's a tropical scene where yellow-footed thrushes, pale blue wood pigeons and crimson-chested woodpeckers perch on trees with roots anchored in a slowly flowing river. From behind giant ferns a long-tailed spider monkey peeks at the viewer, while a little golden lioness relaxes on a thick branch. Meanwhile, a somber thunder-grey Mayan monolith oversees the natural order of the jungle.

"Anita," my voice caught, and I blinked a few times. "I am deeply moved by the image and I am truly humbled by your enormous generosity," I said, overwhelmed by the contextual message in her art.

After dinner we fell into our customary exchange of thoughts and ideas, and I shared with my friend that I had started therapy.

"What made you seek help?" Anita asked intrigued that I had finally taken the step.

"I think one could say that my coping mechanisms were no longer effective. I had to start confronting my complex demons and focus on what I'm about. Or at least try to figure me out," I sighed and continued to tell her about my bouts of alienation and the need to scrutinize my upbringing.

"Your upbringing was impeccable. We know that," Anita reassured me, taking a cigarette and continuing without lighting it. "I have, however, often thought about your mother, and have been wanting to talk with you about my trip to Livingston last year." Then she flicked her silver lighter, put the cigarette in her mouth, held it to the flame and inhaled deeply. She clicked the lighter closed and exhaled slowly, allowing the smoke to escape through her lips as she looked into the distance. It had taken us no time to reach the purpose of her trip to see me. "I marveled at the serenity of the landscape," she continued, "the lush tropical vegetation, the remoteness of it all; mostly, I was moved by the integrity and gentility of the people in the village. I was only there one day, but I spoke to several older people and asked them if they had known your German parents." Drawing again on her cigarette and exhaling smoke, she added, "What has concerned me ever since, and I am relieved we can talk about today, is that two people claimed the Germans had stolen a child." Her deep blue eyes focused steadily on me, wondering how I would accept the terminology.

"When I was there with Fred I also heard I had been 'stolen', but I dismissed it as village talk."

"Maybe you should look carefully at that concept again," my friend suggested. "No mother in a self-contained society such as the one in that village would willingly give up her child." She lowered her voice and chose her words cautiously. "Please try to be fair. If you know what your German mother told you, you should also want to know what your birth mother might have to say."

"No need to be so guarded, Anita, for I lately I've been looking at this more openly," I offered confidently. "Truth remains: I was born out of wedlock. Mutti told me that in Rosa's society, having an illegitimate child disgraced a woman. Rosa knew full well what she was doing when she let Mutti raise me." I smiled at my friend. "No 'stealing' took place there." I was not being defensive; I just repeated what I knew. That's the way it had been. The facts were that I was illegitimate, that Rosa was disgraced by my birth, that Mutti had said she would raise me if I was a girl, that I ended up being a girl, and that Mutti then kept her word by raising me.

Anita ran her fingers through her hair and sighed, "All I can tell you, is that a mother in supportive circumstances does not let her child go. You were her first born," she paused, "...A mother and her first born child have a singular bond. Just look at you and Patrick... You couldn't breathe without him. You must give your mother due credit for losing her child." My friend gazed at me for a moment, and then asked point blank: "Why didn't they adopt you?"

When someone asked me, I had occasionally wondered why

I didn't have the German surname, but I figured it out for myself, and I tended to agree with what I thought Mutti would have answered.

"Mutti had a daughter. Don't you think she would've had serious reservations about that?"

Shaking her head, my friend said, "No, no, dear friend. She took you from your mother and raised you jealously as her own, without committing herself legally. That, in my eyes, is fundamentally immoral."

After a deep, steadying breath, I insisted, "It was the forties; the war was raging and adopting a Black child was just not one of the things anyone would have done." It was clear as I was saying it that I had learned to see me through German eyes: loved, yet inferior.

"Why not?" Anita continued unfazed. "You were raised so completely German. You were so absolutely her child. It's the very least she could have done." My friend's voice lowered. "Commit herself to you, to the world and your parents, that she loved you not only in word but to the fullest extent of her legal and moral responsibility. Given the times, and because of the times, she should have done it. I'm sorry Catana, but I find that omission reprehensible."

We looked at each other in silence, the silence of a failure to communicate. That was terrible language, and I was unwilling to register its inherent truth; those were also the strongest words I had ever heard coming out of Anita.

"She had Ruth," I shrugged.

"That's exactly why she should've strengthened your position. She should've known her own daughter's character. Apart from that, Pablo was not Ruth's father. You were Pablo and Esther's child: their emotional child. That should have entitled you to their name."

Anita had spoken to some of Mutti's friends who were not necessarily Ruth's. I wondered what she had heard, but I didn't ask and she didn't offer. I knew from the conversation that someone must have made comments regarding Mutti's failure to legalize my position. I crawled into my protective shell that with time had become thicker than that of a tortoise. I just swallowed and decided to sit back and change the subject.

As I relaxed, I winced at pain radiating from my right shoulder. "Sorry. I pulled something several weeks ago. In the last day or two I realized I'm in pain," I grinned and added in a wavering voice, "Must be my mental rigidity manifesting itself in my body," I apologized

My friend furrowed her brows, "You are aware that you ignore pain, aren't you?" Anita offered gently.

"When I ache, I do something about it. Saw my chiropractor yesterday. She claimed 'lesser men' would have showed up sooner," I laughed amused. "Pain was something no one talked about as I was growing up. Like money: whether you had it or not, it was not discussed. Simple."

"How about this possibility," Anita looked at me sideways. "How about your Mutti not wanting you to be in touch with your pain... your real pain."

I jumped up, "What do you mean?" And again winced. "I don't understand what you are getting at," I added wryly.

"What I'm trying to say is that you were taught not to feel pain. Not to feel the specific pain of separating from your mother. You probably stopped acknowledging any pain at all when you were quite young."

"That is really heavy, Anita. Where did you get that idea?" I straightened up and gave her a puzzled look.

"You once said that Fred was a hypochondriac, that he hurt here and there. You may dismiss it, but his pain is real and he can talk about it," Anita said simply.

"Really," I laughed nervously. "He's the all time hypo..." But I didn't like one bit what I was hearing.

"All I am saying is this: listen to yourself sometime, and pay attention to what I've dared to say. Above all, consider that it's not normal to go about physically hurting and not feeling it."

I took a deep breath. I had never known my friend to be as candid as she was being then. Of all the people in the world, I would only allow her to confront me so directly. Tears gathered in my eyes. "I now weep sometimes," I smiled through blurred vision. "You know I'm not made for emotions, but lately... I've not been able to keep them from bubbling up."

"There's nothing wrong with that. Nothing at all," Anita said softly. And so we talked until we were too tired and drained to say another word.

The following day we went to the framer, and then drove to Saratoga Springs for lunch. We never stopped chatting but didn't mention my mothers again. When my friend left, she wept as she always did when we said goodbye. Somehow she feared we'd have to wait lifetimes before seeing each other again.

Each time I walked by the painting my eyes were drawn to the peaceful lioness. Guatemala's jungles have sleek obsidian panthers, not furry golden lions. Anita must have chosen ochre for the cat because it complimented the other colors. In the natural kingdom, it is said the lioness is a magnificent mother. The picture was not originally intended for my walls. When it became mine, the inherent symbolism was clear only to me. There's no such thing as chance, I was in the flow, suddenly cascading toward a 'me' I so badly wanted to embrace.

Anita Bucherer Godeffroy's watercolor of
the Rio Dulce

By March 1992, Fred had been home longer than usual. Usual meant he'd be in New York City during the week and upstate on weekends. He'd been home three straight weeks. My professional life allowed little time for the silliness of our earlier years. I looked at my husband wondering how I could have managed to sideline my most ardent supporter, when he was no different than he had always been. At dinner one evening, as we sat over a dish of spaghetti I had prepared with singular disinterest, I watched him eat. Looks like his mother, I thought. I liked my mother-in-law and he had his good looks from her, but I wondered if in coming years my husband's features would sink into the same deep wrinkles. Did all that gray hair come overnight? And just look at him chew!

Fred became self-conscious at the silent attention. "Love the way you made this aglio e olio, Sweetie," he smiled.

"Thanks."

"You could talk to me. Lately, you come home and don't even make an effort to say something."

Cooking was bad enough; I surely didn't feel like entertaining anyone. "Guess I'm overworked," I snapped.

"Yeah, it must be tough being an assistant professor on tenure track," he mocked.

I could take that comment either of two ways and I was inclined to favor the meaner version, so I said nothing.

"I try to help, I do the laundry, I clean the house..." His voice was laced with apology.

"I know, I know." Big Deal, I thought. We finished eating and without another word I began to clear the table.

"It's not my fault work is dead in New York!"

"Well, then do something else!" I said and sucked my teeth.

"Yeah, like what?"

"Like write, or paint! You're the artist here. Go 'n get a life, Fred!"

"You are my life!" He shouted. He was angry. And so was I.

"Don't piss me off, Fred. You know what I mean."

"Yeah, I know what you mean! You think you're so much fun? Who needs all this! It's time for me to get the hell outta here. I'm off to LA. It's pilot season there anyway. Then you can have all the space to rattle around for your committees and conferences. Your boring husband won't be around to suffer through your lousy moods!"

"Yeah, go to California; go to hell, for all I care! I'm taking a walk, damn you!"

At the door I slipped into my sneakers then grabbed my coat and stepped into a cold, clear evening. I walked through the garden and turned right on the street. Right: long ago, Mutti and I turned right when we left Catalina on our walks along the Avenida de la Reforma. Then Mutti held my hand and told me stories and the world smelled of eucalyptus. Now it was dusk and the snow on the sidewalk smelled like slush. I started to jog and remembered how, as a skinny fourth grader, I left sixth graders in the dust. I didn't weep when I raced back then. Now I was running... away from my husband. Tears of confusion blurred the darkening landscape.

TWO DAYS LATER, AFTER DROPPING FRED OFF at the airport, I sat in Connie's office. I'd been sifting through my life with her for more than two and a half years already, and felt I'd still made no headway.

"I'm stressed," I said, "and this therapy is going nowhere. I'm more miserable than I was before. Now I've even chased Fred away."

Connie began to take notes. "First of all, your insights so far have been subtle but profound. You have at least allowed yourself to doubt the integrity of your upbringing. That alone is huge. Now, what's this about chasing Fred away?"

"He couldn't stand my nitpicking, and I couldn't stop it. He's on a plane to Los Angeles."

"To do what?"

"Work. And get away from me."

"So, apart from escaping your moods, Fred's off looking for work? I'd say he has himself in mind, too." Connie gazed at me impassively.

"He's on the other side of the continent and I can't find fault with him non-stop."

"Ahh," Connie mused. "Now, what precisely irritates you?"

"We're too close. Much too close... We're almost one person."

"Let's get comfortable and talk about that. How about some Tension Tamer? It's delicious tea."

She made tea and we settled into our chairs with the aromatic brew in our hands.

I took a sip. "Ummm, good stuff," I smiled.

"Isn't it just?" Connie smiled back, and placed her cup on the table. Becoming serious and taking her pen and pad, she added, "Now tell me about that closeness."

I began slowly, carefully, "Ever since our first meeting, Fred has been as close to me as my skin. Really. We finish each other's sentences. What bothers me is that I feel he controls me, even though I think he needs me more than I need him. When Mutti died he said he'd take care of me. I was grateful he was in my life because I loved him. But after all these years I wonder who really takes care of whom, and which one needs the other more. Know what I mean?"

"Yes. Did I hear you say you think Fred controls you?"

"Yeah. Like Mutti did. It's frustrating, but I see parallels with Mutti in my relationship with Fred. This is about as clearly as I can define it."

I finished my tea and watched her write down what I said.

"Fine," Connie looked up, smiling. "This is wonderful. What you're experiencing happens to all who grapple with their identity. You are looking for your boundaries. You want to know where your partner ends and you begin. You want to see who you are away from the influence of those closest to you: away from Fred's, away from Mutti's."

We were silent.

"I resent the nearness," I grumbled. "There's something else, Connie. When Mutti and I were traveling through Germany in 1960, she made a point of telling me she gave me the right 'frame'."

"What did she mean by that?"

"She implied that people had a better impression of me when I was with her."

"And how did that make you feel?"

"Hurt, I guess, because I remember it so well, and Mutti said it more than once. It was not enough that I acted and reacted like a German, she still felt I needed the attribute of a White partner to 'elevate' me."

"Going back to those days, how did you see yourself then?"

"As superior, of course, and not only with regard to Blacks, mind you," I giggled and smirked.

"Did you believe you needed the 'frame'?"

"I don't think so. But I believed everything Mutti said. It bothered me that she rubbed it in, though."

"What about your White husband?"

I burrowed into the chair. "What about him?"

"Is he your 'right frame'?"

Fred had become my 'right frame', of course. I wouldn't have wanted it differently. "It's not quite the same, but he has always shielded me, Connie. He fears for me like Mutti did. When we moved to California in 1975, Fred's friends also became very protective of me."

"Oh?" Connie raised both eyebrows. "Please tell me why you think his American friends felt that way about you."

"In spite of my aloof attitude, or perhaps because of it, I guess, I was pretty naïve. That must have concerned them. Everyone who was White and liked me, felt they needed to shield me from racist hostilities I wouldn't recognize. In California Fred began to do things by himself that we'd done as a couple in Europe. Like buying our house in Sherman Oaks, for instance. The mortgage company never saw me. Fred brought the papers home and I signed them. It was obvious to me after a while, that in the US - at least that's what it was like in the '70's - if I wanted to live in the sort of middle-class neighborhood I was accustomed to, I needed a White partner to take care of official matters. Times have changed, and so have I, but Fred will always see himself as my protector," I smiled, nodding.

"Be aware of the 'frame' concept," Connie said. "You can

consider it a gift that Fred is away. You now have the space to start identifying consciously what your wants are, and where your needs lie. It's not easy," my counselor smiled. Then added, "You've never mentioned your natural father. Do you know anything about him?"

"I know he lives in Brooklyn."

"When did you find that out?"

"Ruth told me a few years ago."

"Finally!" Connie rejoiced as she began to write furiously in her pad. "This is the first major breakthrough!"

"What's the big deal? I told you long ago."

"Oh no Catana. I'd remember something as important as this, and it would be in my notes." She was grinning so hard it looked like her face would split in half. "When are you contacting him?"

"What on earth for? I'm dealing with mothers, not my father," I countered defensively.

"Yes, but your father, at the very least, can tell you about your mother."

Professor Tully addressing graduating class 1992

PART FIVE

Gilbert E. Reed
1992 - 1994

Initial Contacts

Connie was clear: don't bother to see her again until I had, in some concrete form or other, established a connection to my father. We had exhausted ideas of how to contact him, I just had to muster the courage to do it.

On a Sunday in the middle of March, 1992, with Fred in Los Angeles and Patrick skiing in Vermont, it was then or admit I'd lost my nerve... Again.

Is hi, or hello better, I thought as I slowly marked the numbers on the phone. My mouth was dry as parchment, and by the time I dialed the eleventh digit I had stopped breathing altogether. All senses focused on my left ear. I heard the phone ring at the other end. It rang three times, then came: "Hello?" It was the high-pitched voice of an elderly man.

"Good morning," I breathed. "I'm trying to locate Gilberto Reed."

"This is he."

"Hello Gil," my voice trembled a bit, "this is your daughter Catana." I knew I was his only child, at least the only one he admitted having fathered. "How are you?"

"I am very well, thank you," he said easily. "And how are you?" Wow! What a nonchalant reaction to suddenly receiving a call from a daughter he'd never heard from before. I told him I called because I wanted to learn about my parents, and as a matter of courtesy asked him how his wife was. Mutti had dismissed her as a whining, complaining, sickly woman.

"Vivian's very, very sick," he said. She had serious respiratory problems, and the situation was so advanced no one could help anymore.

"I'm so sorry," I said sincerely. "She's always been sickly, no?"

"She was never really healthy, let's put it that way." He did all the housework, cooked, cleaned, and cared for all her needs as she was on oxygen 24/7, and other than in an ambulance, never left the house anymore. He was grateful for his excellent health so he could do all the needed work. He shared this in an easy, matter-of-fact way. "Mala hierba no muere (weeds are indestructible), as we say back home," he chuckled.

We chatted and laughed like comfortable old friends. I was unbelievably relaxed, incredibly at ease. Forgotten were the nerves and jitters. This day, Gil said, would merit a special entry in his journal.

"You keep a journal?"

"Oh, sure... as did my father. This way I can read about what I was doing ten, twenty, fifty years ago on a particular day."

Mutti used to refer to Gil's father as 'Ole Man Reed.' He represented American and English interests in the area, and was honorary consul of those countries. He was very white, never got a tan, always wore a hat, was always red as a lobster. That was all I knew. Now I learned from my father that 'Ole Man Reed' kept a journal.

"And you Gil? How are you?" I asked, although he sounded fine.

"I have all the physical strengths of a forty-year-old and none of the weaknesses of viejitos," (geezers) he bragged. From the way he sounded, it was hard to believe he was eighty-one. "I always dress my very best when I leave the house, and I get a kick that people think I'm a doctor or lawyer," he laughed. Why did that not surprise me?

I thought it inappropriate to ask about Rosa in the first conversation, but did mention Mutti. Gil's angry reaction took me by surprise. "That woman," he claimed, had caused him tons of grief. He furiously accused her of having set out to ruin his life. It was the first time I heard anything negative about the mother I loved. His was a perspective that would topple Mutti from the pedestal I had her on. Ultimately, he told her off! Set her straight, in a scathing letter so that she never again bothered him. "I don't like being made a fool of," he ranted. "I write to people. I write to Senators, the Governor, I've written to two Presidents. You can read the letters. I'll send you copies, and copies of their answers to me. You'll see. If I don't like something, I make myself heard. I get my typewriter out and let them have it!" That was too funny for words! I burst out roaring with laughter and he immediately joined in, and I was glad his anger regarding Mutti had been diverted to politicians.

We talked for almost an hour. This chatty, humorous, and utterly charming man fascinated me. My father! What a novel realm of familiarity; never before had I experienced such a kindred connection to a man.

"Thank heavens I was sitting when I answered the phone," Gil said referring to my call. "Few people can take a shock like this one on their feet, you know."

"Ah, so I did surprise you," I laughed again. "I was beginning to worry I'd made no impression... I've been postponing this call for a long time... Feared you mightn't answer a letter."

"Don't think about it. This was delightful for me," he chirped.

"I'll call again soon," I promised.

"That would be wonderful; I'll look forward to hearing from you again. I don't like to end a conversation on a serious note," and began to tell me an outrageous joke. Assured I was roaring with laughter, he hung the phone up abruptly.

I called Fred and shared all I'd heard from Gil. It was great that Mr. Reed hat turned out to be a wonderfully uncomplicated gem of a dad.

On Tuesday, two days after the conversation and still giddy about it, I received a letter:

My Dear Catana,

There are many things you should know, and that I am not able to tell you at this time. I have to see you in person and talk, only you and I. You do not know the great harm Doña Esther did to you and to me. She did all this after I got to the

US in 1950. *I have the letters to show you.*

I'd like to come to Albany, but am unable to leave the house as I have my wife under oxygen twenty-four hours a day. There is no hope for her recovery, but I think that by the time I can see you she will be better…

My very best regards,
GEReed

What sort of harm could Mutti possibly have done to us?

Sunday I called Brooklyn again. Gil's wife answered the phone. "Oh, Vivian, good morning," I said easily. "This is Catana. May I speak with Gil please?"

"Who is this?" came a scathing answer.

"Catana…"

"Who?"

I wondered whether she had lost hear hearing. Enunciating clearly, I said: "I am Gil's daughter, and I'd like to speak to my father."

"Mr. Reed has no children," she hissed.

She had not lost her hearing, her mind, maybe.

It had never occurred to me that Gil might not be my father. After all, he legalized me as his daughter and I had proof I was his child. I figured Vivian was alone, and not wanting to upset her, I said in a manageable tone, "All right, Vivian. I'll call again later."

"Your name is not Catana," she thundered. Maybe I had finished with her, but she had not started with me. "Your name is Adriana. That's the name your mother gave you. And you are Edmundo Cayetano's child."

Was she ever abrasive! I knew my name was Adriana. But Edmundo Cayetano? He was the man who later married Rosa. Absolutely: no way.

Then the woman said she and my mother were cousins, had been best friends and had been closer than sisters. When people started saying things about Rosa and Gil, she knew they were lies because it was preposterous to imagine them being together.

"I was one of your godmothers. How could I also have been

your stepmother?"

I paled. "Godmother?" My voice trembled. "How extraordinary, Ruth... You know her. She told me I wasn't baptized because there was no church in the village."

"For heaven's sake! Ruth herself was there," Vivian shot back. "You had six godparents, three women and three men," she popped at me and proceeded to say their names.

I was dumbfounded. Ruth distinctly told me during the visit in 1977 that I was not baptized. Now I heard that she herself witnessed the ceremony. I even had six godparents, for chrissakes! How could this be possible?

Someone was lying. I had the uneasy suspicion it was Ruth. Why? She knew I long ago stopped giving a hoot about organized religions. Baptism was not important to me but for my mother's people it obviously was. My head began to spin at the thought that Ruth was present when I was given the name 'Adriana!' What a shock to stumble on such a blatant lie. Why was I lied to? Was it because Ruth wanted to belittle me in front of my dyed in the wool Catholic husband?

Vivian had no kind words for any of the Germans and said Mutti had tormented a mother who suffered immeasurably at being forced to give up her child. "That woman," Vivian blasted, using the same term as Gil, "threatened Rosa, or anyone else from Livingston, that if they as much as dared to see you alone, she'd have 'em thrown in jail. She was a horrible, cruel person. Ay, ay, ay," Vivian lamented, "no one can possibly understand poor Rosa's pain. No wonder she died so young. Everyone knew she died of a broken heart," Vivian said, releasing another deep sigh. "The sweet woman was only fifty-three. How can anyone take a child away from the mother?" Then her rage exploded again: "Only a heartless German like 'that one' could!" She exclaimed.

My mind was either blank or racing. I should be taking notes I thought. Fascinated, stunned, and slightly dizzy, I wanted to hang the phone up, but couldn't bring myself to do so. "Vivian," I finally ventured, "I know now I behaved badly toward Rosa. I was conditioned to such a reaction, and am really, truly sorry. I've started to look for people who knew her because I'm trying to understand what happened long ago. I want to have an... ah... an idea perhaps, of who she was. I want to know about my relatives..." I rubbed my temples, acknowledging an oncoming headache. "I'm only now daring to... to look at my mother, and perhaps question the things I was told."

"I know how you behaved," Vivian's tone showed no mercy. "You should've seen how quiet, how subdued Rosa was after she'd been to see you. And you," she again chastised me, "even after you left for Europe, never cared to see her when you returned to Guatemala."

"It wasn't often," I countered defensively.

"All the years that woman was sick: '68, '69, '70, and in '77 you talked to Chico Blanco's grandson." For someone who so vehemently insisted she had no stake in my life, it was surprising Vivian knew so much about it.

"How'd you know?" I said, aghast. "I even think you have the years right!"

"Be aware that if one of us hears anything about you, we tell the others."

"But weren't you in the States?" I whispered.

"Yes, of course, but that doesn't change anything," she rifled back.

If nothing else, Gil had been interested enough to keep abreast of my whereabouts.

And then Vivian let me know that she and Gil had been married 56 years. That meant he was a married man when he fathered me. She apparently remained barren and stubbornly refused to accept that her husband had been with the person who was dearest to her. The hair-raising revelations Vivian provided had me thunderstruck, to say the least.

Her exquisite diction and wonderful command of the Spanish language was remarkable, and I complimented her on that. "Oh, yes," she said softening her tone, "my husband and I take pride in our language. We don't want anyone to think we're from the islands." I chuckled at finding two dark people in cosmopolitan Brooklyn, making sure they distanced themselves not only from African Americans, but also from Puerto Ricans,

Cubans, Dominicans, or anyone who spoke a Spanish laced with regionalisms. Vivian's English was almost accent free, and she didn't sound sick, either. Of her illness, she humbly said it was a "terminal condition."

I found myself captivated by her formal dignity and her strong, expressive voice, and her mercurial ability to go from glacial when Mutti and I were on her radar, to warm and gentle when remembering Rosa. The call lasted much longer than the one with Gil. From Vivian I learned for the first time, palpably, how Rosa had suffered at having given me up. Mutti continued her slow descent from the ivory tower. That saddened, as it relieved me, for I was making progress on my journey.

It was my intention to laugh with Gil; instead I got an impassioned earful from his wife and received an education that would force me to look at the situation from a much different perspective.

Ruth had lied. What a singularly scary shock! Why? Who else?

My intention was to jump at my father in anger, but Vivian again answered immediately when I called the following week. If she wasn't sitting on top of him, she was surely cowering by the phone waiting for it to ring. I asked for my Gil. He was home, she said, and proceeded to chat with me as if I'd called her and we were ancient friends. She had me ask twice, before, with tangible reluctance, she handed my father the receiver.

His "Hello," was loaded with discomfort.

"Spoke to Vivian last week," I said.

"Yes, she told me." His voice was low, subdued, stiff. The witty, funny Gil was gone, probably cowering in some dark corner.

"So, what's this about you not being my father?" I blurted out. I had hoped to handle it better. Silence. "Gil, if you're not my father, why'd you stay in touch with the family?"

"I didn't."

Didn't what? "Come on," I said brusquely, "I know I saw you

when I was four or five years old; my best friend Putzi recently told me she remembers you distinctly when we were about nine... And, only a few years ago, when you were in Guatemala you called Ruth and asked her about me."

"I did call Ruth," his voice quivered. "But everything else is not true." Then, as if he'd been jabbed in the ribs he exploded: "It was that evil woman! She caused me so much grief. No one should ever have to endure the anguish she put me through. Oh," he groaned, "the terrible troublemaker insisted that I was your father."

"So you agree that Edmundo Cayetano is my father?"

"That woman didn't like him, so she fabricated the story about me."

"Gil, listen very carefully," I said lowering my voice, "I have documents in which you legalize me as your child."

"That wasn't me. I wasn't there."

"I beg your pardon? Not where?"

"Not in Guatemala, of course."

"Where were you then?"

"In the States. I had left Guatemala."

"Well, for heaven's sake, who signed the papers?"

"That woman must've bribed somebody to sign my name. I tell you, I wasn't in the country when she pulled that one." It sounded as if he was about to cry.

"'That one'? And what's 'that one' supposed to be?" I thundered on.

"The forged signature, what else?"

"Come on! Gimme me a break, Gil! What about Rosa? Tell me she didn't know who the father was!"

"Rosa refused to talk to me," he sighed. "I'm telling you, it was all that woman's doing. She didn't like Edmundo, and she was crazy about me." What? What did he mean, crazy about him?

"Now, what's THAT supposed to mean? Crazy about you?"

"She was in love with me."

Silence.

"D'you wanna know something, Gil? If you want me to take you seriously, you have to act accordingly. You know all this is rubbish."

"It IS true," he answered meekly.

It was all too bizarre and ludicrous. Maybe the old guy was senile after all, or had a touch of recurring malaria and was hallucinating. The man was clearly under pressure, and what little patience I had for moronic shenanigans had run out. I changed the subject and quickly ended the conversation. Lunatics, I thought enraged: two old, whacked out, and absolutely demented lunatics.

Juliette, my kitten, as if sensing I needed comforting, jumped on my lap, arranged herself in a circle and started to purr. I sat back in the chair, eyes closed. What if Mutti had been in love with Gil? Suppose she'd actually fancied him... Remember her secret love affairs? What would've kept her from seducing Gil? Really... What if she loved him and, yearning to have his child, snatched the one he fathered out of wedlock and kept it as her own? Why not? Aren't romance novels full of labyrinthine, heart wrenching kitsch, where crazed women in love overplay their power? And then, too, isn't it common knowledge that European women are notorious for their fascination with Black men? Where was Rosa in this equation? Where Vivian? She was married to Gil at the time! What sort of man was this Gil that every woman in the village fell for his charms including, according to him, the White one in the big house on the hill? She was old enough to be his mother, for God's sake! My little grey tiger was still purring when the phone rang. Startled, I hesitated a second before picking up.

"I couldn't talk," Gil breathed. "When it comes to you, she gets terribly agitated. I'm at the pay phone downstairs."

"I guess I'm relieved you're calling," I answered apprehensively. "That nonsense a while ago was pathetic, you know. I can't help it if Vivian can't handle my being alive..."

"I know, of course, I know," he said softly. "I just want to tell you, that as you've used my name all this time, you might as well keep it. I don't mind you having it."

"I'm drained, Gil; this all is just too much for me. Goodbye." I hung up.

A flood of conflicting emotions was threatening to choke me. Where was the truth? Was there a truth? Tears, hot and furious, spilled from my eyes and ran down my face.

After composing myself, I called Fred and recounted the conversation.

"You want to know something?" He said calmly, "You have to remove Gil from the house. You have to be alone with him and talk, just talk. That's what he wants... He said so in his letter. Vivian has a different agenda, Sweetie. She can say things you about your mother, but not your father. That's for him to do. That's his role."

"What if he really isn't my father?"

"He is," Fred assured me. "Make yourself some lunch... and then have another close look at your papers. There just might be more encrusted in those folkloric documents."

Again I went into the folder and made another discovery: Rosa's name did not appear in the later papers. In 1945, when Mutti had Gil legalize me as Catana, Rosa's name is nowhere on the document. It was all Mutti and Gil. Then I compared his signatures with the one on the photograph: they were the same. On that particular date in February 1945, Gil had been in Guatemala. He lied when he claimed to have been in the States.

"One thing is sure," Fred laughed when I called him back with the information, "your Mutti saw that your papers were in order: she wanted your parents to be accounted for. She did what every responsible parent would do," he said gently, "make sure the child's papers are OK. She was obviously very protective of you." It's when Fred comes out with so much clear logic that he absolutely disarms me. "If Gil said it was okay for you to use his name," Fred added, "he knows why he said it. You'll see... once you have him to yourself, you'll hear the truth."

And so, three months after my first call to Gil, I drove to Brooklyn. He told me how to reach his home and said it was a safe neighborhood. I looked on the map and knew I'd have no trouble finding him.

Meeting Gil

It sounds odd for sure, but I never thought about my
conception. Not even in the back of my mind. Being Mutti's
cherub, fallen from heaven onto a mound of grass, was so much
more appealing than owing my existence to two people having
had sex. As I held my baby in my arms, it did not occur to me to
think of how or when the spark was ignited that brought me into
this world.

That Gil had been a married man when he conceived me
started to intrigue me. Here I was, the product of a secret, passionate
love affair - the sort one reads about in romance novels, where
lovers are drawn together by an irresistible force. I was the result
of bashful stolen glances, whispered longings, tingling fingers,
secret places... Perhaps they conceived me on an afternoon when
torrential downpours trapped them in a moss-covered grotto.
Perhaps, on the sultry sands of a coral beach, my father embraced
my mother under a canopy of trembling stars. Two young brown
bodies fused into each other, embraced in forbidden passion must
have created me.

What would Gil see when he looked at me, I wondered?
Would my lips, as I shaped them into words and smiles, take his
thoughts back to long forgotten embraces? Would my skin remind
him of the texture of my mother's velvet body? Could looking at
my eyes rekindle the spark that lit his soul? In how many ways
would I remind him of my mother, the woman he had secretly
held in his heart?

I drove to Brooklyn to meet my father on a gloriously sunny
June day in 1992. Along the freeway, pines, maples, elms, and
birch trees boasted shiny new green. Here, bushes of wild pink
and mauve rhododendrons; there, yellow forsythias were in full
bloom. Patches of white wild flowers dotted the hillsides, and the
Catskills seemed more beautiful than I had ever seen them. I was
at peace as I raced south on the New York Thruway, over the
Tappanzee Bridge, down Henry Hudson Parkway, through the
Brooklyn Battery Tunnel, along Shore Parkway, to the Rockaway
exit. I made the various turns I was instructed to take and ended

up on a tree-lined street in a courtyard with poplars. I parked next to an elegant, white American car and walked to the building thinking: Brooklyn? This sure is a lot better than I had anticipated. A doorman announced my arrival. The elevator took me to the fourth floor, and I walked to the end of the corridor to apartment 4B.

After bracing myself with a slow deep breath, I raised my hand and rang the bell. The sound of footsteps behind the door made my heart pound so loudly I missed the shift of the latch. He's not six feet at all; he's my height, was my first thought. The hair he had in my photograph was gone. Before me stood a portly, pleasant-looking, elderly gentleman in a perfectly tailored medium blue linen suit, pale blue batiste shirt and a conservative, small print, dark blue tie. Elegant to boot. He was right: he could be taken for a successful doctor, lawyer, or businessman. I was the professor from upstate who had merely taken care to color-coordinate her clothes.

"You're punctual," he smiled mildly. "Did you have a good trip?" I felt his eyes absorbing me as he gestured for me to enter.

"Everything went very well. After all, I had excellent directions," I smiled at him and stepped into the strikingly clean apartment. The living room was to the right, but I was directed left, to the kitchen where Vivian sat at a table. The Haitian woman who came three days a week to stay with her while Gil ran errands was also there.

"Mrs. Tully," Gil said formally, "this is my wife, Mrs. Reed."

"How are you, Vivian? How are you feeling today?" No way was I getting stuck in formal shenanigans, and I handed her the box of truffles I brought for them.

Vivian's illness had reduced her to an ethereal whisper. A long tube attached to her delicate nose connected to a large oxygen tank. Having long lost the vibrancy of health, her eyes were but sad, opaque pools of pale grey. As I held her tiny breakable hand, I was overwhelmed with sympathy for her and wished I could make my strength flow into her body.

"Hello, Mrs. Tully," she said in a strong voice that defied frailness. Turning to Gil she exclaimed, "She looks exactly like

Lucio!" And after looking me up and down, somewhat louder remarked, "It's amazing, she's Lucio all over."

"Who. Is. Lucio?" I asked.

"He's your uncle. He's Edmundo's brother, Lucio Cayetano," she explained.

"Interesting... I've never heard that name."

It was clear I had to get Gil away from Vivian, as she was set to control the content of the conversation. The plan was to meet at his home and then go somewhere to talk. He wasn't making the first move.

"We need to talk, Gil," I said, feeling quite brazen. "How about going for coffee somewhere?"

"Yes, of course," he obliged. I promised Vivian to visit with her later.

On the way out, Gil picked up a folder lying on a table by the entrance. Where'd I get the courage? How great was that! Yes! Without sitting down, I managed to extricate my father from the clutches of his wife.

I had indeed parked next to his car: the newest model of a fancy Chrysler. One glance at my Honda Civic, and Gil decided we'd take the Chrysler. It was immaculately clean, inside and out, and had every gadget that made travel comfortable, including a collection of cassettes with catchy dance tunes. This eighty-one year old geezer seemed to like fun and was prepared for pleasure. "Tell me what this is," he said placing a cassette in the player.

"Guatemalan Marimba," I shrugged.

"The whistle, listen..."

"And?"

"That's the sound of the Ferrocarril Verapaz in Livingston! Isn't it great?" His face beaming all over.

The whistle of the German-owned train that used to bring coffee from the highland plantations to be shipped to Europe had become part of a syncopated rhythm that invited to clap hands, tap feet and swing hips. I shook my head and grinned, as I recognized the makings of a troublemaker in my pedantic father's eyes.

"I WANT THAT TABLE BY THE WINDOW," the hostess

heard as he walked by her and she followed. It was, of course, the best table in the place, and he took the best seat. Then and there, it struck me that he behaved with the natural, uncomplicated, self-centeredness of a White man.

Sunlight filtered through the window softening our features as we sat facing each other. A faint touch of his cologne spiced our booth. I asked for coffee. "Nothing to eat? You've been on the road for hours," he noted, and ordered two coffees and two English muffins. No questions asked. My eyes followed his graceful gestures as he spoke to the waiter. "I don't feel like eating either," he gazed at me, "but you must eat something." I smiled amused at his paternal command.

"All right then, a muffin's fine," I agreed, grinning.

He was assertive, sure of himself... Quite a difference to the man he had been in the apartment. After a few pleasantries - he obviously wanted to get Mutti issues over with - Gil opened his folder. In it were various letters from Mutti (I didn't know they had corresponded for years), newspaper and magazine articles of my days as an actress in Germany, and several photos in various stages of my growing up.

With unnecessary flourish, he handed me Mutti's last letter dated 1955, the one that had prompted his irate response. She had written a little about me and quickly came to the point: she needed his authorization so I could leave Guatemala and study in Jamaica. "Now Gil, I want you to tend to this matter immediately. Don't you be lazy and let time go by! Make sure you take care of it right away." I was shocked at the tone... so unlike Mutti. Apparently she saw no need for any formality on her part. Now Gil, do this; don't be lazy, do it now... Wow, no respect! Had the letter been typewritten, I would have sworn on any Bible that it wasn't Mutti's. Then he handed me with visible pride, a carbon copy of the irate response he'd fired back. It was the letter that had finally gotten her off his back, for good. "There is no proof the girl is my daughter," it said, "and not until I am convinced of that fact will I move in any direction." Who knows who signed what, but I left Guatemala late August 1955.

I brought with me what little I had on Gil: my legalization, name change documents, and the old photo. "You signed the photo on the same date you signed my name change," I stared him down. That means you were in Guatemala on those dates. His shoulders sagged, and for a few seconds he seemed confused.

"It was rough for me then," he murmured. "A lot of people were trying to convince me of all sorts of things regarding you." His expression was grave. Up to that point in his existence, no one had curbed his carefree lifestyle.

"Whatever you have against Mutti, Gil, accusing her of bribery is not only unfair, it's a lie. After all, I resembled you." He looked up at me and I detected a flicker of acknowledgement in his eyes. "And Gil, what about your insinuation that she was in love with you... Did you have an affair with her?"

"Heavens, no! I said that the other day because my wife was right next to me. When it comes to this situation, Vivian turns my life into a living hell. I'd just as soon not upset her, being that she's so frail and all."

"Why did you keep my photos?"

He smiled, his voice husky, "I never really knew whether I was your father or not. But..." he paused smiling shyly, "now I know." His expression was priceless.

The maitre d' came by to greet us. "Well, Mr. Reed, you have a lovely young lady at your table this morning," he said in a rather smug voice.

Grinning broadly at me and winking, Gil answered spontaneously: "She's my daughter."

"I knew it!" The maitre d' said, "She looks exactly like you."

I smiled at my dad. We both knew.

After the maitre d' left Gil leaned toward me, like wanting to share a secret. "There's something you should know," he lowered his voice. "I was with your mother only once. And to tell the truth, I no longer remember when, nor where, nor how."

Once? Oh no... Once? Ohhh... Out the window flew my dream of being the fruit of passionate illicit love, of bringing back to an old man memories of the one woman he had truly loved but couldn't have... Out, too, flew the fantasy of my father looking at me and remembering with tenderness, caresses he had exchanged with my mother. Turns out it was a single forgettable encounter, probably a kneetrembler, that would hang over their heads and follow them like a nightmare for the rest of their lives. Suddenly, I began to laugh and so did he. If nowhere else, here we had to recognize ourselves in the other. We were cut from the same outrageous fabric, had the same shameless character. Someone else in this world did the same type of nutty things as I. But above all, the old man was sensuous. There was such masculine grace in the movement of his hands. His long, slender, delicate fingers ended in oval well-manicured nails. I couldn't remember ever seeing a more beautiful pair of hands on a man. Mr. Reed was funny and disarmingly charming: a man with distinct, self-centered mannerisms whose erect posture and easy movements had the touch of an aristocrat. I could certainly see women falling in love with this tidy well-cared-for man.

"After that one time," Gil murmured, "I never saw Rosa again. She didn't want to have anything to do with me. Every time I wanted to speak with her, to clear things up, she adamantly refused to see me," he whispered, shaking his head. After so many decades, he still looked lost when recalling a time when he was young and deeply conflicted.

"Why?" I wondered.

"I'll never know," he shrugged. "I suppose she must have loved Edmundo, and he'd give her hell if she talked to me."

"Why could Mutti have been so sure you were my father?"

A sly expression crossed over his lips. "That woman protected Rosa. Believe it or not, she never allowed your mother to go dancing. With me, she finally agreed." He kept a serious face but could not conceal the laughter emanating from his eyes.

"No!" I shrieked aghast.

"Yeah! Imagine," he grinned broadly, "I was the only one she trusted with her."

"How often d' you take her to the village?" I asked bemused.

"Once," he grinned.

Well... That's all it takes... Again I burst out laughing. I wiped tears from my eyes and cheeks... gasped for air and laughed until my stomach hurt; I just couldn't stop! Mutti! What was she thinking? She had delivered my young mother to the wolf, the village Lothario! And... there was no question about it: I was the man's daughter for he was laughing as out of control and shamefacedly as I.

"You were drunk, otherwise you'd remember," I finally stammered, gasping.

"Yes, I drank too much when I was young," he paused. "Gave it up long ago... But then, way too much," he shook his head, no longer amused.

"And what was your relationship with Vivian during that time?"

"I had a relationship with her, but didn't marry her until after my mother died in 1953."

Aha! I could see Mutti's mind working overtime. Gil was light in complexion and had a better future, so Mutti figured he'd be the best match for her Rosa... I could almost see how she instigated the whole thing; except it didn't work out the way she'd figured. The one single time she allowed Rosa out of her sight... That's why Mutti knew. Oh, geez, poor Rosa, she must have been sick with shame. Getting knocked up by a partying and drinking kind of guy... Who knows what she told Edmundo, but I was born looking like Gil.

I barely touched the muffin. I was too filled with emotion, admiration, and heaven knows what else to think of eating.

Gil led the way to the car. As he walked ahead of me I had a wild urge to tear his clothes off. I wanted to look at his body, wanted to see if his shape was like mine. Were his legs thin like mine? His feet narrow and delicate like his hands? His toes long and pretty? I observed how he gracefully placed his feet on the ground, how his trousers fell on his shoes. I had a very good inkling that my body looked like his, and from our behavior in the restaurant, I acted and reacted like him. There was no question, I was his daughter, and he knew I was his child.

Gil let Vivian know we were back but didn't ask her to join us. He directed me to the cream colored sofa in the living room and handed me a leather-bound photo album that had been on the coffee table. My father stood next to me, observing me as I studied the contents of the book. In it were two pictures of a young 'Old Man Reed,' dated 1887 and 1888, and taken in a studio in San Francisco, California. No wonder Mutti called him old: one of the portraits was taken the year of her birth. On the opposite page was a photograph of my grandmother, Liberia. Edward Reed, Liberia Espinoza: my grandparents. I examined the two dissimilar people: the conqueror and the conquered. Europe and Africa in America, I thought. Young Edward was even-featured and handsome in a nondescript way. His expression was cool, aloof, a little arrogant, as he looked into the camera. It was a typical pose of early photography. Liberia was already older when the picture was taken. Her face glowed in the sunlight and she looked tired as her large body relaxed into generous folds. She looked solid like a tropical Mother Earth. I sensed my father watching me as he introduced me to his parents. I looked up at him and found him gazing down at me, a deep absorbing expression in his eyes. What was it about my father's eyes? What was going through his mind when his attention was focused so absolutely on me? When I noticed his eyes burning on me, I fell deeply in love with Gil. I fell in love with his knowledge of himself and because he presented me with my heritage. Only then, when my childhood was long over, did I understand that I had missed not having grown up with him.

"Halloo... What are you talking about?" Vivian called from the kitchen.

I couldn't allow her into my magical morning and ruin it. Not making good on my promise to spend time with her, I got up and said I needed to get home. Gil walked me to my car and stood at the curb waving as I pulled away.

It was only 10:30 and I had accomplished much more than I had hoped for. I needed time to digest this spectacular morning. The drive, Brooklyn, Gil's immaculate apartment, Vivian attached to the oxygen tank saying I looked like someone I had never heard of, removing Gil from her clutches, the maitre d' confirming me as Gil's daughter, my less than memorable conception, and seeing photos of my grandparents, aunts and uncles. Above all, Gil's scorching gaze focused on me as I studied his parents. The phone rang as I stepped into my home three hours later. It was my father who wanted to make sure I had arrived well. Gil was in my life.

The next day I called him on the spur of the moment to declare my joy at having found him. Not surprised at my infatuation he responded in kind but then excused himself abruptly. Fifteen minutes later, I ran to the ringing phone. "Please don't call me again," he said hurriedly, "Vivian gets very upset when I talk to you. She's distraught that I didn't reject you. But how could I have, after seeing you?" I smiled and closed my eyes, as a warm feeling engulfed me. This is just wonderful I thought. "I'll call you from now on, on Sundays at noon. I love you," he whispered and hung up.

And so began my phase of writing tempestuous love letters. If I couldn't speak to my father, I would communicate with him in a way that would not be harmful to his wife's frail state.

> *My darling, darling Gil,*
> *I love the sound of your name, Gil, Gilberto. When I hear your voice on the phone or when I write to you, all I sense is profound adoration. I am infatuated with the love that flows between us. Papá, a word I have never said to anyone. It feels good to say it to you; to know you as my father. I want to understand so much, everything, about you. You are that part of me I ignore; and I know that through you I will come to recognize who I am.*
>
> *What fascinates you about me is seeing that in me you continue into the future, and in me, too, you find your parents and all previous generations that carried your genes.*
>
> *My son and my husband rejoice at your being in my life; and when your time and obligations free you up, we will all meet.*
>
> *I embrace you tenderly with all my love and all the love you deserve. I kiss you, papá.*
> *Your daughter who adores you,*

I don't know how he was handling things at home. He said he had become restless since meeting me; that Vivian was aware of it and knew the reason. We communicated in Spanish. English he called "the blunt language of economists and barbarians. "Spanish, on the other hand," he said, "is the language of lovers. Think of corazoncito, such a tender, loving word. But 'little heart?' that's a deformity! Makes me think of hospital, ambulance, emergency surgery. I write to you with the most tender sentiments of my corazón, my adored negrita."

Negrita, or darkie, is similar to Mutti's Mohrle. Had anyone ever dared to say negrita to me, I'd have been profoundly offended. Now, it came from Gil, from a Black man in whose eyes I was authentically beautiful because I was Black, because I was his. For the first time, negrita was a loving term. I became Gil's negrita, and could barely wait to read it in his letters, or hear the word from his lips. He wrote as often as I did: every second day.

I didn't even think to compare Gil with my German father who had been there when I was physically a child. Gil was there as I was a woman, a woman in need of being a child with her father who looked like her, was like her, wanted her and needed her as a daughter.

Uncalled for, Myrna came to mind, that high school secretary whose mere presence had tormented me. She grew up with her father, a man in whom she recognized herself. A father whose eyes lit up with love when he looked at his child and who would tell her she was beautiful. There was no need for further approval from anyone.

In one of his first letters Gil wrote:

> *Negrita Linda,*
> *I received your letter today with the photographs, and thank you ever so much.*
> *It does me good to read your words, and even though I cannot write as eloquently as you, I can read and understand what you say. I am beyond being happy that you are mine, and that for all eternity you will be. I am deeply impressed*

with you. The instant I saw you I loved you, and I cannot
seem to put you out of my mind. I wake up at night, and you
are there, occupying my lonely thoughts.

I' miss you. I can't wait to see you again. Give my love
to your family,

I adore you, negrita mía,
GEReed

⤳ ⤶

Racial Amalgam

In Jamaica, so many years ago, Dr. Dezon was all set to tell
me about shiploads of Caribs who were taken from the island of
St. Vincent by the English and dumped on the Central American
coast. At the time I was not interested in learning about Caribs;
I was studying the Vienna Congress and listening to Waltzes, the
rage of the time, because they were considered sensual. I could
have learned something about my ancestors then, had I wanted
to.

Like all people, mine created an environment that shaped
their culture. They shared a colorful history and were a racial
and cultural amalgam. I have the blood of three distinct races
running through my veins. My dark skin and kinky hair rewards
me with African ancestors, Old Man Reed had been a rather pale
European man and, as a Carib, or Garifuna, I descend from Native
Americans as well.

When I was 28, I traveled to Kenya on a photo shoot. I
studied the faces of people there, hoping to find features similar
to my own because I accepted my ancestral African genes that
had a memory of vast plains, perhaps of the mighty Kilimanjaro,
of stampeding elephants, galloping giraffe herds, of panthers,
lions, hyenas, baboons, hippopotami. Africa was exotic to me,
an exoticism I feared. Beautiful as it was, I mistrusted it. Those
impeccably white coral beaches of Mombasa and Malindi on the
Indian Ocean did not ring familiar. My African ancestors must
have originated from another part of the continent.

Some of my ancestral memory is Garifuna. They were the feisty Arawaks whom neither the Spanish, nor later the British or the French with their advanced technology, managed to subjugate. They were the only island inhabitants who survived the European encounter by retreating to the remote, mountainous Windward Island of Saint Vincent. In the sixteenth century, a slaver capsized off St. Vincent's coast. The Africans arrived with peaceful intentions and the natives on the island welcomed them. In time, word spread throughout the Caribbean that escaped slaves who reached St. Vincent could live there free. That is how the diminutive island became a haven for runaway slaves or maroons.

The Caribs were warriors, the Africans survivors. Upon seizing the island in the late seventeenth century, the British began a century-long effort to suppress and dominate the inhabitants. While the British could not subdue the fiercely independent population, they diminished their numbers to a few thousand. These they deported in 1797 to Roatan, a sandy island off Honduras. From there the survivors migrated to areas that were more hospitable. Settling on the northern fringe of Central America, they proceeded to decorate the Atlantic coast of Guatemala, Honduras, Nicaragua, and Belize with small communities of dark-skinned people.

Mine is the history of a people whose ancestors had great survival instincts and a fierce fighting nature. They had an ingrained sense for liberty and fairness, and demanded an independent, autonomous existence. They would not be subjugated. Die, at the hand of oppressors, yes; live enslaved, never! To be a descendant of Caribs, of a few people who had driven the English and French to frustration for over a century, who never relinquished their right to freedom, is a powerful legacy. My African ancestors had been tricked, imprisoned, enslaved, and still managed to escape their dismal fate by running away and living free among Caribs. My legacy is one of a people who, in the face of European technological supremacy and the blind greed that made them use it, fought to maintain their liberty, their dignity, their autonomy, and won. What a legacy! What joy to have found this unusual

father: part Carib, part maroon, half European. A man who
doesn't back down from anyone!

Gil's Daughter

Two months later, on a balmy August morning, I drove to
Brooklyn for a second time to see my father. After exchanging
enraptured love letters and lengthy conversations on the phone
on Sundays, we needed to see each other again. I had so many
questions for Gil to answer for me; I was a child trying to be with
her dad. If I could, I would have wanted to crawl onto his lap
and have him hold me while I slept. That could not happen, of
course, but it would have been what I wanted. I intended to have
breakfast with him and relive the magic of having found my dad
and having him be as wonderful as he had been in June.

Gil was waiting as I pulled into the parking lot where he'd
suggested I leave my car. It was a few blocks away from his home.
Vivian had become distrustful of his movements and he feared
she might look out the window and inadvertently see me. After
palming the parking attendant a few bucks he came over to greet
me. His lips felt soft and warm as he kissed me on the cheek.
I embraced him and slid into his car, feeling like a wayward
lover on a secret rendezvous. Gil leaned toward me and took my
hand; his manicured fingers felt hard as he squeezed it. His voice
was soft, sensuous, "Where do you want to go?" He whispered
expectantly.

"I thought we're having breakfast." What could he possibly
have in mind? And it occurred to me that though innocent on
my part, my blissful love letters might have given him wrong
expectations. "What do you have in mind, Gil?" My voice felt
small, awkward.

"Cariño, you wrote about being in love with me, about
wanting to see my body, wanting to be with me... I figured..."

Even in the cool, air conditioned car I could feel the fire in his
eyes. I began to giggle like a daft teenager. Geez, look what happens

to your brain when you get old. "There's a misunderstanding, Gil," I said, withdrawing my hand and pulling away. "Everything I wrote and said to you was not meant in a sexual or erotic context. Even though I am a grown woman, my love for you is tender and feels the way a child would love her father. I'm sorry; I'm so sorry you took it the wrong way," I whispered as I tried to arrange my thoughts around the peculiar situation. Gil had no relationship with children, so he saw me as the grown woman I was, with whom he had exchanged lovely words and who might possibly want more.

"Oh, my heavens," Gil apologized immediately, his face ashen, "the fault is entirely mine." His voice was thoroughly contrite. "I did misunderstand your sentiments; I am so, so sorry... it will never happen again."

So, things started out on a completely wrong foot, and it didn't help that the color coordination of his summer suit and shirt was beige and apricot, respectively; not colors I like in a gentleman's wardrobe. To keep the sun from burning his scalp he wore a narrow-rimmed fedora, which I also disliked. The awkward situation seemed to have resurrected my judgmental, critical eye. At breakfast Gil continued to annoy me when he treated the skinny, bottle blonde waitress who served our breakfast with unnecessary familiarity. At least the scrambled eggs and bacon were delectable. No longer shy, I was angry enough to enjoy the food. The shining prince who had swept me off my feet in June had morphed into a mere man in August.

After breakfast we drove to a park by the Verrazzano Bridge and sat on a spacious bench overlooking the silver shimmering Hudson. To our right towered the majestic bridge while leafy shrubs shielded us from the view of a manicured suburban neighborhood. Sitting in nature, just the two of us, relaxed our moods and we began a pleasant conversation that would stay so for the rest of my visit.

"I've been wondering," Gil began, after taking a long restful look at me, "how it was growing up with those people." He still made a point of not using the names of my German family. It was a very complex question and the first time anyone had asked it of me. Not knowing where to begin, I stated the obvious, saying that they loved me, etc. "I never doubted that," Gil murmured, "but how was your experience in school, for instance?"

He found it humorous that I had attended the Jewish-run elementary school and laughed when I told him one kid insisted on calling me 'Hitler.' "I saw me as being German, so I figured it came with the territory. Hitler must still be rotating in his grave," I chuckled. Then I told him that I had been rejected at one school. "What would your family have done had that happened to one of your siblings?"

"Listen, negrita, no day went by that one of us didn't have to deal with a similar insult. We talked about such incidents openly, and after a while, because it was so commonplace we let it go." He put his hand on mine in a comforting way. "It's what we deal with: ignorant people, and there are too many of them around. Know what I mean?"

Had I been in touch with my people's environment I would have known about overt and cryptic racism and rejection. I'd have faced prejudice openly just like all my ancestors who had to deal with White people faced racism, rejection, and oppression. It would have been expected... pedestrian.

"I felt it was my fault that Mutti had been insulted. I was too ashamed to talk about it to anyone in the house." I shook my head feeling sorry, decades later, for the lonely little five year-old and her sense of guilt.

"I suspected such isolation," Gil said softly, "you having no way of dealing with even the simplest rejection. I sometimes wondered how your little heart was beating, all by its lonely self, in the alien European world," he said, shaking his head. "Let's walk a bit, I get stiff when I sit too long."

We ambled out of the park; it was a lovely neighborhood. "I don't think there are too many Blacks living here. We might get chased out any minute!" I exclaimed, feeling honestly apprehensive. The Bensonhurst situation had happened not long ago.

"I have always gone wherever I've darned wanted. No one would consider making me feel unwelcome. Por favor!" Gil said, very much his arrogant self.

"That's what I love about you, Gil, you are sovereign," I smiled at him admiringly. "How did you get like that? You didn't grow up White, while I can sometimes get unsure of myself. Particularly when I'm among a lot of Black people."

"Really?" Gil turned to face me, a surprised expression on his face. "How on earth is that possible after the life you've lived? You'd have to be darn stupid to ever feel second to anyone. You are good-looking, competent, polished, and smart. I'm so proud of you, negrita linda." Hearing these words from my father, I recognized that I had needed someone I could have trusted, someone who looked like me.

We filled the few hours with stories of our histories. It felt unbearable at times to have been deprived of my father's humor, wit, and wisdom. He talked of periods of solitude and alienation, and his misery at his mother's deathbed in 1953 as he promised to make good on a pledge he had given Vivian when he took her virginity. The gravity in his voice underlined the spaces devoid of affection for someone he had fancied in his careless, carefree youth. I was 13 when he married and brought Vivian to the States. He had always been a responsible considerate husband, even after he befriended a nurse twenty-seven years ago. It was a secret not even Vivian knew.

I wasn't ready to talk about his conquests and loves. I wanted to trigger his memory toward Rosa, but it didn't work. Try as he did, he couldn't fill any gaps regarding my mother. While Gil made a point of distancing himself from "those people," Vivian, through friends, kept abreast of the movements of the Livingston Diaspora. "As a matter of fact," Gil said spontaneously, "Rosa's oldest daughter lives in Brooklyn."

What? I knew Judith. She came to see me in Guatemala when Mutti was sick. I beseeched Gil to get me her phone number. His eyes darkened as he frowned, displeased at having revealed too much information. Now he'd have to ask Vivian and she would know he was in touch with me. "I'll try but can't promise anything. People move around a lot in that community, and their numbers change," his tone was subdued, unsure. I reassured him I could wait to receive the needed information.

My grandmother, Liberia Espinoza, moved into Edward Reed's house in his old age. She brought Gil, the youngest of their five children with her; he was the only one to have lived under his father's roof. My grandfather was ahead of his time, for he legalized his racially mixed children. They all obtained American papers and attended schools in the States. Gil received a degree in engineering from Tuskegee Institute and worked for decades as an electrical engineer for Consolidated Edison Company in Manhattan. While he experienced institutional racism and discrimination in the States, he was most bitter about the personal racism that is prevalent in Latin American societies.

As a youth, while working in an office in Barrios, a larger port on the Atlantic, a clerk once came to him saying a barefoot Black woman claiming to be his mother was asking to come into the building. The clerk refused her entrance. He informed Gil of the situation. Given Gil's light brown complexion and wavy hair, the clerk, who was not from Livingston and ignored the family dynamics, disbelieved the dark woman's claim. Gil yelled at the "ignorant Indian" and, after a barrage of swears and insults, demanded he escort his mother to his office.

Not that there was a similarity with what I did, but I shared how I had told Patrick not too long ago, that if it would ever suit his purposes, he should not reveal that he had a Black mother. My father's reaction was such that I feared he'd have a stroke. "How can you ask your child to deny who he is?" He raised his voice at me; the fiery look in his eyes was frightening. "How insensitive are you?" I'll never forget his appalled reaction.

"I felt that in this racist world, Patrick could take advantage of passing for White," I tried to clarify. "Why load the burden on of being Black if you don't have to," I mumbled my excuse.

Patrick had reacted the same way. He was deeply hurt and shocked that I would expect him to deny me. "Don't ever say anything like that to me, ever again!" My son issued a stern warning. "I find it offensive, insensitive! I will never say I'm White. You are my mother and I love you! I am your only son, Mom. How can you say that to your child, to someone who loves you?" And he hugged me so tightly I feared he might crack my ribs. My child, and now my father, made me understand the tragedy of disavowing one's mother. Yet, I had been conditioned to do away with mine. I denied Rosa... and I could never have passed for White.

Among her people, the corpulent woman I saw in the photographs had been a generous village matriarch, a natural queen with impressive organizing skills who left nothing to chance. Not even death: her coffin and the clothes she would be laid out in were ready and waiting for her in the attic, years before she died. "I've never heard of anything like that," I said bemused and impressed at the foresight.

The morning that had started so awkwardly could not have concluded better. I learned about my father's people, his village, about a grandfather who color-coordinated all his files and a grandmother who was a respected village matriarch. I learned about a protective son and similarities Patrick shared with my father and grandfather. I had news for Fred who always said I was so German, so clear, orderly, and reliable. It was not the German in me, at all; it was my Carib grandmother who had formed my father's most telling characteristics and he in turn, without my ever having lived with him, passed some on to me.

Gil's Visit in Albany, NY

In January 1993 Vivian was relieved of her long suffering, and Gil could again travel at leisure. Six weeks after the funeral, in early March, he came upstate to spend his eighty-second birthday with us. Patrick was in his freshman year at Oberlin College and missed meeting his grandfather. Fred was his usual charming, handsome self, except he was so nervous he might have been on an audition for a coveted part in a movie. He wanted to be the ideal son-in-law, and although that was his part with my German family, this was different: he would meet my father.

Gil arrived with Grace, his woman friend of twenty-seven

years, and stayed in the best hotel in town. The first evening
they came to dinner in our home. I prepared one of my staple
tried and true meals, chicken in white wine sauce, dill rice,
gingered zucchini, and crème caramel for dessert. It was light
food, appropriate for the type of eater I had observed during our
breakfasts in Brooklyn.

My father complimented us on having a charming, warm
home. Grace liked the paintings, particularly the large one of
Indians on the steps of the church in Chichicastenango. We
settled in the living room to chat; Fred offered aperitifs, and Gil
asked him a few questions about our life and how he had managed
to end up with a monster of a wife.

I went to the kitchen for final preparations and left everyone
laughing, enjoying each other's company. The mood apparently
shifted for I heard Gil shouting nasty things about Rudolf. I
quickly returned to the living room to see Gil having a disdainful
look on his face. He acknowledged my presence with a passing
glance and was set to continue the tirade, "Anyone with his
peculiar behavior..."

"Don't you dare, Gil," I interjected. "He was no Nazi. Ruth
would never have had anything to do with him... How would you
know what Nazis were like anyway?"

"Then, I might not have known," he grimaced unfazed, "but
I've lived since! Now I can smell them."

"You've seen too many Hollywood movies!" I glanced at
Grace and Fred and laughed uncomfortably in an effort to make
light of an offensive situation. This guy was nuts! Where was the
charm? What was going on with him?

I looked at Fred who opened his mouth to speak. "Don't! Just
keep it to yourself!" I snapped at him. Turning to Gil I whispered,
enraged: "Just dare to say Pablo was a Nazi, too!"

He laughed a short wicked laugh. "No. That old guy was not
a Nazi. He was a bastard though," he added in a derisive tone.
Things were certainly not going the way I had anticipated, and
the evening just continued to deteriorate as Gil persisted in
telling stories that ridiculed every member of my German family. I
was struck dumb and speechless at what I was hearing. The man's

mouth was unstoppable.

Grace and Fred complimented me on the meal. But my father, heaven knows what devil rode him, was either deeply upset or not liking the food, left most of it untouched. From our breakfasts I knew he ate little, but leaving the food to be thrown away was insulting and hurt my feelings. After he finished playing with what was on his plate, he resumed telling jokes that would ordinarily not be shared in the company of women. Fred looked at me from time to time and eventually burst out laughing, not at the jokes but at the embarrassing situation. He could just not keep a straight face. THIS was the man of his wife's dreams?

For the life of me, I'll never know what got into Gil. What liberated him? Was it the context of our home? Did he feel safe with Fred - safe enough to reveal such fury? Was I being too critical? I'd been so in love with my father! What had happened? How was this man seeing me? Was he seeing me at all? Did he care for me as a daughter, or was I only a woman who liked him. I could not have been more disappointed, more heartbroken.

It was a restless, fitful night. My heart was shattered to pieces. I tossed and turned and tossed again, as my unforgiving critical nature kicked in. When I finally fell asleep - did I sleep? – I don't know, but I sensed Rosa's eyes on me. I could feel her at my bed caressing me with her serious gaze, slowly relaxing me. She was so real, so clear. I wanted to touch her but didn't for fear the ghost might vanish.

> *"How could you have liked that man?" I breathed.*
> *"I didn't, hija mia. I didn't."*
> *"What happened then? What happened that you were with him?"*
> *"He forced himself upon me."*

I sat up slowly. Tried to focus, to look at her, but she had vanished.

Had I slept? Was it a dream? "He forced himself upon me." I heard it. She said it. The information rang true by the way the feeling resounded within me. Date rape? Date rape! Fifty, twenty

years ago it was not a term. Then it was the girl's responsibility to
avoid a stupid situation where a man could take her against her
will. Mutti gave me a car at nineteen so I'd not have to rely on a
ride home with someone who'd had too much to drink and might
make me do things against my will. If Gil had forced himself on my
mother, Mutti knew it. She was the one who let Rosa go out with
him. Gil said himself that he couldn't remember when, or where,
or how; that he always drank too much when he was young. He
said he had been the only one Mutti allowed Rosa to go out with.
And that Rosa, after that one time, flatly refused to honor his
attempts to contact her. That bastard! He'd been entrusted with
my mother and he abused the privilege. No wonder Mutti treated
him like a snot-nosed brat. Mutti knew, Ruth knew, Agatha knew
what he had done. You son of a bitch, I thought. Just you wait,
you damn jackass, son of a bitch!

The following day was Gil's birthday. I was sore about the
previous evening and wanted to cancel having dinner with them.
"We're both disappointed about last night, but they made the
effort to be with you today," Fred said quietly. "The least we can do
is have dinner with them." I didn't tell Fred about my realization
during the night, and reluctantly agreed to honor the invitation.

Gilbert E. Reed had reserved the best table in the most
private and elegant restaurant in the hotel, where formal dress
was expected. The ambience was intimate, expensive. In the
far corner, a red haired woman in purple played tunes on a baby
grand. People stopped their conversations as we entered the small
dining room. Three Black people and a White one, all dressed to
perfection, who moved with the blasé airs of eastern potentates...
We attracted attention in upstate New York in the early 1990's.
Most eyes were on Fred, which amused me, as it was the first
time in our many years together that he found himself being the
minority.

But I was not my charming self. In fact, I had trouble being
halfway civil.

Fred and Gil fancied jumbo shrimp. Grace ordered green
pepper steak. I chose venison chasseur with wild mushrooms and
spaetzles. If it wasn't the most expensive choice on the menu,

it was close to it. Then I asked for the wine card and ordered a bottle of fine French red wine. "A bottle is too much for me; why don't we share it?" I said to Grace and she happily agreed.

When my order came, I picked at it. "Such a shame, that they don't know how to cook the food they offer," I said with disdain. Instantly the waiter was at my side asking if everything was to my satisfaction. "The mushrooms are burned, venison should be well done, the spaetzles are mealy and the condiment expected with this meal is cranberry sauce." The waiter apologized profusely and offered to serve me a different dish. "No, thank you," I responded, in the most nonchalant manner. "I'll just have some butter on the roll, and wine."

Fred couldn't believe it. He'd seen me in action before, but it all paled compared to this. Gil ate his shrimp, proving to me that he did eat dinner. The men talked while I conversed with Grace who was genuinely pleasant. I liked her.

"Tell me," I said to Gil in a loud stage whisper, making sure to crank up the tension, "was it your grandparents or great grandparents who were slaves?"

Gil turned to stone. "We were never slaves. There was no slavery in Latin America," he whispered, a grave expression in his eyes.

"Don't be ridiculous!" I continued in a resounding tone and, pretending not to know better, added, "Then how come there are such distinctive African features in Latin American Blacks?"

"Ouch! My arm!" Fred cried, grabbing his right arm, trying to divert attention. He grimaced as if in pain, "Enough now!" He whispered to me, "For heaven's sake, stop it." Everyone's eyes were on us while Gil crumpled into his suit. Grace gave me an affirmative nod: of course, there had been slaves.

I petulantly took one or two sips of my wine, leaving my glass practically untouched and the bottle half full. For dessert I ordered poire Helene and a double crème de menthe on ice. Again, I only nibbled and sipped. The dinner cost Gil several hundred dollars, which he paid in cash. That's for the dinner you should have bought my mother, you bastard, I thought.

I was heartbroken and glad to see Gil leave. I had news: my

fascination for him was over.

He called the next three Sundays. The conversations were brief: of course, he noticed the difference in my responses. "Me quieres?" (Do you love me?) He asked, and I changed the subject. I had done what I was great at doing: I had dumped him. Totally.

UPSET AT THE SITUATION WITH MY FATHER, I wondered why I cut him off so completely, so unforgivingly. Why was I so repulsed, so angry? I had only met him three times and each time I gained a different insight. At our first meeting I felt like a little girl, loving and trusting him unconditionally. Everything about him was admirable, perfect. The second time we met, when he had misunderstood my sentiments and was hoping for a romantic rendezvous, I didn't like the color of his clothes although I had to admit he was impeccably set out. That time I saw and related to him as a man rather than a father. That could have been a pre-adolescent stage, when a child is more critical and tends to question the parents' judgment and motives. And in Albany? I rebelled like a seasoned teenager. No forgiveness; Gil got a dose of real adolescent rejection.

A FEW DAYS LATER, as Fred and I were finishing our breakfast and discussing my emotional plight with Gil, Fred said, "You'll need to see if you want to leave the situation as it is now. Give yourself time to grow up, as it were. Then you'll contact him and begin a relationship of acceptance and respect. Like the one you have with Patrick."

"I don't know; can't think that far ahead. You make it sound so easy. But you're right, when it comes to the relationship with our son. What's special there is that he is the adult. Patrick is an old soul, for sure," I managed to crack a smile.

"Don't sell yourself cheaply on your relationship with the kid," Fred followed up calmly. "Once you recognized your inclination to control, you stepped back and allowed him his space. He may only be nineteen, but you already have an adult relationship with him. It's remarkable what you have accomplished with him." With that Fred came over, pulled me up from the chair, took me in his arms and hugged me tightly and kissed me on the cheek.

"OK," I said, pulling away from him and grinning, "provided Gil lives long enough, we might end up developing a relationship. Eventually. I still have something I want to run by you." I sat down and pointed Fred to sit. "Mutti told me she would not have kept me had I been a boy," I didn't care. I was a little girl and I was hers.

"Why was that? Why would she have put such a thing in your head? She must have adhered to some negative stereotypes," Fred's voice was low, husky. "I was in the Marines and hated how the White Southerners made a point of segregating Blacks. Blacks, like Whites, are not a monolithic group. Have you ever thought about how your Mutti reacted when she was scared?"

"Why?"

"I think that like most people, she generalized. Remember the tiff you had about that secretary at the high school, Myrna? It was all Blacks, before you acknowledged that it was only that woman that upset you. Now there's something wrong with all Black men. It's only Gil who has hurt you, not all Black men." Sometimes the simplicity and clarity in my husband's insights floor me completely.

I tried to find a time when I might have seen Mutti deal with a fearful situation but could not discover such a moment. It's plausible that she feared Rosa might win my love and loyalty. Could Vivian have been right when she acidly said Mutti had threatened people from Livingston who came to see us? Did I learn to fear Black people because I'd been taught to fear Rosa? I thought I was scared of Blacks because I grew up without seeing any.

"Do you think it's possible you were taught to associate the stereotype the White world placed on Blacks?" Fred offered a tentative question. "Remember how in California, when you felt threatened or intimidated by a Black individual, your reaction was: 'Watch out! They're bad news'."

"Its a logical sequence, because I don't relate to other ethnicities as monolithic groups," I said, as I tried to clarify my jumbled thoughts. "You know I try to be fair and give everyone the benefit of the doubt."

The longer I though about it, the clearer it became: when Rosa came to see me, and I was left alone with her, I was uncomfortable and anxious. I wonder now, did Mutti and Ruth also feel that way because they had me, when I belonged to her? I think so. Could that mean that my fear of Blacks became a condition I learned by observation? I wonder...

Birthfather G.E. (Gil) Reed,
Guatemala, 1945

Gil with Catana in Brooklyn, 1994

PART SIX

My Mother's Family
1994

Rosa's Children

How do I find Judith? She came to see me while I was visiting
Mutti many years ago. Did she marry the athlete she was in love
with then? Was she really in Brooklyn as Gil presumed? The
phone numbers he provided after Vivian's death did not pan out;
as he said, "those people move around."

It occurred to me that although unlikely, Ruth might know
something about her. That also meant engaging her in my search.
What reactions - my own and Ruth's - should I prepare for? How
would I begin to formulate questions about my Black relatives
when they had figured only as concepts, not individuals? And how
would Ruth react? Would she be hurt that after a lifetime of being
her family, I would now, so late in life, ask about my people?

"Just a second, I have Judith's information right here in my
phone book," Ruth said when I called her. "I don't have her
number, but here's her name," and she proceeded to spell out
Judith's married name. I was pleased at the ease of Ruth's response.
I called the Guatemalan information system, was given a few
numbers, but none worked. Reluctantly, I realized I'd have to go
to Guatemala if I wanted to find relatives on my mother's side.

Fifteen years had passed since I swore never to set foot in
Catalina, at least never to sleep there again. Now I planned a trip
for early June 1993, so Patrick could join me during his summer
vacation. My son made me understand in the most natural way,
that my past was also his and mattered to him, too. Fred had to
work in New York, so we left with his blessings.

On the balcony of the airport in Guatemala, waving excitedly and calling out to us was Ruth, her sons Thomas and Andreas, their wives and five children aged 3 to 11. In a caravan of four cars, we arrived at the home of my childhood.

Hidden from view by a tall white wall and even taller pine trees, Catalina stood as always, solid as the Rock of Gibraltar. The house had survived in elegant style many earthquakes and revolutions and gave me a sense of eternity, for my earliest memories of a home go back to that simple, single story house. The birdbath was still in the center of the lawn; the flat stones in the grass still marked the path to the entrance, and the drive to the garage was bordered with blooming Asian lilies, as always... I planted the two pines from seedlings when I was six. Now they towered majestically over the garden, their lower branches heavy with baskets of flowering orchids. The heavy bamboo verandah chairs were still there, unchanged after forty-five years. Before the carved mahogany door with polished brass knocker and doorknob, were the same old retractable iron bars that allowed the entrance to remain open while obstructing passage to the house.

At 84, Ruth lived alone as the enduring family matriarch. In spite of our previous differences, I looked forward to seeing her again for I was always touched by her intrinsic gentility.

Patrick slept in what had been Vati's room, now a sparsely furnished, light and cheerful space where Ruth kept her collection of succulents and African violets. A host with a different spirit resided there now; not the one I remember of Vati's day when, in my child's eye, it appeared somber and slightly foreboding.

I stayed in my old room at the end of the corridor. The bedspreads and curtains were purple with yellow stripes, not cream as in my time. A scented breeze blew through the open window bringing back long forgotten memories of falling asleep with the scent of roses. I felt comfortable being back in the home I left exactly forty years ago, returning occasionally, and always grudgingly.

Thomas and Andreas lived in houses in Ruth's gated community, immediately behind Catalina. The three homes formed a close family cluster with well-defined boundaries.

My primary objective was contacting my Black relatives, but the urge had faded once I was with Ruth. The first week and a half I showed Patrick my childhood haunts in the once quiet residential neighborhood. Now it was an upscale urban district filled with boutiques, restaurants, and banks. We drove to the lakes, Chichicastenango, and Antigua. Patrick got to know the younger generation, which delighted in correcting his German. Four months with those kids, he claimed, and he'd be fluent in German and Spanish again. In the evenings, when Ruth returned from her day at the art gallery and before dinner, we sat in her salita (private living room) sipping red South American wine and talking. The walls were still graced with the same old paintings of foggy, lantern-lit streets and shadowy figures trapped in landscapes where gray covered the ground for months. I knew the works well, and studying them again brought back the nostalgia that had seduced my imagination and drawn it to fantasy.

Like a pale violet in the shade of weighty trees, Ruth did not come into her own until late in life, and then did so with tremendous grace. Vati, Rudolf, Mutti, had to leave this earth before she could blossom at all. After her husband died, she reluctantly accepted a partnership in a gallery and became successful at something she had never dreamed of doing. Her work has sustained her mentally and emotionally. "Without the gallery," she said, "I'd have died long ago, or I'd be sitting in a chair in the sun where someone forgot about me."

As we sat in the salita reminiscing, I told Ruth how Mutti's astrological chart had all planets on the partner's side. Ruth reached for her wine, took a sip, and after enjoying its taste, asked me what that meant.

"That she pretty much depended on others to do her work," I looked at Ruth from the corner of my eyes.

"Well, that she did." Ruth took a cigarette and held it to her lighter. "That's why she got along so well with people. She never knew if she might need them, so she never alienated anyone," and she blew the smoke out the side of her mouth.

"To have been that way, she must've been manipulative," I ventured.

"You're realizing that NOW?" Ruth laughed heartily.

"Only 'cause I dared to look at her critically," I added defensively. "I'm trying to find out why people can manipulate me."

"Really? You of all people, being manipulated?" Her eyes were steady on me as she took the cigarette to her lips and inhaled again.

"Oh, sure. My mother-in-law, for instance."

"How so?" Ruth raised an eyebrow.

"Her children say she's a master manipulator. At first I didn't get it. Through therapy, however, I saw she had me dancing on a string."

"And all this time I thought you had a good relationship with her..."

"I do, but now I know how to keep her at bay. Therapy's been great. Believe me."

"It's interesting," Ruth said pensively, drawing on her cigarette and exhaling again, "that we were both unable to see how mother controlled us... To make her chart, didn't you need her time of birth?"

I told her how I got it from the Records office in Landau, and how she was found as Emma, not Esther. "Emma!" Ruth laughed joyfully. "That's true. Emma! Right! How absolutely typical! That name was simply not sophisticated enough for her." Ruth's eyes danced with mirth.

"You didn't know that?" I said surprised at her reaction.

"It's just that it's been so long since I've heard Emma in relation to her." Ruth became serious as she sucked on her cigarette. It upset her, she said, to think how Mutti had controlled her deep into her old age. "You at least..." she shrugged, "you, she allowed to do whatever you darned well pleased."

"She didn't approve of my becoming an actress."

"Of course she did," Ruth exclaimed. "It made her look good. Mother wanted to attract attention: to be different. She liked to set herself apart from regular people."

Was that why Mutti kept me? To have a child that was different than the rest, to have a conversation piece? But I had to agree: Mutti glowed with pride when I was little; and later, during my interviews with magazines in Germany, when she received much attention as my mother. I felt she was prouder of me than parents were of their genetic children.

"I guess this is what sisters do. They gossip about their parents," I chuckled, changing direction.

"Indeed, in moments like these, you feel like a sister to me," Ruth smiled.

"Except, of course, that I know nothing about your childhood, other than that Vati wasn't your father. Mutti said your dad was a kind man, and I think I met him in 1960, but I'm not sure."

Ruth's expression darkened as she told me how she found out that Mutti had taken off with Vati. In all her fabulous stories, Mutti never mentioned anything about abandoning her child. "When did you see her again," I dared to ask.

"Mother came back after three years. All that time I was bounced around from one disinterested relative to another. In the process they baptized me and I attended seven different schools."

"Three years? Baptized so late? Seven schools? This is terrible," I murmured, hurting for Ruth. I couldn't believe she was treated so badly. "How did you feel when she came back?"

"I didn't care." Ruth gestured with her hand as if shooing a fly away. "It didn't matter to me whether she was there or not. She must have felt bad at having left me, I guess. I was thirteen when I came to Livingston."

"And in spite of that awful treatment, you never rebelled against her and always complied with her wishes." Ruth only shrugged while my mind began to spin. "What did you think about Mutti keeping me?"

"Dead set against it," she answered honestly. "Imagine, those two were over fifty, we had been expropriated and were in danger of being deported... and here Mother decides to keep a baby."

"What if something had happened to them? Had she prepared for that?"

"Of course not." Ruth's tone was edgy, angry. Then her expression softened. "Once I realized, however, that nothing would change Mother's mind, I committed fully to raising you.

I never again challenged her decision. We'd have to make it, I figured. And we did." As she said those words, she embraced me with one of her disarmingly gentle looks.

"Thank you," I said, moved and humbled by her generous acceptance of me.

⤺

We spent the first weekend with Thomas's family in Punta de Palma, a small resort on the Atlantic not thirty minutes by boat from Livingston. Saturday Thomas rented a motorboat for the day and with packed lunches we set out to amble along the coast. At one point my nephew suggested going around the promontory into the mouth of the Rio Dulce.

"Would you like to go Livingston?" he asked me.

"Hmmm. I don't know," I said, meaning 'no', but Thomas nevertheless instructed the boatman to cut across the estuary. We approached the sleepy hamlet over choppy river waters. Thomas pointed to a house and explained that it had been Rudolf's. The Casa Grande was no longer, he said, pointing to a higher elevation where it had once stood. He turned to me, and shouting over the motor's roar, asked again if I wanted to go on land. "Naw," I said slowly and looked at Patrick, who eyed me impassively. He knew it was my call, and if I couldn't muster up the courage, I wasn't ready.

"O.K., then," Thomas shouted over the drone of the motor, "let's head up river to the Golfete; maybe on the way back..."

The boat turned left and we moved up the Rio Dulce. Dense tropical vegetation grew into the water. Here and there was a lodging made of woven palm leaves. Through the open entrances we could see hammocks hanging inside. It was idyllic, peaceful. Nothing in this area's changed in a thousand years, I thought. Farther up river, Thomas had the motors stopped. "Listen, hush," he said holding a finger to his lips, "listen to the sounds of the jungle." When our hearing adjusted to the quiet, we heard a hum that became a murmur. Then a chirp became audible here, a screech there, a call, a flutter, a splash; the cracking of a tree's limb led to orchestral sounds of teeming life concealed under the dense green canopy of the wilderness. It was delicious, the heat, the breeze, the colors and sounds. Farther on we stopped at a hot spring on the shore of the river and jumped into the water to enjoy a natural spa. I became conscious of sitting in a hot spring near the place of my nativity. Had my parents also bathed there? I wondered.

It had been enough to sail on the river and see the village from afar. I was not ready, emotionally or spiritually to set foot there. I had a glimpse of Livingston, seeing it as I saw myself: still very much in the distance.

Jennifer, Willie, Marta

I was back in the world of my experience with an ambivalent willingness to revise it. Surrounded by the objects of my childhood and being with Ruth returned me to the womb of my Germanic security. The two weeks of my stay were coming to an end. It was already Wednesday; we were leaving on Saturday and I had not even tried to place the all-important phone call I had traveled so far to realize. On the way to my siesta, I saw the phone book lying on the table in the hall and briefly wondered if I really wanted to follow through with my objective and contact my relatives. Did I truly want to find them? Why hadn't I opened the thing before? I felt its draw, felt it daring me to walk by without opening it. If I looked and still didn't find Judith's name, I could at least say I tried. So, I sat down on the stool by the phone, placed the book on my lap, opened it and leafed to the letter S. To my surprise, there were seven names, one of which belonged to the name Ruth had given me as Judith's husband. I dialed the number and soon heard a young woman's voice:

"Si, dígame?"

"Hello, I'd like to speak with Judith," I said in Spanish. "I'm her older sister, Catana."

"She's not here," the woman said, "but you can talk to her

daughter Jennifer. Just a moment," and she left me hanging.

There was no time to fret as right away an angelic voice on the other end of the line said: "Hello?"

"Hi, Jennifer," my voice quivered. "You don't know me, but I'm your mother's sister, Catana. I'm in Guatemala and am trying to contact Judith."

"Oh, I'm so sorry, but she isn't here, she's in New York. I know who you are," she chirped excitedly, "my mother told us about you. You're here now?" She seemed thrilled, while I was thoroughly surprised she knew about me.

"I'm here only a few more days. Where in New York is your mother?"

"Brooklyn. My mother and my aunt Adela have been in the States for several years, now," Jennifer offered happily. I asked her for the address and phone numbers, and after dictating the information, the girl added, "Where are you staying?"

"Here at Catalina, on the Reforma," I said, knowing full well she wouldn't know where it was, and frankly, not caring if she knew or not.

"I'd so much like to meet you; I've heard so much about you. When may I see you?"

Cripes, this Jennifer was direct. She was attending a nutrition school, she said, and tomorrow after classes she would visit. I'd made a simple call, and in so doing plainly overwhelmed myself. I looked for Patrick to tell him I finally made contact... and now his cousin Jennifer was on the way to see us!

"Can't wait," was my son's reaction, as his face lit up with the brightest smile. "Wonder what she looks like, Mom! A real relative of ours! Imagine that," and his embrace crushed the air out of my lungs.

It struck me in an odd way, that I had come to find my sister, but would instead see her daughter. Honestly, I didn't care to meet this Jennifer even though her sincere joy in talking to me was disarming on a certain level. But why would she want to see me? What's more, what had she been told about me?

"She's only a little niece," Patrick said, sensing my alarm. "It's not the whole family crowding in on you. A little girl is hardly an invasion," he added embracing me again. "She said she knows about you," he grinned, stepping back and looking at me, "which means that while you may not consider her family, she has always included you. Mom! This is exciting. You came for this, remember?" But his joy was not contagious, and it was clear that I was suffering under a solid dose of anxiety. In the morning I told Nola, Ruth's maid, that I was expecting my niece.

We had barely finished breakfast when the bell rang. Can't be her, I thought, it's only nine-thirty. I looked out the living room window and saw Nola walk toward the gate and open it. A small dark girl entered. She wore a white blouse and dark blue pants, and smiled as she approached the house. Patrick stood next to me, his hand resting on my shoulder. "Smile, Mom. You look great when you smile," my son said, tightening his grip and flashing a bright beam at me. What a beautiful face my son has, I thought, ever so grateful he was with me. We walked toward the door and waited for Nola to retract the iron accordion bars. My niece stepped in, and I took her in my arms. It was the most natural reaction.

Jennifer barely reached my chin. Where does this tiny being come from I thought. Her body was warm and smelled like flowers. She gave me a joyful, somewhat bashful look.

"Good to see you, Jennifer," I said, smiling broadly. "This is my son, Patrick."

"Hola, prima," (Hi cousin) Patrick said, giving her a hearty hug.

"Tía," (Aunt) Jennifer turned to me, "I didn't know I had a cousin." Then, with a flirty smile for Patrick, she asked him, "Have you been to Guatemala before?"

"Once, when I was four," Patrick answered, all smiles. "But now, you two get to know each other. I'll be back in a bit," and he went to the garden to play with Ruth's Airedale.

My niece accepted a glass of lemonade, and we settled down in the living room.

Two thick braids framed Jennifer's fine-featured face. Looks good, I thought, as I realized she was aware of my observing her.

"I don't remember my grandmother Rosa, but they tell me I look exactly like her," the young girl said, looking at me intently as I studied her features.

"So... aha," I mumbled. So that's what she looked like. I no longer remembered my mother's face. If I had ever looked at Rosa, really looked at her, the way Jennifer's eyes were on me now, her image would probably have remained with me for all eternity. But I hadn't cared to imprint in my mind the face of my mother. The few times when I might have tried to recall her, some ten years ago perhaps, she had long been erased from my memory. Sometimes, on seeing a round-faced dark woman, I wondered if Rosa looked like her. But I didn't know, of course.

Even though Jennifer seldom looked directly at me, I knew she scrutinized me carefully; our meeting would be reported in detail, as many times as necessary. I learned about her studies, the trips to Brooklyn to see her parents, their work in the States. She was twenty-two and had two younger brothers. Archie was nineteen and had just begun studying medicine at the university in Guatemala, while Anthony at thirteen was still in school in Belize. "I brought pictures of the family to show you," my little niece offered, as she took photographs from her purse. "My parents," she said, handing me a picture of Judith and her husband. Both looked radiant. "This is my aunt Adela, and her son Benji and her daughter Heidi. These are my brothers, Archie and Anthony. That's all of us," she giggled.

Patrick peeked in and quickly sat next to me to look at our family. "These are great pics," he exclaimed admiringly. "How clever of you to have brought them!"

"I don't have anything on my uncle Willie; tried to call him last night to tell him you're here, but he must've worked late, and I had to get up early today..." she shrugged apologetically.

Yes, of course, there was my brother Willie. I had never seen him. "Tell me, Jennifer, where do you live?" I asked.

"On the way to Antigua."

"That far? How did you find this house?"

"My mother brought me once," the child said simply. "She brought me here and said that this was the house where you grew up." Looking at me out of the corner of her eyes, she added with a serious expression, "We didn't come in. We stayed outside of the gate."

"Your mother brought you? Judith did?" I asked wide-eyed, puzzled.

Jennifer nodded. "When you said you were in Catalina, I knew where I had to go."

I just stopped thinking and sat there feeling deflated. Patrick and Jennifer picked up the conversation as if they'd been friends all their lives. On leaving, I thanked the tiny girl for the pictures, for having come. I held her in my arms and took a good, long look at my mother's face.

Patrick and I accompanied Jennifer to the bus stop. On the way she commented that I walked like Judith, and that I was a lot like her mother.

I could only smile at the thought that this little niece who looked like my mother had been comparing my every move to my sister.

It was an emotionally exhausting morning, and I soon developed a headache. It overwhelmed me to realize that the Universe had seen fit to show me my mother's image first and by itself, before seeing other family members. And then, that the child knew where Catalina was because Judith had made sure the next generation knew one of their own had been separated from them. I didn't want to think anymore.

By dinner, all I learned was stored. I was tired early, however, and about to excuse myself, when Nola came in with the phone. "Señora, the call is for you," she said in Spanish. "The gentleman says he's your brother Willie." I left the room with the phone.

"Sí..." I said.

"Jennifer just told me she saw you today," I heard my brother's pleasant, silky voice. "I'd love to meet you. Would it be possible?"

"Sure," I said, surprised at being happy to hear him. "When?"

"It'll take me fifteen minutes to get there," he said and I could hear the thrill in his voice. I had meant tomorrow. The evening was young in Guatemala, and who knew how I'd feel tomorrow?

"Okay, Willie, right away is fine."

He came with Archie, Judith's oldest son, who was staying with him. Archie and Patrick liked each other instantly. Willie and I looked at each other and smiled and smiled and smiled. I couldn't help but smile at such a darling face. He was fifteen years younger than I, and we looked alike.

"I never thought I'd get to know you," Willie said, "never expected to ever see you." He was serious, his voice gentle as he looked intently at me. "I had hoped against hope that I'd get a glimpse of you before I died." He plain couldn't get over me sitting next to him.

I knew I loved him, and I didn't know why. Not knowing him at all, I already loved him. Is it familial similarity that creates love within families?

Ruth came in briefly to greet and soon left. It was good that way.

What I remember best of that evening, is Willie not taking his eyes off me, and repeating over and over that he couldn't believe we had finally met.

And then, Willie remembered the inside of Catalina. "You've been here before?" I asked, intrigued.

"Sure, I played with two tall boys. They built a landscape with electric trains. It took them a long time to put it together. I think it was there for three years." No one had ever mentioned to me that they knew Willie, when he had actually visited several times with my mother.

"You mean Ruth's sons?"

"I don't know whose sons they were, but they lived here." Pointing, he said: "Over there's where the landscape was set up."

I wondered if Thomas and Andreas remembered my brother. Other than Willie, there would have been no other Black boy they could have played with. I lay awake trying to figure out who could confirm what I heard from Willie. Ruth conveniently pulled blanks. Marta! The maid who had been with us as long as I could remember... she would know.

Marta began to work for us when I was five and she was only fifteen, and through the years she, too, had bathed me, combed my hair and made sure I took the hated daily dose of cod liver oil with lemon and salt. She was the one who pulled me off the roof as I was delivering Shakespeare's speeches to the Romans. Honoring our life-long acquaintance, Marta came by late in the evening. We sat in the living room. Her hands were in her lap, and her posture upright as it had been on evenings long ago when Ruth was out and she would proceed to tell me detailed indigenous monster stories. She probably got even with me then for some mischief committed earlier in the day. I still remember the tulun, tulun... ya voy llegando (pealing bells... I'm coming to get you) and the ensuing tale that would keep me awake till dawn.

But things were different now. "Marta, my brother Willie was here last night," I sighed and cleared my throat. "He told me a few things I hope you can help me understand."

"Ah, Doña Catana, you are looking at your family. At last," Marta smiled approvingly.

"I did things I'm ashamed of now. Better said, I didn't do what I should've done." Each apologetic word was hard to formulate in these tough moments. "It's difficult to piece everything together after so many years, but do you remember Rosa coming here with my brother? Last night he said he played in the hall with Ruth's boys."

"Si, señora, it's true. Doña Rosa brought him. Her husband, el señor Edmundo, was here too," Marta's eyes were glowing. "I would serve them lemonade on the veranda," she noted.

"You make it sound as if they were here frequently."

"Well, Doña Rosa came to ask about you. She had to know how you were and where you were. And what you were doing."

"I didn't know. I thought once I was in Jamaica and Europe, she'd no longer come by."

"She sometimes brought the children, and she visited Doña Esther after she had the stroke." It was clear that Marta empathized with the anguished mother who needed to know about her child. "Doña Rosa knew you were in good hands, but she still wanted to be reassured that all was well."

Marta had been the one who called me to the living room to see Rosa. She had seen me ignore my mother. "I feel bad for having behaved so poorly," I said meekly, wishing to be a child again and have Marta embrace me as she did when I needed comforting.

"It wasn't your fault," she said softly, reaching for my hand. "I don't know if you were taken or given, but in the end there was agreement among all. You were la Señora's child. Everyone wanted it that way."

"I've never treated anyone as badly as I treated Rosa. You know that. But why, why, Marta?"

"Look, niña Mohrle," Marta said, calling me as she did when I was little, "your mothers were always very proud of you. Everything you did was perfect. Believe me." She looked at me intently, as if trying to burn into my consciousness the truth in her words. "I don't know of anyone who's had more people love her and be concerned about her than you. You can't blame yourself for having acted as you did."

"How do you mean that, Marta?" My voice began to crack.

"You were not encouraged to know your people," Marta shrugged. "When you were fearful, there was no one to help you. Most of the time you didn't even know you were scared. You were deeply loved and just as deeply, isolated." Her look was urgent. I had to, for my peace of mind, understand what she was saying.

I thanked Marta for having come, for having shared so much of my life with me. She had always been a person of utmost integrity. Catalina, my childhood, and Marta all went together.

Thank heavens I'm leaving in the morning, I thought. I need distance and space to think.

As we waited to go through customs at the airport, I felt a tap on my shoulder. "Hola, amor." It was Willie. "I always come to say good-bye to my sisters when they leave. From now on, I'll do the same with you," and he kissed me on the cheek. What beautiful soft, full lips! My brother did things that were plain touching. His presence alone was moving. He was like Patrick: gentle, yet serious beyond repair. Their eyes zero in on you, and you feel they can read your mind. Patrick, even as a baby, sitting in his carriage, had stared people down. No one could make him smile if he didn't feel like it. Now I found my brother having the same, unblinking, intense look as my son.

The plane lifted up and flew northward, and the landscape

below became smaller. "I had a great time, Mom," Patrick smiled. "Thanks for letting me tag along." Then he reclined in his seat and put his earphones on.

⤙ ⤚

Rosa's Daughters

It appeared that getting the information of their whereabouts was easier than making the initial connection. Of course they'd heard from Jennifer and surely would've already called me had I given Jennifer my details. There was so much about me I questioned, from my appearance to my personality. I was a far cry from Mutti's pampered child, from the actress, the model. I now was a professor going crazy with self-analysis, wondering how my sisters were expecting me to be.

Insecure with my appearance and afraid I'd seem too stiff and distant, I also compared my life with what I knew of theirs. I felt guilty at having dissipated the money I earned and blown what I had inherited. After worrying if they'd like me, I worried if they might need money and I'd not have any to give them. It also occurred to me that it was petty of me to think like that. They probably had more than I did anyway. My pitiful sense of inadequacy was again hitting rock bottom. After all the effort I put into finding my sisters, there was no one with me in whom I could confide my pathetic fears. Patrick was already at Chautauqua for a summer of music, working on the piano with his professor. And Fred, who understood so much of my pain, was in New York City during the week. It was Wednesday; I was at home alone. Not wanting to deal further with my angst, I picked up the phone and dialed Judith's number.

A woman answered in perfect English. I asked for Judith. She hesitated an instant and then shouted: "Thelma, pick up, it's for you!"

Thelma? There was a click and a sunny voice said "Hellouuu..."

"Hi, Judith this is Catana." I had hardly said the words, when a loud "Uyuyuiii" came through the receiver.

"Mujer! Como estás! (Girl, how are you) I heard you were half way 'round the world trying to find us, and here we are, right in each other's back yard!" She sounded vibrant, bubbly, bursting with joy. Her amazingly delightful spontaneity dissolved my fears.

"It cost me a ton of courage to call. You know how 'presumida' (conceited) I was..." I said. "I need to see you, we need to meet and talk. I want to ask you many things about my mother."

"I'm always there for you," Judith voice was now calm and low, "you must know that! Had I known you were this close, I'd have contacted you long ago."

It took no time for me to feel as if we'd always known each other, as if we'd grown up together. Thank you God, I thought, thank you for darling Judith. We talked about Jennifer, Archie, Willie; and how well Archie and Patrick liked each other. We also mentioned that Jennifer looked so much like our mother.

"Exactly like our mother," Judith underscored. "It's uncanny to see her doing things and moving around just like her grandmother..."

Jennifer had told me Judith worked as a nanny for a wealthy family in Manhattan, "taking care of other people's spoiled children." So I knew Judith was sacrificing herself so her children could create a better life for themselves. She had married the soccer star she was in love with when she saw me at Mutti's. It appears that Judith became the primary resource for regular family income and secured the studies of her children.

After a few days I called Adela; I had only seen her the one time she was six before my departure for Jamaica. Jennifer said she was a friendly but bold woman; someone better not to "mess" with. In other words: someone from a different mold than her mother.

"Thought you'd never call me!" I heard Adela's low, raspy voice coming through the phone. "You've called and seen everyone except me. It's about time I hear from you!" Her delivery was sharp, direct! If there's a shortcut, this one will take it, I thought. She didn't giggle much but added in a gentler tone that she was delighted we were talking.

Without speaking a word of English, but with the guts of a scout focused on a better future, Adela was the first to come to the States. She was now a nurse, working the night shift in a retirement home, so she could be with her children after school.

We decided to meet in three weeks in Greenwich Village, in the apartment a colleague, who spent her weekends in Connecticut, had offered me. It would be only the three of us, undisturbed by husbands or children, just Rosa's three daughters spending time together. The day our mother had lived and died hoping for had come: her children had found each other.

JULY 31, 1993, A SATURDAY, began as an unhurried, lazy morning in the city that never sleeps. I hardly slept during the night and was filled with the anxiety and expectation of an eight year old awaiting the visit of important people from afar. At first the hours seemed to crawl. If I looked in the mirror once, I looked in it a hundred times. One who rarely looked at her reflection, I was now constantly checking my appearance. I noticed in passing that it was a year, almost to the day, that I'd sat by the Verrazzano Bridge with Gil. I hovered by the window looking at the traffic below hoping, by chance, to see Judith and Adela as they approached the building. Then the doorbell rang. I glanced at the clock: eleven, on the dot. I walked down the corridor thinking: good luck kid, this is it... I removed the latch, turned the knob, and there they were: Judith with an armful of the most luscious pink roses, Adela behind her with an interesting arrangement of dried flowers.

Judith's arms fell around me in a tight embrace. "At last, at last, at last," she said, tears spilling from her eyes. "It's wonderful to hold you in my arms! At last!" She held me and rocked me and had no intention of ever letting me go. When we separated, tears dropped from her face making me aware that I wasn't weeping, and immediately I wished that for once I'd stop observing me. Judith tended to her tears while Adela and I exchanged a much shorter and, thankfully, less emotional embrace.

After arranging the roses in a vase and helping ourselves to iced tea in the kitchen, we relaxed in the comfortable living room chairs and began to exchange stories about what had brought us to the States.

Adela was indignant that she ended up marrying "a guy from back home," when she had tried so hard to get away from them. "There's no choice for us because even here we still only associate with people from our region." Both had applied for citizenship and had no intentions of ever living in Guatemala again. "No way will I live back there again," Adela said, crossing herself and kissing her thumb.

I observed my sisters, looking for shared physical similarities. Dark as my complexion is, I am lighter than they are. My bone structure is finer and my body less muscular; my legs are thinner, and my feet and hands more slender than theirs. Judith and I have similar facial features, but not Adela. While Judith is gentle, and submissive, Adela is direct and quite uncompromising, and in that way a bit more like me. Judith wore a bright orange dress that contoured her shapely figure in the most complimentary way. I would never have dared to wear such a bright, sexy outfit. But it suited her perfectly and she looked as radiant as the sun!

Without having a single harsh word for "la Señora," they told me how they saw our mother take an early morning bus to the city with the sole purpose of seeing me, only to return in the evening dejected at having failed in the effort. She was told I was not there. They felt our mother had been wronged, and it bothered me hearing about a depressed Rosa having been denied me. She instilled in them that although there were only three children at home, she had given birth to four. Every year they celebrated my birthday with a cake and a piñata and were reminded, indoctrinated, that if I ever needed any one of them, together or alone, they were to be there for me. "Always, and at any time," Judith underlined.

"I was incapable of understanding my mother's longing for me," I said, stirring uncomfortably in my chair.

"She wrote to you regularly when you were in Germany," Judith continued the torture, "but she never heard from you."

Letters from Rosa sent to me? "I never received a letter from her," I said, astounded. "Never a letter, or for that matter, anything from Rosa. Where did she send them?"

"To the house in Guatemala. Our mother didn't have your address in Germany." Judith's eyes filled with tears. "I can't believe they could have done that," she said wiping them away with the back of her hand. "Our mother wrote to you every two or three months... then she'd wait, and resigning herself that she wouldn't hear from you, she'd sit down and write to you again. She never gave up hope that you would one day send an answer."

What was I to make of that? Would I have answered her? Would I have responded to what Rosa might have said to me in writing? We'll never know because the choice had been taken from me. No contact must have seemed the best solution all around. Everyone in Catalina knew how I felt. They could not keep her from coming to see me, but they certainly could interfere with her correspondence.

"After our mother died, I went to Catalina one more time to inquire about you. I was told they were moving to Germany and were in the process of selling the house." She looked at me from the corner of her eyes, trying to gage my reaction.

"Really? I never heard about any such plans. What was that about?" I asked Judith, knowing full well she didn't know either.

"I was surprised when Jennifer told me where she saw you."

"And I was surprised she knew where to go," I added, still reeling about the withheld letters.

I could only figure that Ruth must have brushed Judith off. Neither Mutti nor Rosa lived any more and she probably didn't see the point of having this family prolong my mother's discomforting habit. What better way to stop the visits than by saying they were moving to Europe? Was that why Willie kept looking at Ruth in a peculiar way? And why she soon excused herself from the company? Was I reading too much into this? Fact is: Rosa brought Judith, and Judith brought Jennifer to Catalina.

As my sisters talked, Rosa grew into a personality of many dimensions. It felt as if I could see her in their house, tending her blooming potted plants or sitting at the machine sewing her own and her children's clothes. Once a month, when Edmundo brought home money, she bought groceries to feed the family for the next four weeks. Rice, beans, ground maize for tortillas, flour and sugar for pastries. She had a rooster and laying hens for eggs and chickens. When staples ran out, and she needed to supplement the income, she baked tarts and cookies for sale. As soon as my sisters had learned to add and subtract, she placed a small table in front of the house and had them sell her desert treats. "From the age of four or five, if we wanted to eat, we had to help; it was as simple as that," Judith laughed.

How different things had been for me. I was called to meals and sat at the dining table waiting to be served. It never crossed my mind that there might not be enough food for everyone. And I only offered my time in the kitchen when it was fun, like helping with Christmas cookies or arranging hors d'oeuvres for cocktails, not that my help was ever asked for or needed.

"When I dream of my mother, I put jasmine blossoms in a vase by her picture," Judith interrupted my thoughts. "In my mother's house, jasmine bushes bloomed outside our bedroom windows, and at night the delicate scent lulled everyone to sleep." Rosa died while Judith was pregnant with Archie. Shortly before the birth, during a nap, she dreamt Rosa at her bed. The scent of jasmine was strong in the dream as the spirit promised a swift delivery. When Judith awoke the room smelled of jasmine. She stood up, her water broke, and Archie was born two hours later in an easy birth. "We know our mother is near when the scent of that little white flower is strong without it being around. She gave us the sign with Archie." Hearing that, I shared that I'd had dreams of Rosa's spirit being at my bed.

"Back home we believe that there is no death, that when life in the body ends we return to our real essence: that of being spirits," Adela commented.

"I imagine that's a Carib perception," I said intrigued. "I've been reading about Caribs in anthropology books. Are you able to speak the language?"

"Yeah," my sisters laughed in unison.

"Who taught you?"

"Hey, who do you think? Our mother, of course!" Adela

laughed louder and I could see her gold tooth sparkle.

"Ruth said she didn't speak Carib."

"Well, she did. How could she not have known how to speak the language of her people when she grew up among them?" Adela shook her head and looked at me as if I were nuts.

I knew she spoke German, Spanish, and English. I suppose Carib was too primitive for Mutti to give it linguistic credence, and Rosa had to be superior to those in the village.

Among the things that were difficult to talk about was Rosa's submissiveness and docility. She was not a radiantly happy woman and a pervasive sadness accompanied her even when she laughed. She never displayed her feelings, never let off steam to voice what weighed so heavy on her heart. She would have lived longer, Judith said, had she not kept everything inside, had she perhaps sometimes imposed her will. They did not infer anything in the slightest, but I felt accused. Was it the situation with me that had contributed to my mother's enduring sadness or to the reason for her subservience and early demise? I observed how Rosa's memory saddened them and wondered if I could learn to share in that sadness. They knew the woman who brought me into this world. The three of us had, at some time, lived in the same womb. Before sensing the air or seeing the sun or hearing a bird, we felt her breathe.

WHEN I MENTIONED HAVING MET MY FATHER who lived in Brooklyn, their reaction was one of shock. I had to explain that we only shared our mother.

"We've heard about this man claiming to be your father, but we know that's a lie," Adela puffed.

She had a friend who knew his wife, and the general contention was that the guy was an awful man and a big liar.

"He appears in my papers as my father. And we look alike," I said, my tone sharper than intended. "I was born out of wedlock, before Edmundo married Rosa. That's why Mutti could keep me in the first place. She would not have had power over parents of a legitimate child. If Edmundo had been my father, he would at least have come to see me, don't you think? I don't know what he looks like, I've never seen him in my life." It was the truth; I had never seen their father. And why would I lie to them anyway?

"No, our parents were married when you were born," Judith said immediately, refusing to acknowledge what I had just told her.

So I detailed the missing father's name in my original birth certificate. There you go, I said to myself, they were told stories, too. Lies on one side; fibs on the other. All families must have secrets, but as I saw it, it was time to end the farce. "Morality has nothing to do with it," I said in a voice that oozed frustration. "We are adults now, and the facts are quite clear. It really doesn't bother me." My tone was softer, mellower, "and I hope it will eventually be OK with you, too, because it's the truth."

"In an article that appeared in the newspaper, about you being an actress in Germany, you mentioned that man as your father and our mother became very upset." Judith reflected.

"I never mentioned a father in interviews. Rosa must have read my name as 'Reed Cayetano,' and what upset her was the Reed in my surname. I eventually dropped that name," I said, realizing that after so many years, Edmundo must still have given Rosa hell.

＜

"You love the painting I gave you?" I responded, my mouth full with food. We were having lunch and Judith belatedly thanked me for her wedding present I gave her. "I didn't know you married, how could I have given you a gift?"

"It's a watercolor of a red hibiscus," Judith explained. "Ruth told us you painted it in school in Jamaica. She brought it when she came to my wedding reception."

I sputtered and gasped and my mouth dropped open. "Ruth was at your wedding reception? Ruth was there? I don't believe it! I know nothing about this!" I was hanging at the edge of my seat. How could that have been? My mind began to reel again. "Judith, when you married," I said, once my thoughts began to unscramble, "Mutti and Rosa were both still alive, right?"

"Yes…"

"Say it again, Judith: Ruth was at your wedding?" The thought alone seemed outrageous. My eyes widened at the realization that Ruth in her loyalty to Mutti, could well have gone to the reception. But why? To represent me? How come no one had ever told me anything about this?

"She was there," came her answer, "and one of her sons was there too." Seeing my even more stupefied expression, my sisters burst into roaring belly laughs while I fell back into the folds of the chair and broke out in perspiration. This was too much. Ruth and one of her sons had attended Judith's wedding! This was the first time I felt, palpably, the deliberate interference that had taken place when it came to my relationship with my family. What else was there like this I didn't know? What else had been done 'for me,' or 'in my name?' Hell, how could I have developed a relationship with my family, if Mutti and Ruth dealt with them and systematically kept me out? The more I learned from my siblings, the more I felt the pain from the wedge that was driven between us.

AND THEN JUDITH TALKED ABOUT the time she and my mother visited Mutti, about two years after her stroke. It was the last time my two mothers would be together. "From the moment we walked into the room and she saw us, the Señora began to weep, but so bitterly that her entire body shook. She sat in a wheel chair, crooked and crippled, holding her wilted right hand. To my last breath on earth," Judith sighed, "I swear I will never forget the scene: my mother standing next to the withered old woman, gently stroking her arm and talking to her in German. It gives me chills to think about it," she whispered, looking down at her hands. Her expression was somber, sad even. "Our mother spoke German, you know," my sister said slowly, looking up at me. I nodded. "I couldn't - for the life of me - understand what my mother was saying, but her voice was gentle and sweet as she spoke to the old lady."

Marta had mentioned that visit. But Judith was revealing volumes about a relationship between the two women. I don't remember ever seeing them interact.

"All I felt at witnessing them caught in such tender emotion is that they had shared a history. What history I don't know, but the speech-impaired Señora weeping inconsolably during the entire time we were there, is indelibly ingrained in my memory." Tears had welled up in my sister's eyes.

"Did you ask Rosa what she told her?"

"I wouldn't have dared. What happened between them was sacred."

What had they shared? What where their secrets? How had their paths crossed, influencing the outcome of their lives and mine, forever?

"Rosa died shortly after Mutti, didn't she?" I asked, although I knew the answer.

"Yes, isn't that odd? They died within the year."

"Almost to the day," I added.

I heard names of aunts and uncles, cousins several times removed; it seemed there was a family Diaspora spread over the US, with some relatives living as far away as Australia. But I was most intrigued to hear that a sister of my mother's, Tia Justa, was still alive, as was my mother's best friend, Alicia de Garcia. Both resided in Livingston. When evening came, and it was time for them to leave, we held each other tightly when we said good-bye. "You will come to visit me upstate," I said to them. And they were ready to leave with me that very minute.

MY WORLDS WERE COLLIDING. Why the lies? Why the intrigue? These were honest, sincere people. There was no reason to have feared them. Why was I restless and confused, and despite all the joy, unhappy?

I understood, in my torment what my mother's legacy had been: to remember her courage in the face of insurmountable adversity. All I have of her is the fragmentary, elusive memory of her visits. All she could give me was the example of her courage and the wisdom that lay in her fortitude and in her unwavering love for me. At the base of her infinite faith was the knowledge that I would one day recognize how much she had loved me.

Her power lay in her silent perseverance. If she was not allowed to interact with me, no one could keep me from having to look at her, even if I didn't see her. She came for all in Catalina to recognize how she had been wronged. She never accused, she only came to see her daughter. Sometimes her long trip was in vain, but that didn't deter her from coming again, and again, and again. Her bequest to me was LOVE.

I prepared a cup of tea and curled up on the sofa in the corner where Judith had sat. I wanted to look just as pretty surrounded by the colorful floral pattern. I raised the cup and inhaled the warm scent, and realized that for the rest of my life I would not be able to hear the word jasmine or smell the fragrance or see the flower without thinking of my mother. Nor would I be able to erase from my mind the image of my two mothers' last encounter.

I was in touch with a part of me that was new, but I could not think any more. I had many tomorrows for reliving the memorable moments of today.

Then, enraged at the injustice done to her and blind with fury, I actually cried for my mother. Out loud, without shame or restriction, I wept. I hurt. My face, my eyes, my heart ached because I had wronged the woman who had endured so much to claim me. Had I loved her? Had I? I felt that in some form, at some time, I had. I longed to regain the elusive memory... When did we separate? How had it been when we separated?

Helplessly, I wept.

To Livingston with Willie

Nine months after the visit with Patrick, I was in Guatemala again. I sat on Catalina's veranda waiting for Willie to pick me up for the drive to Livingston. The air was cool that foggy March morning in 1994, and moisture hung heavy on the branches of the old pine trees. I loved to inhale the serenity of morning in the Guatemalan highlands, to feel the heaviness of dawn, witness the dance of fog and sunlight before breaking into a crystal clear day.

As I collected my thoughts, I checked my feelings. How would it be with my little brother? What would the village feel like? What would the people there reveal to me about Esther, about my mother, my father? I was free of emotions, empty, as I faced the void.

"Como estas, hermanita?" (How are you little sis?) Willie said giving me a kiss on the cheek, and helping me to my seat in his spacious, and practically new white Ford truck.

As we drove out of the city and headed through the mountains, I felt an indescribable love for the landscape: the stark silhouetted volcanoes, ragged ravines and gently undulating hills against the pale golden light of the heavens. I felt the change in vegetation in every pore of my skin as we left the temperate forests and drove through dry brush and desert, to reach the coastal jungle. In five hours we dropped from five thousand feet to sea level.

Puerto Barrios is located on a natural harbor, protected from winds by low mountains. It's the port from where Mutti and I had sailed to Europe decades ago. Willie parked under a breadfruit tree and gave a boy some coins to watch his truck. Lunch was grilled, freshly caught ocean fish, fries, and avocado.

I would reach Livingston without the apprehension and disdain I had 16 years ago, and without last year's reluctance to go on land. I was with people who came and went to the village regularly, who belonged there and who, to reach it, sat for an hour or more in a metal hull with an outboard motor. I was and wanted to be where I came from, with my brother whom I already loved and trusted fully.

"I must look like hell, Willie. Look at how the ocean air has unruffled my hairdo," I shouted over the drone of the motor.

"What's wrong with it?"

"What's wrong with it you ask? Look at it! It's a royal mess!"

"Looks fine to me," Willie answered nonchalantly, smiled and shrugged.

"Hey, Willie! The heat, the humidity! How does my hair look?"

"What's the problem? Everyone's hair is like that," he laughed a wide-open happy laugh flaunting his immaculate pearl-white teeth.

In other words, shut up Catana, you look like everyone else. You'll arrive at the place of your birth with a head full of frizzy hair, just the way God intended. And guess what? I actually didn't mind.

Livingston appeared in the distance and I marveled at its tiny size. As we approached, I could see long-legged dark children playing soccer on the beach. Where the land rose stood several houses and an impressive estate that I don't think had been there when we visited with Fred. "That's the hotel we're staying in," Willie said, pointing to it. Good, I was reassured of acceptable accommodations.

Livingston was picturesque, tropical, and smelled of ocean, salt, and heat. The hotel was sophisticated for the village. All rooms had terraces covered with bougainvilleas and faced the Atlantic. A slow moving, lanky chambermaid brought drinking water and sweet-smelling fresh white towels. I flipped a switch and the fan over my bed began to rotate as I lay down to rest and listen to the breeze in the palms and the ocean waves unfolding in the distance. Tropics. Oh, yes, it felt good to be in the heat. After freshening up, Willie and I set out for a walk. The village had two main streets that met in the center at the top of the elevation. One began at the mouth of the river, went over the hill and down to the ocean, crossing the little peninsula; the other cut across the peninsula lengthwise from the tip of the promontory into the jungle.

We strolled along one of the few paved streets and came to a solid house made of stone. Sitting on a bench in front of it was a dark, rather corpulent woman with gray hair. Three small children lay motionless on a mat by her broad, thick, bare feet that had never seen the inside of a shoe. The woman's eyes moved slowly as she saw us approach; the rest of her did not move at all. Willie pushed the gate open.

"We're here to see you, Tía Justa," he said smiling at her. "This is your niece Adriana. She wants to talk to you."

Oh wow! What a sight! So that was Justa Nery, Rosa's half-sister, my aunt. She grunted and looked at me with opaque disinterested eyes. How could this be my mother's sister? Willie motioned for me to sit on the bench next to her and positioned himself by the gate. What was I expected to do? What was I supposed to want from this freak of a being? The three children on the mat in the shade were perhaps ten, six and the baby a few month's old. They, too, barely stirred. It must be terribly hot, I thought, but they should be accustomed to heat. How could they just lie there in the shade and do nothing?

Sitting down, I said, "Hola, Tía Justa." I smiled at her, feeling really out of place.

"Uhu."

I could tell this was not going to be fascinating. "How are you?" What else do you ask when you have the distinct feeling the being before you does not understand?

"Uh," she nodded affirmatively. I figured she meant 'fine.'

I tried not looking at her directly and smiling more broadly; perhaps I intimidated her. I really couldn't think of anything to say. "Your grandchildren, Tía?" I then asked.

"Uh huh."

Jesus, Mary, and Joseph, have mercy on me, I thought. Then the oldest child got up smiling a shy little smile and asked if I'd like some tamarind juice. I thanked her smiling, but declined. No way was I drinking anything that didn't come in a bottle with a factory seal on it.

"You are mad, aren't you?" I asked the middle one who had a furious look in her eyes. She neither looked at me nor answered, but covered her eyes with the back of her right hand revealing the lines of her hand. The central line was long and ended in an upward curve with a sharp point, indicating keen intelligence. Her dagger-throwing eyes also proved she had a quick mind, and I wondered if I were to take her away from having nothing better to do than lying in the shade, and sent her to a good school... could she still develop ambition and goals for a better life, or would she, after six years of this torpid existence, become a disinterested, immobile creature like her grandmother?

There was nothing I wanted to know from anyone like Justa Nery. She was completely removed from anything I could remotely deal with. I motioned to Willie that I was ready to go.

"I thought you wanted to talk to her," Willie said, as we walked away. "I should've warned you... She's one of few words."

"You don't say? Have you ever heard her do more than grunt?"

"Well, she's the only one from mother's side who is still here, so I always pay her a visit when I'm in Livingston."

He didn't answer my question. "Family is just about everything for you, isn't it, Willie?" I said, marveling at his loyalty.

My brother showed me Livingston landmarks, and at one point said we were in Barrio Barique, the area where the Caribs lived. In my birth certificate it said that I had been born in Barrio Barique. So that's where I was now. We reached a plot with banana trees and tall green grass. "This is where you were born," Willie said. "Our mother's house was torn down several years ago. See the blue wooden boards on the house over there," he pointed. "Those boards were taken from our mother's house; this way," he smiled, "the memory of our mother's house continues in the life of that new one." I shook my head, and just looked at him. What could I have said to such a sweet observation? "Our mother showed us where each of us was born. You are the only one of her four children who was born in Livingston." At that I smiled at him and gulped through the lump that was growing in my throat. So this is where the hut stood where I first saw the light of day...

We continued our stroll to the elevation overlooking the ocean and reached a house on a broad, tree-lined street. Willie pushed the gate open without saying a word and led the way through the garden to the back porch. "This is my sister Adriana," he addressed a woman and, turning to me and gesturing with his hand added, "Alicia de Garcia, my godmother." There was no protocol, no need to announce one's intent to visit. I probably would have liked a little time to prepare mentally for the encounter with the woman who had been my mother's best friend and presumably knew everything about her.

Alicia de Garcia's expression was seriously unfriendly. Good thing I no longer looked as if I could be reprimanded like an insolent child. I had questions for her, and was not going to be intimidated by any strong words she might want to hurl at me. After looking me up and down, Alicia de Garcia directed us to some chairs under a palm tree that faced the ocean breeze.

"It's about time we see you," was her brusque greeting once we settled down.

"If it weren't for my little brother, I wouldn't be here. Thanks to Willie, I have finally made it to this distant corner of the world," I responded with honey-coated words.

"Yes, Willie... he's a good man," she said, her expression softening as she looked at him.

"Judith and Willie tell me you were my mother's best friend," I cut to the chase. "Perhaps you can help me find answers to questions about what happened in my life long ago."

"I was your mother's best friend, certainly!" - Did she ever have a gruff way about her! - "Your mother yearned for you every day of her life. Every year on your birthday she drove to the city with your piñata."

I hadn't asked about that. "Curious," I said, "I don't remember having had a piñata."

"Certainly! Of course! Your birthday falls on the 26th of August. I will always remember that date." Her pose and gestures were those of one who knew more than anyone else in the universe.

"The date is right," I agreed. The piñata was not. But I didn't feel like letting her know that she had lost some credibility. She could not have known that I had few birthday parties, the last when I was ten. They had been European-type parties, where everyone played organized games. There might have been a "Happy Birthday to You" song, but no Guatemalan mañanitas, no marimba, no mariachis either. No piñatas. Judith said Rosa celebrated my birthday with my siblings. They were the ones who had a piñata on the 26th of August.

"I recently met Gilberto Reed," I said, changing the subject. "What do you know about him and his relation with my mother?"

"I know that he's a drunk and a liar!" She shouted, and got so agitated she almost fell over in her chair.

"He's my father," I said, beginning to enjoy my deep dislike for her.

"That man is nobody's father! She flailed her arms. "Your father is the father of all Rosa's children: Edmundo Cayetano."

"Gilberto's name is in my papers," I threw back at her. "And I believe it because I look like him." I cocked my head to the side and glared at her, which made no impression.

"Do yourself a favor and forget that lie. He is not your father. Rosa would have told me. I was her best friend."

Okay, next thing. "Do you remember when my mother left for Guatemala City?" This was becoming a crucial question. Ruth had said something that intimated Rosa having been in Guatemala right after the German's departure from Livingston.

Alicia was very clear: "She left with the Germans, she left with them. She left when they did."

That confirmed Ruth's words, but differed from Mutti's version - the one I had always believed - that I was the only one who came to the city with them.

"How long did she stay in the City?" was my next question.

"After the city she moved to Tiquisate, where Edmundo was."

I knew that, but when? She couldn't narrow it down. This woman was presumably my mother's confidante. For that her answers were not good enough. What's more, I disliked her intensely. What could my mother have had in common with her? She looked like the last person I'd trust. Someone who had an answer before she heard the question. When I discovered that she ignored how many and who my godparents were, I knew she had nothing to tell me. Moreover, the woman didn't say she knew me as a baby. Rosa provided responsible godparents for her children and Alicia served that purpose fifteen years later when Willie was born.

The meetings with Justa Nery and Alicia de Garcia had been the most important part of my trip to Guatemala. They were over and had not produced anything useful.

My body was telling me I needed to rest. The long trip, the heat, and, yes Tia Justa and the many levels of emotion related to her, had worn me down. It was time to shower and unwind under the ceiling fan in the hotel. Time to lie down and wait for the day to cool off.

In the early evening, when the temperatures had moderated, I tapped on Willie's door ready to visit some people he wanted me to meet. On the way he pointed to a grassy path that led to where the Casa Grande had once stood. As nothing remained, we went straight to see Lucio and Josefina.

"Who are they?" I asked distractedly, and gathered from his look that he was surprised at my question.

"Lucio Cayetano. He's my father's brother, an uncle," Willie explained.

I didn't care. Cayetanos were not blood relatives. I had seen the people who interested me.

"Ave Maria," my brother called, using the customary greeting when entering a home.

"Ay, bendito!" (Blessed be) A woman exclaimed as she came out of the shadow's diffused light.

"Tía, I bring you my sister Adriana. She has come to visit Livingston."

My eyes almost popped out of their sockets, as I stared at a singularly beautiful face. What beauty, and that in Livingston! I had only seen such delicate porcelain features in Rome when Fred and I lived around the corner of the Ethiopian embassy. She could be Ethiopian, or maybe Nefertiti herself, I thought. She was very slender, almost frail. Her caramel colored skin glowed golden, and curly hair crowned her head like a filigree halo. The teeth were perfect alabaster. How old is she? I wondered. What had been her name again? Ah, yes, Josefina...

"Mucho gusto, Josefina," and I extended my hand.

Then Willie greeted Lucio. As I was about to shake hands with a diminutive fine-featured man, my brain suddenly snapped into gear. This was Edmundo's brother Lucio, the one Gil's wife had claimed I looked like! She must have been delusional, for not in the wildest stretch of any imagination could I resemble him.

"Bienvenida, bienvenida," Lucio said in a soft baritone and reached out to embrace me with both arms.

The house soon filled with Lucio and Josefina's children, grandchildren, nieces, nephews, friends... anybody, everybody. All wanted to see the woman who'd been taken away as a child. I was in the middle of a nest of Cayetanos, and there wasn't one of them whose face was as round as mine, or whose body was built like mine. Willie led the animated conversation until he sensed my social skills had run their course. After the round of good-byes, we moved on.

The sun had set and the few village lights were turned on by the time we continued our walk. On the outskirts of the village, already in the jungle, we ambled into Raimundo Cayetano's bar. People sat outside the hut at tables around trees drinking much and eating little. A slender man came out with bottles of beer for his customers.

"Tío, look who's here," my brother shouted.

The uncle hugged his nephew, embraced me, and made us sit at the bar inside. From an icebox he took out two bottles of ice-cold beer and handed each of us one. His wife, a diminutive, round, cream-colored woman, made skinny quesadillas for those who ordered something to eat.

Raimundo recalled the era of the Germans as a great time, when everyone in the village worked, and no one had to leave in search of a livelihood. Livingston then wasn't a crummy village at the end of the world, he said. There were no drunks or bums. "It was beautiful then, and it's a damn shame," he added pounding his hand on the bar, "that those days will never return." I was grateful to finally hear something good about the people who were so dear to me, and I was glad Willie heard it too.

We left Raimundo and ambled to the beach where we walked on the sand. It was quiet but for the enduring breeze in the palms and the waves. The stars were out, all of them; the new moon a sliver on the horizon. Livingston's beach was quiet at night, and I wondered if I had been conceived there.

The village was another story: it was bustling with Saturday night activity. Naked light bulbs with bugs buzzing around them brightened the porches and storefronts. Side streets were dark. Everyone had something to do, someone to see, somewhere to go. Hippiefied European and American tourists dined on the balconies of shacks that called themselves restaurants. I wondered if after a dinner in this village at the margin of the world with no television, any of those eating would be alive in the morning. Loud music floated out of radios and boom boxes. Livingston was warm, colorful, exotic, poor. Its existence reminded me of the surreal world of Gabriel Garcia Marquez' Macondo, where a simple story could become a bigger than life reality, and a brown baby born in a hot, lost jungle, would grow up German.

At the hotel we ordered a shrimp dinner served with pan de coco, and Willie began by telling me about his daughter who looked exactly as I did as a child. He spoke of our mother; how she had loved and spoiled him. How his world ended when she died, and how his father, who never paid much attention to him, told him to go to the city without offering him any support. He learned to survive on the streets and became a man at 14. My little brother wept as he remembered how sweetly our mother had touched his life; she had loved him, he said. He was a serious, gentle, emotional man who was not ashamed of his tears. I hated having to sit there and see him weep like that. It was something I could never do, bring myself to cry like that with someone looking at me. Judith wept when she talked about our mother, now Willie. They were always overcome with emotion when they talked about her. And again I thought that if I had known her, perhaps I, too, could weep at her memory.

"What does it say of my mother, that she knew a man before she married my father?" Willie asked, his eyes clouding over.

So, my sisters had left it to me to fill him in. I had to tell a thirty-nine year old man, who wanted to behave like an adolescent when it came to his mother being female, not to judge her! Heaven knows why, but it was clear now that lies had been flying all over the place. Willie looked straight into my eyes and didn't blink. Nothing moved in his face as I said so many things to him. I knew he wanted to doubt every word. How could I be considerate of his feelings in this frustrating situation? More than anything, I stressed, I needed to understand why my mother could walk away and leave me. Getting to the bottom of the lies had now become my quest.

"All I know," Willie said quietly, "is my mother telling us over and over that she gave birth to four children and that we are always to be there for each other. She raised us, but you were the one she longed for."

My nose began to tingle and I swallowed hard, but managed to keep the tears from welling up. "No power on earth would have allowed Esther to keep me without Edmundo's consent," I said succeeding in blinking back tears. My brother finally looked away. His eyes were dark, his mouth drawn. He was torn between my words and the ones he had heard from his parents.

"The way you say these things..." he said humbly, his head bowed, "it could be possible."

We learned much, that day. I learned that part of what I'd been told as a child regarding my growing up with the Germans had been true to a significant degree. What Willie had to deal with was more difficult to swallow: that my mere existence cast a shroud over the image he had of his mother. He and his sisters had been told stories, and it was our mother who told them.

I WOKE UP WELL BEFORE DAWN and sat on the balcony waiting for night to turn to day. It was quiet and cool. Occasionally I heard a breaking wave, a pelican's wing, or a cricket's chirp. The perforated canopy of the heavens, the muted sounds of nature, the salty smell of ocean, the breeze on my skin... I was in communion with all that was around me; I was at my source. "Thank you Universe for the gift that is my life," I whispered into the breeze.

As the black of night slowly changed to gray, I dressed, left the hotel, and walked up the grassy path to where I spent the first year of my life. Only one of the six Egyptian palms of long ago remained on the empty grass-covered plot. I opened the barbed wire gate and walked through the property trying to see if I remembered the Casa Grande and the sweeping view. I looked at the Rio Dulce and wondered where Mutti decided she saw the jungle leaf with the brown baby on it. What would Vati, Mutti, and Ruth say if they could see this now? Just as well it's gone. Their era was over and time had erased the Livingston they knew. Village roosters welcomed the new day as they did on the morning of my birth. I was conscious of being somewhere at the outer border of the periphery of a peripheral part of the world, reconnecting, or trying to, with the child that left over half a century ago to become an actress in Germany and a professor in New York. I felt Mutti's spirit near me and thanked her in my heart for having raised me. There was no shame in my birth, I whispered to her, no shame in Livingston. As I acknowledged my heritage, my spirit embraced hers in forgiveness. We understood then, Mutti and I, that forgiving could only soothe the pain and comfort the wound. Did she take me? Was I given to her? Whose was I? The scar of the separation would remain indelible.

Livingston: I liked the smell of heat, the sounds of nature, the gentility, passion and compassion of the people. Everyone knew the other in this world of simple pleasures. Fish was fresh, fruit was sweet, eggs the size of fists were eaten still warm from the chicken that laid them; black beans, pan de coco. How do they make pan de coco?

As I walked down the hill a stray dog limped along, tail tucked between its legs in fear. Dogs in the tropics get beaten a lot. In the distance a woman balanced a metal container on her head. She had gone to the well to fetch water for the day. There is little to want in Livingston, and less to have. It was Sunday morning in the village. The morning after a night of drink and dance and senses responding in the heat. I am the product of one of those sultry tropical nights, of youth and sensuality, of liquor, rhythm, and sex. Of midnight passion and whispered promises that turn to lies at dawn. I was born at dawn in the heat and palpitation of this sensuous culture. But I grew up so removed, so distant from the blood and gristle of this sort of life - so cool - that I learned not to perspire. I had accomplished what I had set out to do. There was no more to ask, nothing more to say.

After breakfast Willie and I walked once more to the plot where I was born. Barely a leaf moved in the early morning quiet. A lone rooster serenaded the moment, and it seemed that this spot on earth stood still so I could honor the place of my ultimate truth. I inhaled the warm air and smiled at my brother who observed me gravely and in silence. I could hear my heart beat; I sensed the blood in my veins, the pores on my skin. I was alive and deeply moved, sad and happy, empty and filled to capacity. I turned and embraced my brother. "We can go now," I said.

Edmundo

We returned to Barrios in a hull with an outboard motor, climbed into Willie's truck and by mid morning were in Morales to pay Edmundo a visit. Rosa's husband had worked most his life for the United Fruit Company as electrical engineer. Years after my mother's death, to believe my sister Adela, "he lay down with a woman who could have been his granddaughter," and proceeded to "infest himself with children." He married the "lazy woman," and now had five little ones. My siblings were furious with him, particularly Adela, who would have liked her father to live out his years in her care. "But no, he had to load up on new kids, and now has to work until he drops dead," were Adela's bitter words.

We pulled up in front of a small yellow house on a quiet road where tufts of grass grew between cracked pavements. A horde of boisterous children ran around laughing and playing tag. Their joyous laughter and beautiful smiling faces belied their obvious poverty. Willie brushed by, barely looking at them.

Our mother, he stressed, kept her children clean; and his father would have lost his job had he walked around the way he did now. In his eighties, Willie said, the old man was worse off than he had ever been at any time in his life.

As we approached, I observed a short man, shorter than I, and very, very dark. He was not wiry like his brother Lucio, though they looked alike. His jaundiced eyes had a gentle expression; he seemed genuinely happy to see me. "Welcome, daughter," he said as he extended a broad calloused hand.

He called me his daughter. Had my mother told him I was his? Did she tell him anything? She was not promiscuous, but had she been with him before Gil? Or did she seek him out after she found herself with child? Not to say I am light, but I am fairer than either my mother or he. Was it his male ego, or was he naive? He was loyal, that is true, for he stood by my mother as she presented to the world a story of having lost me to the Germans.

Edmundo's new wife is young and her skin is the color of pale honey. Her nose is narrow, her lips thin, her hair is brown and straight. The five young ones are all exactly as honey colored as she, have her features, and straight hair. "As straight as Montezuma's," Willie agreed after I mentioned it. She says she loves him and for that he houses, clothes, feeds, and cares for her brood, wherever she may have acquired them. And the kids are all over him: papito here, papito there, papito this and papito that. He sits down, and two jump on his lap. He won't tell them to go away but places his arms around them. He is an old man surrounded by young voices and many beautiful faces that smile and laugh and look up at him with joyful eyes, and call him: papito. Willie says he was nowhere as lovable with them when they were growing up.

Here is a man who fathered three children, but there are nine who carry his name. Six are not his, not the oldest, and in my humble opinion, not the five youngest. To him, all are his children because the women he loved said they were his. He made his home at the end of the railroad tracks, where the banana companies prepared their loads for shipment to the United States. God willing, he will not have to conclude his life there.

We sat in a room with several chairs and a sofa that doubled as a trampoline. The walls were bare; two light bulbs dangled from the ceiling on crooked electrical cords. At least they had electricity and running water. One of the children offered lemonade and Willie accepted.

"We have always wanted to tell you something that was very important for you to know, but we never had the opportunity to do so," Edmundo said to me with a faint smile. His tired eyes, yellow and gray with age, lingered on me gravely as he spoke. "Bad tongues said we gave you away because we didn't love you. That's not true. We loved you very much, but we knew they would offer you a better life than the one we could have given you." I felt a lump building in my throat... I looked at his thickly callused hands. Just don't cry I said to myself, biting hard on my lip. Not now, just don't cry now. "You were so bright," the man continued gently, "and you were accustomed to being with them. We knew they loved you so much... We knew they'd take good care of you."

I drew air into my lungs and sighing, forced a smile. I swallowed and again bit the inside of my lip, hoping the pain would keep me from dissolving in tears at this humble man's sincerity, his simplicity. He took the first opportunity to tell me what had weighed heavily on his soul for too long. Did he really believe I was his? I thanked him and let him know I regretted not having known him sooner.

"But you have come now," he said, "and I can go to my grave having seen you again. Your mother too, would have wanted to see you." His eyes filled with tears. He missed her, he sighed, letting his tears run down his cheeks, and his new companion added that he always wept when he thought of my mother. She wasn't jealous of his grieving and his memories.

What humility and what emotion Edmundo had. He wept without shame, just like Willie, Judith, and Adela. They all laughed easily and were not ashamed to shed their tears.

"I've been wondering when my mother went to Guatemala," I said after a moment.

He answered, "She left with them; when they left Livingston."

Now I knew. All of us: Vati, Mutti, Ruth, my mother and I, left for Guatemala together. "Do you remember how long she stayed in the city?"

He thought, and shaking his head said, no, he didn't really know. She didn't return to Livingston, but came to Tiquisate where he was working.

Why could no one remember how long my mother had stayed in Guatemala before leaving to be with Edmundo? Maybe he took work in Tiquisate, which was in the south, so Rosa wouldn't have to face Livingston without me?

"My mother was in the Casa Grande a lot, wasn't she?" I asked Edmundo.

"All the time. She was with Miss Agatha, the godmother who raised her."

"I thought Tina was her godmother," Willie interjected surprised. "Tina always said she was the one who raised our mother." He had been at the edge of his seat, his eyes dashing from one to the other as we spoke, poised to pick up any nuance that might be new to him.

"Tina was also a godmother, Willie. But it was Miss Agatha who your mother grew up with. That is why your mother lived in the Casa Grande."

"I've never heard that name," Willie said looking at me, alarmed at discovering there were indeed things in his mother's life he ignored.

Edmundo took the children off his lap and went to a cabinet, from which he removed three photos and handed them to me. I looked at the spotted, withered pictures that Ruth must have taken. In one I am perhaps half a year old; my mother holds me toward the camera and smiles proudly. In the second I'm about three and am standing next to my mother who holds me by the arm and presses me against her side while I try to free myself from her grasp. We are laughing and are happy. When I looked at the third picture, I paled and almost dropped it: an image of Rosa when she was perhaps eleven or twelve, sitting on a swing with Mutti on the porch of the Casa Grande. Mutti's arms embrace her tenderly, and my mother has an arm around the German woman. What a wonderful exchange of tenderness between my two mothers. How had they related to each other, then?

"These are treasures, Edmundo. I don't have a single picture of my mother where I can see her face. May I have them?"

"Please. What would otherwise become of the pictures?" he answered humbly.

Were those the only pictures my mother had of me? I had an album of photos that were taken of me since I was a tiny baby. Why did my mother not have more pictures of me? Gil had more! I wanted to live the moment and not lose the intensity by wondering if leaving Rosa without pictures of me had been intentional.

We wanted to visit her grave, but the cemetery was locked. That, on a Sunday, at two in the afternoon! "They don't want weekend drunks sleeping their stupor off in there. It's nice and cool," said two women sitting on the curb with flowers. They had already sent someone to the warden's house for the key. We decided to wait. Then a message came that he was too drunk to walk, and someone should go to his house to get the key. "Let's do that," I suggested, "otherwise it'll be midnight before we get back to the city." We rang the bell and tooted the horn, but no one opened. Then a lad on a bike drove by saying the cemetery was open. We returned, only to find that the women were still sitting outside, still waiting patiently for the key to come.

I decided to leave without seeing my mother's grave. As we pulled away, the scent of jasmine filled the truck. I held my breath and looked at Willie who grinned winking at me. He also knew that we were leaving with Rosa's blessing.

Catana with brother Willie in
Guatemala, Spring 1994

Sisters: Judith, Catana and Adela in Greewich Village, NY, Summer 1994

Mutti with Rosa in Livingston, 1932
A picture Ruth took, and Edmundo gave me

PART SEVEN

Sharing Treasures ... and Truths

Being with Ruth

I returned from Livingston to resume the format of evening exchanges with Ruth, repeating the routines of my previous visits that consisted of retiring to the comfort of her salita to sip wine and talk before dinner. At times, particularly when we discussed Mutti, we felt each other as sisters who compared the monsters our mother had created in our lives.

One evening I asked her point blank about Judith's wedding. She furrowed her brows as if trying to remember. She was clearly set to pull a blank. Even after I reminded her that Judith had told me one of her sons had been with her, she just shrugged and shook her head. Fortunately Thomas, who always checked on his mother before retiring, came in at that precise moment and kick-started her memory.

"Sure," came the unencumbered response, "I went with you. It was in a district on the way to Antigua. She married the famous soccer player. What an athlete that guy was!" His face lit up with admiration.

"Aaah... yes, now I remember," Ruth said, not even embarrassed. "We framed one of your pictures and gave it to her as a gift," she volunteered freely. Suddenly, it was back, and so clearly!

"Why didn't you tell me about the invitation?" I snapped, frustrated at her continued attempts to avoid coming forth with information. "And why didn't you tell me about giving her one of my hibiscus paintings? And cripes, Ruth, you attended the reception and I knew nothing about that?" I stared at her.

"It was unimportant," she immediately said in the most matter-of-fact way. "You were in Europe and we took care of the situation."

Now it's a situation. "But never to even say a word about it, ever... Not one single word..."

"Catana, for heaven's sake," Ruth leaned forward to take a cigarette. She lit it and inhaled. "You didn't care about them, the whole thing would only have upset you," she let the smoke escape slowly through the side of her mouth. "This way, at least there was a semblance of your presence."

With the perspective I had at the time I might not have responded: she was right. But it was Judith after all and so, who knows what I might have done. The real thing remained that, without involving me at all, they had taken care of a 'situation' that should have been my responsibility to deal with.

"Did you know," Ruth said, preparing to blind-side me the following evening, "that Mother had a secret lover and traveled with him around Europe?" My mouth dropped open. I wanted to disappear in the chair. That had been one of the secrets Mutti had confided in me, and I had taken an oath never under any circumstances to breathe a word of it to anyone, least of all Ruth.

"I swore I'd never mention it," I stuttered, stupefied.

"So she told you..." Ruth said, looking at me from the corner of her eyes with glee at her own cleverness.

"Well..." I attempted. "I thought you didn't know. She made me swear on all that's sacred never reveal any of this to you."

"Of course Mother never told me. But she told you! Typical! Aaah, hahaha," Ruth burst out laughing. "Just like her to think I was so dense not to notice! I was studying at the Letter House in Berlin, and she made me return to Guatemala, presumably to keep Vati company." Her dark eyes turned darker with every word. "She gallivanted around Europe for months and wanted to travel unobserved... Mother wasn't as clever as she thought she was." She sounded angry although she was grinning, probably at the dumbfounded look on my face.

"If she weren't dead already she'd die now," I squirmed, smiling uncomfortably and thinking how hilarious it was that Ruth, who Mutti always claimed to be a little slow and somewhat dense, was actually astute as all hell. Early on in her life, she had figured her mother out at every step and turn of the way!

"Mother was a free spirit and did whatever she felt like doing, whenever she felt like it. I resented it when she returned from Germany after visiting you," Ruth again changed the subject and this time seemed really pissed. "All she did was talk about you and your accomplishments. Mohrle here and Mohrle there and Mohrle all the time. I just got sick of hearing about it. You were living the existence she'd wanted for herself, and she loved the notoriety that came with it."

"When I was little, Mutti told me she wanted to join a circus. Maybe she had really wanted to be a performer."

"See, now, that's another thing she never told me," Ruth frowned at hearing something new.

I think we reckoned that Mutti had played each of us against the other. And because we had both been trapped in her maze, we spent years practically as enemies.

⌒

During dinner, the night before I returned to the States, our conversation revolved around my academic research regarding paintings by Antoine Pesne that were in the Charlottenburg Castle in Berlin. In some depictions, Frederick I's children play with an African youth, a court moor, who had a silver band around the neck. The representation of Blacks in Western Art deeply fascinated me, and Ruth was most interested by what I was discovering in my studies.

After dessert, Ruth went to her bedroom and returned with a purple velvet pouch that held two shining silver bands. They were one inch wide and two and a half inches in diameter. "Agatha gave these to me," Ruth said handing me one. "Apparently her grandmother wore them on a plantation. Imagine how old they must be; Agatha herself would be over a hundred and twenty by now. They must have historical value," Ruth said admiring a shiny band.

"It's so small, it could only have fit a child's wrist," my brows creasing as I studied it. "The enslaved did not own jewelry, and this is nice and heavy. It could only have been worn by a child, a little house-slave the owners loved; that's my guess," I nodded.

I was leaving the following morning. Was Ruth making sure I'd come back again? I knew about Rosa and Agatha... But what had Ruth's relationship with Agatha been?

In my hand was a solid silver bracelet, buffed to a bright shine. A little enslaved girl, a little house slave had worn it. "You may have them," Ruth said, her eyes veiled in gentleness. I nodded smiling back at her; we both knew they needed to belong to me.

Ruth and Agatha... My stay had been too short. I needed to be with Ruth and learn more about her. She also held the key to what tantalized me from the edges of my memory. Although she liked to pull blanks, I knew we could talk. It was time we did more of that.

There were still crucial pieces missing in the puzzle. I wanted to know when my mother left me. What had our separation been like? There was more, but later... I'll work on it later, I thought as I reclined my seat on the plane, closed my eyes, to wake up several hours later in New York.

Diversity in the Classroom

In the course on cultural diversity I taught at the University in Albany, my students came from practically every racial and ethnic group in the United States. I presented the topic from a strictly academic perspective - similar to earlier having been a cerebral actress. In the fall of 1994, however, I incorporated some of the personal insights I gained in my lengthy process of self-discovery.

"Cultural and personal identity is a topic that's very close to me," I informed the class in the first week of the semester. "Not long ago, I began to search for my roots, my history. It's not as easy as it looks because I grew up German in Latin America, and as you can see, I'm Black." I stopped for a second to see who was paying attention and who was fidgeting. "What might surprise you, is that for most of my life I hated being dark. I hated who I was: a Black person." That got their attention. "It took years before I could look in the mirror and say, 'hey lady, you're OK'!" Now all eyes were on me; I was on stage again, except that this monologue had not been memorized. I walked around the desk to close the gap between students and teacher.

"It took courage and a lot of mind and soul searching, before I could look at my beginnings. I didn't want to appear ungrateful to the German family that gave me a privileged, loving childhood. But at some point, when my hair was already turning gray, serious issues of misplaced identity began to surface and cramp my style. It became an urgent need to learn about my early history and see if it synched with what I'd been told by my German family." I could hardly believe the intensity of their attention. It was as if they were holding a collective breath. Then one student ventured forward.

"Like Alex Haley, professor? Like he wrote in his book Roots?" The book, a seminal work on the search for the ancestry of Haley's enslaved African ancestors, had been a sensation.

"I did not pursue my African origins but the history and culture of the people of a tiny community in which I was born. I needed not only to understand who my immediate parents were, but more than that: I had learn to honor them." Some students were gaping at me, open-mouthed.

"Everyone should be proud of who they are," one of my usually quiet students in the back row contended, "particularly if they are a minority."

"Absolutely," I agreed eagerly. "All history is valuable. But the victor's perspective is recorded while the contribution of the vanquished is deemed insignificant. That applies not only to the history of nations but to personal histories as well." I looked around the class, "Pay attention to this: Minorities in all populations... Algerians in France... Jamaicans in England... Blacks and Hispanics in the States... sooner or later suffer from an internalized sense of self-rejection. Let's call it internalized colonization." I stepped to the board and wrote the term down, and underlined it.

"But Algeria is no longer a colony nor is Jamaica, and as for us, we experience prejudice, but we are basically free," a student from Puerto Rico interjected.

"Well observed," I noted smiling. "But what I'm referring to relates to peoples living among victors. They have to absorb the victor's values in order to survive." I walked to the window and looked at the parking lot below. "The reason I mention my personal history, and why it is valid to do so in this class, is because a few months ago it occurred to me that I had a colonized mind." I turned around and looked at them, then smiled. "Think about it," I furrowed my forehead, "dominated like someone living in a colony who thinks White people have all the right answers. As a child, I wanted to be White and be an integral part of the ruling society in which I was growing up."

"That's part of the oppressor society," a young woman murmured under her breath.

With a friendly, unthreatening smile I took two steps toward her and asked, "Now, how do you think I behaved when I was among Black people?"

"Ugh, huh," she glared at me rather disdainfully. "You must have been a snob and given us a hard time," she said, looking up at me through her eyelashes.

"Not so at all." My smile broadened as I said, "I was too scared of Blacks to be able to deal with them at all." That was an answer no one expected. I returned to my desk, turned to face them again, adding, "When among Blacks, I became unsure of myself." Some started talking to each other about the issue.

"Were you like that with all minorities or only when among Blacks?" a young Dominican asked.

"Excellent question. No other minority bothered me, I did not see others as a monolithic group."

"If you grew up with White people, you grew up middle class, right?" Another offered, and someone else added, "Man, you probably had every advantage in the world. How can that make anyone insecure?"

"Consider that someone can look different to how he or she feels. Someone who does not identify with his or her outer appearance. That was me. I had no racial or ethnic frame of reference. I was dark, but felt White." I gave them a few seconds for that to sink in. "What do you think I should have marked in the American census, for instance?"

"Look at you Professor, you are Black. Black is where you put the little cross. That's a no brainer," a student from St. Barts said, gesturing exaggeratedly.

"Why, no," said another, turning around in her seat to face the classroom. "She's Guatemalan, and that's Hispanic. I'd give Hispanic the mark."

"My guess is: if you feel European and identify European," a Chinese student in the back said, "You could mark the White box."

"No way, man," someone I knew was from Canada volunteered. "Mark 'Other', because that's what you are, you are 'Other,' Prof., there's no box for you!"

I laughed at the engaged participation. "See the dilemma some face when coming to the States? Elsewhere, I never really thought about who or what I was: I had a nationality. Here I was forced to see myself racially and, or, ethnically... for socioeconomic and political reasons. I eventually did settle on 'Other,' but that was not all..." Scanning their attentive faces, I asked them, "Can you figure out what I added on the line next to 'other?' I wrote 'African Hispanic' on the little line."

Everyone cheered. Three even clapped their hands, as if that had been the ultimate coup. Then someone said laughing, "That sounds like you're denying that you feel European, doesn't it?" And they all had a good laugh again.

"Not denying it completely," I grinned, amused at their gaiety. "And thank you for reminding me about it! It just shows how complex the issue of identity can be. And then... the whole European thing is no longer important because I have succeeded in claiming where I came from. I learned to value my own history and that of my people - from their perspective and not what others had to say about them as if they were specimens to be studied in a lab. Now I can do what I would never have done before and that is stand right here," I pointed to the ground, "and talk about having hated being dark... and not feel threatened by you all, because you are secure in your cultural cradle." I looked at the beautiful young faces wondering why I suddenly felt they were beautiful. "I no longer feel inferior to someone who grew up with a Black mother."

After the brief introduction I sat on the desk and began to discuss the semester's curriculum. In addition to covering the assigned reading material I wanted them to talk about themselves. On Fridays each one would have fifteen to twenty minutes to teach the rest of the class about their family's experience in the United States and how that story fit into the country's larger society and history. "On Fridays," I said, "you will be the teachers. Through your stories we will learn what this course is about: diversity."

That was the most successful class I ever taught, particularly with regard to class participation and attendance. At the end of the semester we had a party and everyone brought a typical food prepared in their home. We made sure there were no duplicate dishes; those who shared a communal ethnic identity prepared one favorite dish. We had a buffet of cheese pirogis, chicken empanadas, sesame noodles, rice and peas, apple strudel, fried chicken, caramel flan, falafel, vegetarian sushi, chocolate fudge. I am sure I missed some... but you get the picture: foods from very distinctive cultures.

I had worked my way through self-rejection and found myself in a deliciously comfortable space: all the time. And when I walked by a mirror, I would stop to look at my reflection and smile at me. 'You look just great,' I'd tell my reflection, 'you're quite a pretty woman'. Time and again, it surprised me that I liked my appearance. There I was, thirty years past my prime, sporting white hair at the temples and twenty pounds heavier... and I liked me. My world had shifted and certainly seemed to be in order.

January 1995

It was mid December 1994. The first winter storm in the Northeast left a slick, icy, carpet. Trees glistened in the sunlight; the world was quiet, clean, and cold, and the season had people hustling in preparation for the holidays.

Winter invariably rekindles childhood memories - this year begging to appease the urge to be with Ruth. I had left Guatemala eight months before, knowing full well I'd have to see her again soon. In the course of a recent phone conversation, she told me of a dream where she was driving in a car with Mutti and five other friends who had all passed to the other side. "Tell me," she said sounding a bit aggravated, "what am I doing with all those dead people in my car who are constantly scolding me and telling me what to do?"

A nervous chill ran down my spine when I heard that. Could they be telling Ruth to come clean with me and fill in the details she's been avoiding? Oh horror, are the dead perhaps coming to claim her? A deep sense of sadness came over me. I knew so little about Mutti's daughter; I should know more about the woman who lathered my body with baby oil so I'd grow up having soft skin. She clipped and creamed my fingernails and toenails. My teeth are straight, thanks to Ruth who helped me massage the gums each morning, who drove me to the dentist and paid my dental bills. She played with me, read me stories at night and taught me prayers. I made all those countless wishes with her at my side. The thought of her dying was unbearable. I needed to be with Ruth and tap into the reservoir of her perfect memory; she was my childhood haven, my security.

I booked a flight for December 29th. That way I'd spend the holidays with my men, and visit Ruth for a few weeks before spring semester began.

I'M IN CATALINA, SITTING at the desk where I used to do my homework, going over the list of questions I need to have answered. I'll sleep again in the bed where I curled up as a child. My clothes are in the closet where my girlhood dresses hung; my shoes on the same old shoe rack. This room is my cocoon where I can retrace my steps, become younger again; feel protected, invulnerable. Ruth is here, my room is here: I feel safe. A few hours ago I heard her on the phone saying to the Lutheran minister, "My sister Catana arrived from New York. It's only when she's here I feel the family is complete." I've been part of this family all my life, and yet, why does it touch me to tears when Ruth includes me today? Is it because I never wanted to return after Mutti passed? Or because there had been such bad blood long ago? Mutti and Rudolf, the cornerstones of discord, were out of the picture. Ruth and I were left behind to mend the fences. We were Mutti's daughters, after all. We were sisters who had at one point loved and hated, only to regain love for each other in old age.

IT WAS DURING MY FIRST LUNCH that Ruth's six-year-old granddaughter confronted me. A brilliantly intelligent, but most inquisitive, and therefore rudest questioner imaginable.

"Where's your mother?" The fresh little face asked.

"She's dead, you know that. Ruth's mother is dead," I said, already sensing this might become uncomfortable.

"Not that one. I mean your mother, your real mother," her dark eyes pierced mine.

"She was my real mother," I answered unfazed... This was going to be a challenge.

"I mean your mother when you were born," the girl insisted, and everyone began to chew more slowly. Obviously, the kids had asked before and were given an answer. But that hadn't been enough for this little monster. She wanted me to say that my mother was so poor she couldn't take care of me and gave me away. That way her great grandmother and grandmother (and by extension, she) were magnanimous heroes to whom I should forever be indebted.

I wasn't going to be bullied into telling a little kid things I myself was, as yet, incapable of understanding. So, I offered her the story of the big leaf on the river. She was quiet while she played with the peas on her plate. Then, with a little crooked I-know-the-real-story smile, she said:

"Who was the woman who gave birth to you, and then put you on the leaf to float down the river?" Her smile was pretty condescending for a six year old.

"I was a miracle," I said patiently.

Her eyes flashed poisoned daggers at me; she was losing her patience with so much stupidity. "Everybody's born from a woman," she contended defiantly.

"I can't help it," I shrugged and calmly added, "That's the story I was told."

"That's not the way things happen... And, she wasn't your mother!" The little dragon voiced triumphantly.

"You mean to tell me that your grandmother told me lies?" I blinked a few times as if shocked at the possibility.

Her eyes softened as she looked at Ruth, not sure if she should say her grandmother was a liar. After all, she knew about babies being born: her pediatrician father had allowed no room for flights of fantasy.

"No," she mumbled, a bit uncertain. "My granny tells the truth." She chose a diplomatic solution and began to eat her mashed potatoes.

The ensuing conversation among the adults was a bit forced.

Suddenly, the high-pitched voice rang out again: "You," the young inquisitor said pointing her index finger at me, her pretty face beaming broadly, "are a cabbage patch baby!"

Thanks to American enterprise, her scientific mind had allowed for imagination, after all. Children are born, but cabbage patch babies... are probably left on big leaves.

"You're going to be a brilliant scientist," I grinned at her.

"Nope," she answered resolutely, "I'm going to be a doctor, like my dad."

"When I was little and told my story," I said to her and the other children at the table, "all the kids were jealous because they were born in a boring sterile hospital, and I had floated down a river on a big jungle leaf," I shrugged, smiling.

"Well," she replied, looking at her father. "It's just that today everyone knows how babies are born."

"Now really," I said giving her dad an admonishing look, "you, of all people should know what babies are," I laughed.

He grinned, and winking at the children concurred: "Absolutely, all babies are remarkable, wonderful miracles."

With that, the questioner remained quiet. From time to time, she looked at me out the corner of her eyes, but she got it: from me, the answer she wanted was not forthcoming.

THIS SORT OF SITUATION HAD tormented me throughout my life: I was unable to ward off unwelcome questions. I couldn't tell people the personal questions they asked me were none of their damned business. I answered as truthfully as I could even though I felt thoroughly invaded, my boundaries breached. Those asking came across as having the authority to know. This little girl was only six, but whether six or sixty, questions about the birth mother are insensitive to a child who did not grow up with her. Somehow, natural children (and adults, too, mind you) set out to make adopted ones feel inferior. Our birth mother is not as good as theirs, because we did not grow up with her.

I had a cramped feeling in my stomach and ate little at that lunch, but having worked through it, I was pleased to have crossed that threshold. I could never again be pushed into that uncomfortable place.

⌒

And then there was the issue of my name, which I tackled with Ruth one evening before dinner. I have never heard of anyone being called Catana. Yes, the Japanese ceremonial sword and a motorcycle, but both are spelled with a K. So, one evening I asked Ruth how I came by my name.

"Rosa named you Adriana after Edmundo's mother," Ruth contended, "but Mutti felt that, as you were no relation to him, you should also not have that name. After all, according to Mutti, Catana was much more exotic and sophisticated. Mother read your name in a novel," Ruth shrugged, and I practically choked. In a novel! "She liked it, and chose it for you," Ruth glanced up at me unaffected by my shocked expression.

I always thought Catana came from Mutti's own Katharina, that she had named me after herself. "Which book, what kind of novel was it?" I stammered, hurt.

"It's among those of fictionalized history in the hall." That surprised me even more! Good grief, the book was still in the house! "It's up there, somewhere," Ruth pointed.

I looked in book after book, but couldn't find it. After dinner I didn't relax in the salita, as usual, but renewed the quest for the origin of my name. After days of searching, I eventually I found it, and speed-read the work from cover to cover. It spoke of Spanish adventurers, of valorous, sometimes brutal, impassioned men and submissive, unfulfilled, enamored women. They had come from Spain, had conquered what they saw as a simple people a world removed, and imposed upon them their medieval rule and medieval morality. Again and again, reference was made to the anthropophagous vegetation, the heat, only second to the passion that consumed men and women in an alien merciless environment. There she was Catarina Ana, a beautiful Spanish woman living the romanticism of nineteenth century Naturalism. Her beauty was her trademark, as was the fact that Catarina Ana was called Catana for short.

In typically Mutti style, she replaced the name my mother had given me with a name she read in a novel. How like her, I thought. I was hurt beyond words that she gave me a name she read in a stupid romantic novel! At that moment, it didn't matter that it was indeed a beautiful, unusual name.

⁓

On my list of questions for Ruth was one that sometimes weighed on my soul. I only thought about it when my friends asked. Each time I considered approaching the issue, however, I couldn't get my mouth to follow through. Ruth seemed more open this time, more willing to talk and share. So, on one of our evenings I mustered up the courage, and said, "Do you know why I wasn't adopted?"

"No," Ruth snapped back. "But neither was I."

Huh? What?

"But you have Vati's name," I shook my head, stupefied.

"Catana, those two (meaning Mutti and Vati) didn't do anything right. When I first arrived, Vati went to some office in Barrios and declared himself as my father. That's all he did. He never legalized me with any proper authority. Not in Guatemala and not in Germany."

I just looked at Ruth. "Well then, how'd you manage to end up with his name?"

"My passport had expired when I was leaving to study in Berlin. I was nineteen and the German Embassy in Guatemala was taking time with extending a new one. Someone may have wondered why I had a different surname. But I was under time pressure so I threatened them to either give me my papers immediately, or I'd go to the Guatemalan authorities and change my nationality," She grinned and I burst out laughing. "When I opened my new document, I had Vati's name. He was the German Consul and without looking further, they assumed he was my father," she concluded.

That's how things are done at the outer edges of nowhere. Ruth may have figured that if I'd have been astute and interested, I could have done something about my legalization. As she had nothing stating she was legally entitled to carry Vati's name, it would also have allowed me to I outrank her in the family hierarchy. That's why she and Rudolf were glad to see me stay in Europe: the farther away I was from friends (including Mutti) having me look into my legal situation, the better for them.

What bothered my friends never really mattered to me. I knew I was Mutti and Vati's emotional child, in each and every imaginable aspect.

And so, as the list of questions decreased, the answers piled up and things began to make sense.

"When she came for me after three years, Mother told me it

was hot in Livingston. I thought it was like the Sahara, all sand and dunes," Ruth recalled. "But then I saw the rich green vegetation and the many flowers. I was very happy; I liked Livingston. Most of all I was glad to be with my mother again." There was no one to play with her, and no one - other than the adults - to talk to because she only spoke German. Mutti may not necessarily have been a loving young mother who spent time with her child. It was the housekeeper Agatha, with whom Ruth whiled the hours away, and Agatha who became her teacher, friend, and confidante.

"I liked the old woman..." Ruth said, taking a sip of wine. "She was from Belize, and let everyone know she was British. She didn't want to be a subject of such an inferior nation as Guatemala. So much so," Ruth laughed, "that she refused to learn Spanish, which she saw as the language of primitives." Agatha took pride in speaking the King's English and had a remarkable knowledge of British affairs and history. As the German Consul's housekeeper, she felt obliged to read about German, particularly Prussian history: the Hohenzollern's, Frederick the Great, Bismarck, and just about everything since German Unification. Agatha taught Ruth English and gave her a solid academic foundation that made the transition to boarding school in the States, a year later, easy. "I learned from her more than I could ever have learned in a school, anywhere. She told Vati which books to order, and what I needed to have for my American curriculum," Ruth said with more than a glint of admiration. Agatha's only son had drowned long ago; our houseboy James was her grandson. James took much pride in his appearance and work, always wearing an immaculate white steward's jacket with brass buttons and white trousers.

"When did Agatha start to work for the family?" I asked.

"Oh, dear," Ruth said, taking a cigarette. " She started to work for Vati way back in 1907 or so. She worked for him and she stayed with us until we came to Guatemala City."

"What happened to her when we left Livingston?"

"Agatha came with us," Ruth said in the most simple of ways. "Agatha, James, and Rosa came to the city with us."

Not that I had asked her, but I vaguely remember Ruth mentioning quite a while back that a German couple overheard

Rosa speaking to me in German. They thought it fascinating: a Black mother and child speaking German in Guatemala. That's why I knew Rosa had been in the city early on, perhaps on a visit. I now held my breath as my heart rate increased; we were starting to get somewhere... "They lived with us in the house in Santa Clara?" I asked tentatively. I didn't want Ruth to notice how eager I was to hear further details, so I did my best to keep an impassive exterior.

"They lived with us, at first," Ruth continued, "but Agatha was getting old, and we felt it would be best if we moved her to a retirement home."

"Oh? I thought social services were non-existent, atrocious at best," I said raising an eyebrow.

"That was not the case," Ruth assured me. "We found a lovely home for her, but she didn't like it there because people called her 'negrita'."

"I can understand that," I nodded, feeling terrible for the poor woman who must have been distraught at being called a term that even without malicious intentions was insulting. The diminutive of 'negro' underscores the notion that Blacks are childlike, simpletons. There is no way the term, coming from a White person is acceptable to a Black one.

I strongly feel that Christian symbolism is devastating to peoples of color, particularly Black people. According to Christianity, white represents purity and goodness, black stands for evil and all its ominous associations. The connotation that darkness is sinister, is nefarious to those who are dark. That's why most peoples of color don't have a White god. They worship the earth, which feeds and sustains them. They honor life and where it begins: in darkness, in the womb. In agriculture, the new moon begins the cycle of growth. For Whites, evil lurks in Hell, which is below the earth: exactly where life, in the form of food and nurture, is sustained. Dark people release evil spirits to the heavens, where the White God with his host of angels rules.

In Latin America, for instance, firecrackers are blasted into the sky to release evil despised entities. Although the reference to Biblical Blacks initially referred to Jews, Christian suggestive use of color has been disastrous for Jews for two thousand years, and in the past five hundred for Africans and Native Americans as well. They literally became the incarnation of suffering and oppression at the hands of those who selected themselves as 'chosen' because of their Bible and their pale skin.

"Negrito or negrita," said by someone who is not Black, is just as offensive as "negrote or negrota." The suffix "ote" changes the subject from the inferred simplicity of the diminutive, to a grotesque brutish being.

"Everyone was actually very sweet and kind with Agatha," Ruth said, "but she couldn't get them to stop calling her negrita. So, after a few months she returned to the coast."

"When did she die?"

"I don't know," Ruth's voice was brittle. "One day we heard she had died."

"When was that?"

"Don't remember, Catana, we just heard," Ruth shrugged.

The war - the constant fear of impending deportation - had focused the Germans' concern on their own survival and ability to cope. By the time peace came and the fear was over, Agatha had died.

"And James," I continued my interrogation, "what did he do?"

"He was the houseboy, as he had been in Livingston."

"How did he handle the city?"

"At first he managed, but once Agatha left he, too, longed for Livingston. He had no one other than Agatha, and with her gone..." Ruth shrugged. "He took off."

"How long after her departure could he have left?" I asked, throwing the question away to conceal how crucial the next answers would be.

"Probably less than a year, yes, sure... Certainly less than a year."

All three had arrived together; two succumbed to the isolation, the insults. Rosa stayed longer, because Mutti had me.

"With Agatha and James no longer there," I said calmly and going for the jugular... the one that had been eluding me, "How much longer did Rosa stay?" I held my breath as time hung suspended around us.

"Rosa stayed about a year and a half, I would say..."

There! I had it! I could exhale. A year and a half! I was one and a half when we arrived. One and a half and one and a half makes three. I was three when my mother separated from me.

"I was three when Rosa left," I murmured with the little breath I had left. But I was breathing again, breathing hard. I could feel my hands getting sweaty, then cold. My heart burned and pounded so hard it hurt my chest.

"Yes, that should be right, you were three," Ruth said without looking at me, a pensive expression on her face.

"At three, Ruth," I said leaning over to her, wanting her to look me in the eye and lowering my voice, "I must have missed her." I felt my heart constrict and another lump begin to build in my throat.

"You didn't miss her," Ruth said plainly, still not looking me in the eye. "She left, and all we did was roll your bed from her room into mine."

My mind reeled, my vision blurred, my head spun; all the breath was sucked from my body again and I was about to faint. Tentatively, my voice quivering, I said, "I slept in her room?" and almost choked.

"Yes, of course!" Ruth's voice was soft and must have been filled with disquieting memories.

"I must have missed her, Ruth," I said, looking up at her, "I was three, I shared her room..."

Ruth regarded me impassively. "Catana," she said gently, sure of what she was telling me. "By the time Rosa left, you were so accustomed to me that you didn't miss her at all."

We looked at each other in silence.

I had been under the impression that as all single children, I slept in my own room. I also believed the earlier story of having been placed next to Mutti's bed right after I was born. Now I heard that I had not been in Mutti's room at all... I had been with Rosa, and shared her space for my first three years.

I was soaked in perspiration. We had taken the final hurdle.

A LITTLE FIGURE STOOD AT THE DOOR with his arms crossed. He was all business: "Ya etá tevido," (dinner is served) he said. It was Marlon, the maid's two and a half year old boy, announcing to us that Nola, his mother, had served dinner.

Perfect timing, I thought. I'd had as much as I could take for a while.

We stood up and I embraced my thin, dear Ruth. "Thank you," I gulped, and kissed her on the cheek.

When the two weeks came to an end, I was again happy to leave... I like being in Catalina. No, I like knowing Catalina is there and I can return any time and still find Ruth moving around inside. But my life is elsewhere. Two weeks away from elsewhere and I become impatient to get back to my husband, my son, my cats, my things.

"Come back again soon," Ruth said the morning I left.

"Of course," I answered, and meant it.

In the airplane, I looked out the window. This time the route took us over the city. Through the trees, I recognized the roof of Catalina. I followed the topography of the land for a while. "We are flying over Lake Izabal," the pilot announced, and I followed part of the course of the Rio Dulce. "We are now over Belize," he commented soon after. Livingston was behind us. Soon we were over the Gulf of Mexico.

The morning after my return, I called Judith.

"Hi, hermanita, guess where I've just been?"

"Sounds like Guatemala?" I could hear her smiling.

"Yup. And Willie sends his love. I have another of my direct ones to ask you."

Judith laughed. "All your questions are direct. What is it?"

"What was Edmundo's mother's name?"

"Her name was Berta, why?"

"Ah," I said. "Willie was right. He just wasn't sure. Do you know who Adriana was?"

"I asked my father the last time I saw him," Judith said, her voice serious. "She was his youngest sister. He told me she was his favorite sibling, and that she died during the birth of her first child."

"Oh." I felt I was receiving sacred information. "When did she die?"

"A few days before you were born."

I fell silent. Mutti and Ruth had it wrong. My mother had named me after someone who had been special to her and to the man she loved. The name Adriana was a gift of inclusion, of family.

"Do you know anything more about her?"

"Only that she was a sweet girl, that my dad loved her, and that she was too young to die when she did."

My mother could have named me Esther, or Ruth, or Agatha, or Berta, but she chose Adriana, after a real, warm person, not some fictional character in a harebrained romantic novel of conquest and passion and lust. I like both names. One kindled the European imagination; the other was a Carib reality. Catana Adriana. Adriana Catana. Adriana.

Three years old

Marlon misses me. Marlon is the two and a half year old son of Ruth's maid, Nola. He is a happy, free spirit, and interrupts any conversation Ruth and I are having by joining in and pointing to his socks saying, "tengo taltetines." He has learned so many words that his mother uses him as her messenger. "Go tell them dinner is served," she says to him, and off he goes looking for us to tell us "Ya etá tevido." Then he doesn't stay because that's business. After he's delivered the message, he crosses his little arms and goes back to the kitchen.

Sometimes during breakfast, the door opens and Marlon barges in with his cereal bowl. He places it next to Ruth without a word, goes back to the kitchen, leaving the door open, and returns with a container of Bulgarian yoghurt and one with granola. He puts them on the table and says to Ruth with a serious face: "Tíveme" (serve me). Ruth asks him if he is hungry. "Tí?" he answers, for si (some of his consonants are not quite right yet). Ruth scoops three heaping spoons of yoghurt and two of granola into his bowl. "Gatia," he says, for thank you, all very business like. He takes his little bowl and, closing the door behind him, ambles back to the pantry to eat.

He came into my room as I was arranging clothes in my suitcase and asked me what I was doing. I said packing, as it was time for me to go home.

"Adonde te vá, Tatana?" (Where are you going, Catana) he asked me, and answering his own question he said: "Te vá a lo etado?" (Are you going to the States?)

"Yes, but I won't forget you. I'll send you the photos I took, and a little surprise," I said seeing his little eyes cloud over.

"No te vaya, Tatana," and he hugged my legs with all the strength of his little arms.

I called Ruth the other day. She told me Marlon had been asking where I was. For the first few mornings he'd run into my room and would come out disappointed saying, "Tatana no etá." (Catana is not there). Ruth said she explained several times that I left, and still he asks. The next question follows, "cuando viene?" (when will she be back)? I left Guatemala three weeks ago, and the little boy still asks for me.

AMONG THE THINGS I FOUND OUT from Ruth on the last trip was the crucial question no one answered before. Not

Ruth, not Alicia in Livingston, not Edmundo. All said Rosa came with the family, but no one was able to tell me how long she had stayed in the city. Before my last two trips to Guatemala, I was under the impression that Rosa had remained in Livingston. Now I know I was with her for three years before she left me.

Vulnerable and confused, I asked Ruth, "Tell me, did I ask about Rosa? Did I miss her? At three years old, I must have had a connection to her."

"No, Catana, I don't remember you ever asking for her," was Ruth's answer.

One is able to remember incidents that occurred around the age of three. My counselor told me that. She also told me that children tend to block out traumatic incidents and later have no memory of what happened during the entire period.

I do know that when Marlon's mother leaves for the market without telling him, he goes around the house looking for her. "Y mi mamá?" he asks. "She went to the market," we tell him. "Ah, cuando viene?" (When will she be back) She only leaves him when she's in a hurry. He understands she'll be back soon because he knows how long it takes to go and come back. Reassured, he either joins us to talk about his 'caltetines,' or he goes to the garden where he waits to see her as she returns. Then, he runs to her shouting: "mamatita, mamatita!" and embraces her legs, happy to be with her again. Marlon is a little over two and a half years old.

This little boy showed me that it would have been impossible for me not to have missed my mother. How many times did I ask, "Where is she?" or "when will she be back?" How many times must I have worried about her not returning, that something had happened to her? How many times was I distressed knowing she had forgotten me? Did I cry for her at night before going to sleep? I know we never included her in my prayers when I prayed with Ruth.

I rejected her because I didn't understand her leaving me. It was two of us who were dark. She was the first and the last dark person I had contact with in my young life. I was accustomed to Ruth, and she indeed took excellent care of me and all my needs, but she was not my mother.

When Rosa left me, alone and saddened, I began to see her as a flawed mother. She was not a White mother, for all White mothers I knew had their children with them; and she was not a brown mother for all brown mothers had their brown children with them, too. She was different because she was a Black mother and she didn't have her Black child with her. I must have rapidly and bitterly concluded that Black mothers are bad mothers because mine could walk away and leave me. I was too young to understand a mother's sacrifice, a mother's yearning for her child; too young to see that she had been driven away, and that I had been lured, seduced, by Mutti.

Mutti and Ruth never said a mean word about Rosa; they just never talked about her. When she came to visit, they were uncomfortable and I became uncomfortable too, though for completely different reasons. I associated their discomfort not with their consciences, but with the one obvious reason: Rosa was Black and might steal me. In their hearts, they knew what they had done, certainly with the best of intentions for me, but the worst of outcomes for my mother and my relationship with her.

When they first arrived in Guatemala City Mutti did not engage new servants. She had James and my mother. The status of servant was new to Rosa. That had not been her position in Livingston. When James left, a new houseboy took take care of the housework. But who cooked our food, washed, and ironed our clothes? That must have been Rosa who, because of me, became the maid.

⌐⌐

"Why are you always tired, Mami?"

"The days are long, little girl. I have to do the laundry, cook the food and clean the house; iron the clothes, feed the dog, wash the dishes, prepare dinner. When it rains, I have to polish the silver. I don't have time even to go for a walk with you. I have to work a lot, my love, that's why I'm tired."

"You were never tired before."

"Before, we were in Livingston and I could play with you."

"I don't want you to be tired, Mami, I want you to sing with me the way we used to."

"Maybe tomorrow we can play when I finish my work."

...MY MAMI IS CALLING ME. I don't have to go when she calls me. I am doing things with Mutti. We are busy. I love being with Mutti, she always has time to be with me. I don't care if my Mami calls me. I don't want to eat. Why else would she call me...? Mutti doesn't say I should go to her. Mutti doesn't hear her either. Ruth doesn't hear her, nobody hears her when she calls me. See...? She stops calling me. If she comes to get me, I'll scream. Really loud, like the other time, when I hollered and embarrassed her. Afterward I felt bad about it; I don't think she'll come get me again, though. She doesn't like it when Mutti looks at her when I scream. Mutti always protects me. I heard her tell Mami if she goes away to be with Edmundo, she can't take me with her. She also told her to remember that when I was a baby she almost killed me when we went to the village and gave me food that made me sick. My Mami loves me, but she doesn't know how to take care of me. Mutti knows everything better and loves me better.

"Your bath is ready, Mohrle. Come, it's time to bathe."

"I just want to look at this picture here. Then I'll come."

"Please, Mohrle, you need to bathe and eat. After that you can come and say good night."

"Hum, hum, hum..."

"Come, baby, let's go!"

"Hum, hum, hum..." (I'll scream if she touches me!)

"Rosa, let her look at the pictures. Only a few more minutes... it doesn't matter."

"I've drawn her bath water, she should come now."

"You must be tired, Rosa... Why don't you let Ruth bathe her?"

I wanted Ruth to bathe me, anyway.

I heard my Mami crying in her bed. In the morning she played with me as she dressed me, the way she did before.

"Why were you crying in the night, Mami? Why were you sad?"

"I'm sad because I have no time to be with you. I'm tired and sometimes my body hurts."

"Don't be so sad, Mami, I can help you." She dressed me in my favorite yellow dress, and as she sat next to me and was about to put my socks on, she took my foot and looked at my toes.

"They are like little pearls, these tiny toes," she said to me, "my baby has such beautiful little feet."

She put my socks on, then my brown shoes. "After breakfast we'll go for a walk," she said.

"I am going for a walk after breakfast with my Mami," I ran and told Mutti.

"I'm going to the Zoo," Mutti said. "Do you want to come along?"

"Mohrle, do you want to go to the zoo, or do you want to go for a walk with me?"

"I want to go to the zoo," I said, climbing onto Mutti's lap.

"You take her for a walk in the afternoon, Rosa." Mutti said, embracing me.

WHEN WE CAME BACK FROM THE ZOO, Mutti called my Mami, but she didn't come. Lunch was ready and the table was set with a place for me, too, but where was my Mami? Ruth and Mutti talked in the living room, and then we sat down to eat potato pancakes with applesauce. I love potato pancakes, but where was my Mami? After eating, Ruth brushed my teeth and we went into her room. My bed was in her room. She laid me down, kissed me and covered me and I fell asleep wondering where my Mami was, and why my bed was in Ruth's room.

"Well, little sleepy head," Ruth smiled at me when I woke up. "You're finally awake! Here, let me dress you; we are having afternoon tea. I made lemonade and cookies for you."

I didn't say anything while she dressed me; my eyes just followed everything she did. I had the feeling I had done something bad that my Mami was not there. Ruth took my hand and we walked to the living room.

"You are so quiet, Mohrle," Mutti said. "You are still half asleep! Wake up, little dreamer!" And she tickled me, but I didn't feel like laughing.

"Where's my Mami?" I asked her.

"She had to go away."

"Where did she go? When will she be back?" I looked at Mutti and then at Ruth.

"We don't know, she had to go far away," Mutti's face was very serious.

"Where did she go?" I asked again.

"To Tiquisate."

"Where is that? Why did she go there?"

"She wanted to see Edmundo."

"Why did she leave me here?"

"Because you will now stay with me. Everything will be just as it always was. You know that you are my little Mohrle." Mutti stood up and came over and picked me up and hugged me. I put my arms around her neck and kissed her. "I love you, little girl," she added, hugging and kissing me.

"I love you, too, Mutti," I whispered.

That night, after tucking me in, Ruth took my hands and placed them together. "Repeat after me," she said softly, covering my hands with hers:

"Müde bin ich, geh zur Ruh'
Schließe beide Äuglein zu,
Vater, lass die Augen Dein,
Über meinem Bette sein. Amen."

(I am tired and ready to rest. As I close my eyes, I pray God will watch over my sleep.)

We didn't pray for my Mami, but I wished she'd come back.

In the morning, we got up. Ruth washed me, brushed my teeth, combed my hair and put pretty ribbons in it.

"Is my mother coming today?" I asked.

"No, Mohrle, she only left yesterday."

At night, after the prayer, I asked for her again, "Is my mother coming tomorrow?"

"She only left yesterday, Mohrle, you know that."

"Yes," I said, "I know."

Ruth kissed me and secured the blankets, and turned the light out. She left the door open so that the light from the hall fell into the room.

The next morning Ruth said, "Mohrle, look at you! You've been crying all night."

"Where's my Mami?" I asked. But I knew she had not returned. She abandoned me. It hurt so much that she could just go away and leave me. When I thought about my Mami my chest hurt. I knew she would never come back, so I stopped asking about her.

One day Ruth returned from work and called me. She was really excited. "Mohrle, Mohrle, come here, I brought you something." Her face had the biggest smile. "Here," she handed me a box with a bow. "I hope you like it," she said and sat me on her lap and helped me open the present.

The box was filled with cotton. I took the cotton out, and there, right in the middle, was the most beautiful brown baby. I said nothing; I only looked at the beautiful baby, and leaned my head on Ruth's chest and smiled.

"Don't you want to pick her up? That's your baby, Mohrle."

I saw my arms reach into the box and both my hands picked up the doll. She had her eyes closed, but when I held her up she opened them and said "Mama." Her eyes are brown and she moves them from side to side, and her eyelids have eyelashes. Her mouth is slightly opened in a faint smile showing two tiny bottom teeth. I held her close to me, and her little voice again said "Mama." Loud and clear, she said "Mama" to me.

"Thank you," I said to Ruth, my eyes sparkling, my face lighting up in a broad smile.

"What are you going to name her?"

"Lulu," I whispered.

That night I held Lulu close. I had a baby to take care of, a little brown baby like me that would live with me forever. I kissed my doll and fell asleep holding her soft body close to me.

LULU HAS BEEN WITH ME ever since. I never traveled anywhere without her until recently, when I prefer to leave her home. Her body, which is made of mesh, has become brittle and can no longer be mended. The porcelain face is as beautiful as when she was new. Lulu was made in Germany, at a time that country was wracked with racism. Yet she is the prettiest brown doll I have ever seen. How she found her way to Central America will forever be a mystery. But one day, in a department store named La Paquetería in the Guatemala of the early forties, Ruth happened upon her. She was expensive; the family was in no position to spend money on frills, but it was important to Ruth that I have the doll. Knowing the owners of the store, she gave them whatever money she had with her and promised to pay the rest at month's end.

The carpenter made a wooden crib for Lulu; the seamstress sewed the mattress, pillow and bed sheets. Every time a new dress was made for me, one was made of the same material and style for Lulu. My doll wore what I wore, ate what I ate, and slept when and where I slept. Lulu was at my side always.

"I will never leave you," I whispered to Lulu every night after prayers, "I will always be with you, I will always take care of my baby, I'm a good Mami." Lulu is the one who knows more about my thoughts and feelings in my early years, more than anyone ever will, including me.

I have an album with lovely childhood photographs of me; Ruth took all of them, also those of Rosa and Mutti. There are none of me with Ruth because she was behind the camera. She was my Mama who watched over my wellbeing with tender love. Prior to the forced departure from Livingston, she told me, she gave me a little bag with a banana and a cookie to hold while we walked to the river. We got into a boat and she then peeled the banana and gave me half. While we ate the fruit we waved goodbye. Goodbye house, goodbye hill, goodbye palms, goodbye bright red trees. Then Ruth gave me the cookie to eat while she paddled the boat down river a little bit. "I gave you something to eat," Ruth said, offering me one of her disarmingly gentle smiles, "so that the departure would seem like an adventure for you."

In context I can now tell the rehearsal prepared me for leaving with them, but more importantly, that I would not return, and that my fate was sealed to theirs.

The feelings accompanying the fragments of my memory as they returned were difficult and increasingly painful to bear. I looked in my album at pictures taken when I was about three. In one, I'm wearing a dark blue coat with white collar and four large mother-of-pearl buttons. I'm holding Lulu. Mutti told me I was awfully proud of my new coat. "Now I'm a real little cypress," I said, meaning I'm a little princess.

I used to like these pictures; I look so perfect in them, well groomed, never a speck of anything on me, always very serious and slightly aloof. Looking at them again, however, disturbed me. I recognized, with goose bumps on my arms, that the serene little princess looked sad.

BEFORE RETIRING I TOOK LULU from her drawer, removed the flannel that covered her, and sat cross-legged on the bed, my back against the headboard. I turned the light out and cradled my doll as I had half a century ago. What artist's hand made you? Whose idea were you? I knew she was smiling at me in the dark of night, as always, immobile.

I held her firmly against my chest and closed my eyes and sat motionless for what seemed hours, trying to ban from my mind the guilt that in the past weeks plagued my soul. The more I rejected it, the larger it loomed over me. I had chosen Mutti over my mother. I was the one who chose the German woman.

I may have been lured, but it had been my choice to fall for the seduction. I wept. Heavy hearted, I slid down and lying on my side, holding Lulu tightly, I bathed her with tears as I must have done when we were young.

"Did you know, Lulu," I whispered, "how I felt when my mother left?"

"I did," Lulu's answer resounded within me.

"I was the one," I whispered, "who could have been with my mother, but I chose not to know her." I wept, and knew then that for the rest of my life I would never be able to forgive myself for having rejected my mother. My heart ached, my lungs burned. At times I could not breathe; I hurt so badly.

"Notice your pain, feel it," Lulu whispered. "It shook your body as a child when you longed for your mother. You decided then, never to feel such pain again, never to think of her again. Your mother will always love you, Mohrle. You don't have to punish yourself. Your mother forgave you long ago. That's what mothers do."

Rosa is at my bed as I sleep. She has the fragrance of youth and the radiance of a young woman. She looks at me now as she looked at me long ago. Her serious, gentle eyes rest on me. I, her daughter, with my hair graying at the temples am now older than she.

Have I died? If I haven't, why am I observing this scene?

"I am glad you have reached out to me." I feel my mother say. She smiles faintly as she holds me in her gaze. I sit up to have a better look at her. "You are beautiful," I hear myself whisper. I reach for her hand and she lets me hold it. I recognize the hand that had cleaned, had sewn, gardened, cooked, had handed over the family's last money for a bus ticket to the city. I recognize the fingers that had longed to touch me but had not felt free to do so. Good hands, strong hands, artistic hands... my mother's hands.

"There are many truths, my child," I feel my mother whisper. "I never left you Adriana; I was always with you. I always understood you and I am proud of who you have become."

My spirit embraces that of my mother. I feel her heart beating softly in her chest. "You are on the other side, why does your heart beat?"

"There is no death," her Carib soul whispers. "I will love you eternally, for in the infinity of the Universe, there is only the pulse of infinite LOVE."

A few months old: in my mother Rosa's arms:
Livingston, 1940.
A picture Ruth took and Edmundo gave me.

Fred and Catana, 1995

EPILOGUE

Sedona, Arizona
Autumn, 2012

In 1995 I completed the first draft of *Split at the Root*. There would be four re-written drafts and then the manuscript just gathered dust for 16 years.

It is my intention that the memoir concludes in a dream or a phase of split consciousness such as is characteristic of dream states. By 1995 I had been in therapy for years and intellectually understood the conflicts within me; I had found the concluding answers to begin writing the story.

Also, by 1995, Fred had successfully undergone surgery for cancer. The prognosis at the time was excellent so that we expected a full recovery and continued our lives with little, if any preoccupation for seven years. Then, late 2002 the illness returned in spades. The answer to the question is it terminal this time, was year and a half, perhaps more, perhaps less.

I heard it. Fred heard it but he walked out of the doctor's office as if assured a magic bullet to target and destroy his cancerous cells would be found in time for him to outrun his fate.

"When you retire," he dreamed out loud, "we'll go to France once more in spring and walk down the Champs Elysées, we'll

dine on a bateau mouche as it carries us down the Seine past a lit
Parisian cityscape; we'll drive through the blooming fields of the
Provence and sit by the beach in St. Tropez at sunset; and while
we're at it, let's drive along the Riviera to Portofino and spend a
week at the Splendido, as we did in 1971. Yes, Sweetie," Fred was
hopeful and full of conviction, "when you retire we'll go to France
again, for sure."

By August 2003, the treatment was destroying him faster than
the illness. One morning, as he lay in bed sick as a dog, I declared
I was ready, then and there, to retire. "If you had only one more
year to live," I asked him point blank, "what would you do in the
last year of your life?" He had not expected I'd ever so directly
point out the inevitable. His eyes revealed the anger he tried to
conceal as his lips narrowed to a thin line. I sat down on the bed
next to him and waited for his answer.

Eventually, and quite haltingly, he said: "I'd get rid of all this
and move to Antigua in Guatemala." He wanted me to be in the
fold of my family at the time of his leaving.

Said and done. We sold the house, had our household packed
and stored for shipment, and mid-December 2003, with Juliette
our little cat, we boarded the plane for Guatemala City.

Ruth invited us to stay in Catalina until we found a suitable
home in Antigua. At 95, she was in exceptional physical and,
above all, mental health. Late February we moved into a house in
Antigua, at the foot of the imposing volcano named Agua.

At first I didn't have time to see how I felt about residing in
the country I had so often sworn I'd never live in again. Despite
the family's generous welcome, despite the help, despite enjoying
a privileged environment, it became impossible for me to adjust
to a place where social conditions were far worse than when I
had left them over half a century earlier. Ultimately, too, the old
rivalries with Ruth and her need to control began to reemerge.
She would never bring herself to see past Mutti's consummate
love for me. But I was, as I had always been, beyond her reach for
I coveted nothing; she could thus not punish or reward me. Our
relationship would remain as convoluted and complex as ever,
where jealousy and rejection intertwined with an intense and

tender love for each other.

Through his remarkable humor and ever-present grace Fred, who in healthy times had complained of aches and pains, stoically concealed from everyone the misery his deteriorating, brittle body was putting him through.

In December 2004, our son announced his sudden marriage to someone with whom he'd only been in love with for a short time. They honeymooned in the Southwest and decided they had to live in Sedona, Arizona. In another rash decision, they rented a house with a small guesthouse, and in less than a month moved from Los Angeles to Sedona. Patrick urgently wanted us in the States and he will tell you that, like the Magician in the Tarot, he manifested our return.

Like one hanging onto a raft on the rapids of the Colorado, with merely blind trust in the current, I again dissolved our home and shipped our remaining household to Sedona.

It is said the veil between the worlds is thin in Sedona, and that the inhabitants of old came here to transition into their next existence. Like the ancients of bygone times, Fred's earthly existence concluded in this strikingly beautiful landscape of red rocks. At home, with Patrick and me at his side, early one afternoon in May 2005, he glided peacefully into eternity. His was a gentle death, a moving experience beyond anything we could have imagined.

That same afternoon I received a call from Willie who was in Belize. "How are you, sister," he said. "I feel the need to know how you are." Not ten minutes after the conversation, the phone rang again. It was Judith, and later Adela called. Both sisters offered to take the next plane and be at my side if I so desired.

Patrick and wife, whose marriage began under the most somber of circumstances, returned to Los Angeles a month after Fred's passing. Sedona is not for career-minded people.

There I was, stuck, without Fred, in a place where I knew no one. So I reconnected with Empire State College to work part-time in the College's Center for International Programs. I would teach blended courses (partly in the classroom, mostly on line) in the Lebanon Program, from the comfort of my home in the desert.

I believe in the eternal life of the spirit and recognize that, from beyond, Fred put me on a track to meet an extraordinary man: Farai.

En route home from a trip to Lebanon, I stopped in Paris to visit my childhood friend Putzi. There I met Farai. At first we exchanged friendly emails, but then he came to Arizona and began to seriously proposition me. I absolutely rejected his advances. After all, (and I shared this with him) I had never as much as had a lengthy conversation with a Black man, much less was I interested in exploring a relationship with one. But this man, deeply steeped in his African culture, with his mind-blowing intelligence and eye-popping list of lifetime accomplishments, began to intrigue, indeed fascinate me.

I shared with Patrick my confusion at being deeply aggrieved at Fred's death, and simultaneously finding myself drawn to another man's attention so shortly after losing my soul mate. My son neither judged me nor was he surprised.

"I am partial to Dad, and will of course always be," he offered solemnly. "He was my greatest ally, and is my constant companion now that he is on the other side. But in your life, in Catana's life, Farai completes Fred. From what you tell me, all that Fred was, Farai is not; and all Farai is, Fred was not. In the infinity of Spirit, Mom, which we as humans don't have the capacity to understand, Farai and Fred are one. I believe," Patrick's wise old soul informed me, "that Fred travelled the Universe to find that spirit to complete him in your life. Farai is Fred's ultimate gift of love to you."

Awed by my child's words, I was humbled at being liberated in such a gracious, noble way. The loss of one beloved man did not forbid the encounter with another; I was free to engage in a new relationship. "You may eventually learn to love Farai as tenderly as you loved Fred, because in spirit, they are two sides of a whole. And, Mom," my son concluded chuckling, "you must know that you are, for lack of a better word, a 'wowable' woman. You will always be."

The Black skin neither Mutti nor Fred could give me, I now own with pride when I walk with Farai, when I sleep with him and awake to rest my eyes on his peaceful face, when I feel his tender lips eagerly searching for mine. The simple comfort in our being together does feel as if we found each other in the farthest recesses of the Universe, to complete an interrupted existence. If there was someone who understood the depth of that primal wound: the degree to which I must have missed Rosa, it was Fred.

Therapy helped me assimilate my emotions intellectually. But the culture I was taught as a child as being superior would have remained as such in my emotional framework, were Farai not teaching me the poetry of his Sub-Saharan language, the beauty and complexity of his African music, showing me the grace in the movements of his African body, the rhythm in his walk, and yes, joyfully awakening my desire for the roundness of his sensuous buttocks.

2010:
July 15 - At 98 years of age, Gil faded into Eternity.
August 8 - Three weeks later, Ruth, aged 100 years, 8 months and seven days, followed Gil.

2011:
In summer, I retired from Empire State College to rededicate my time to writing. It took months before I could wrap my head around this story again.

2012:
May - Thomas, Ruth's oldest son and his wife came to Sedona. Upon leaving Thomas reminded me that with the exception of Rome and Mexico, he had visited me in all the places I had lived. It was an observation that in a touching way again underlined the family ties. For Ruth's children and grandchildren, as for Judith's

and Adela's, I am quite possibly the elusive, eccentric family member who separated from the fold to lead an eclectic, colorful, conflicted life.

June - Patrick released the first CD of his own original piano compositions.

September - Farai, after almost seven years, remains a fixture in my life, continuing to support my rewarding hermit's existence in Sedona.

A bloom from a centenarian rose
bush in Antigua, Guatemala